# DIVORCE LAW MADE E-Z!

**E·Z LEGAL FORMS®**

Deerfield Beach, Florida
www.e-zlegal.com

> **NOTICE:**
>
> THIS PRODUCT IS NOT INTENDED TO PROVIDE LEGAL ADVICE. IT CONTAINS GENERAL INFORMATION FOR EDUCATIONAL PURPOSES ONLY. PLEASE CONSULT AN ATTORNEY IN ALL LEGAL MATTERS. THIS PRODUCT WAS NOT PREPARED BY A PERSON LICENSED TO PRACTICE LAW IN THIS STATE.

Divorce Law Made E-Z™
Copyright 1999 E-Z Legal Forms, Inc.
Printed in the United States of America

**E·Z LEGAL FORMS®**

384 South Military Trail Deerfield Beach, FL 33442
Tel. 954-480-8933 Fax 954-480-8906
http://www.e-zlegal.com/
All rights reserved.
Distributed by E-Z Legal Forms, Inc.

1 2 3 4 5 6 7 8 9 10   CPC   R  10 9 8 7 6 5 4 3 2

This publication is designed to provide accurate and authoritative information in regard to subject matter covered. It is sold with the understanding that neither the publisher nor author is engaged in rendering legal, accounting, or other professional services. If legal advice or other expert assistance is required, the services of a competent professional should be sought. From: *A Declaration of Principles jointly adopted by a Committee of the American Bar Association and a Committee of Publishers.*

Divorce Law Made E-Z™

# Important Notice

This product is intended for informational use only and is not a substitute for legal advice. State laws vary and change and the information or forms do not necessarily conform to the laws or requirements of your state. While you always have the right to prepare your own documents and to act as your own attorney, do consult an attorney on all important legal matters. You will find a listing of state bar referral services in the Resources section of this product. This product was not prepared by a person licensed to practice law in this state.

# Limited warranty and disclaimer

This self-help legal product is intended to be used by the consumer for his/her own benefit. It may not be reproduced in whole or in part, resold or used for commercial purposes without written permission from the publisher. In addition to copyright violations, the unauthorized reproduction and use of this product to benefit a second party may be considered the unauthorized practice of law.

This product is designed to provide authoritative and accurate information in regard to the subject matter covered. However, the accuracy of the information is not guaranteed, as laws and regulations may change or be subject to differing interpretations. Consequently, you may be responsible for following alternative procedures, or using material or forms different from those supplied with this product. It is strongly advised that you examine the laws of your state before acting upon any of the material contained in this product.

As with any legal matter, common sense should determine whether you need the assistance of an attorney. We urge you to consult with an attorney, qualified estate planner, or tax professional, or to seek any other relevant expert advice whenever substantial sums of money are involved, you doubt the suitability of the product you have purchased, or if there is anything about the product that you do not understand including its adequacy to protect you. Even if you are completely satisfied with this product, we encourage you to have your attorney review it.

It is understood that by using this guide, you are acting as your own attorney. Neither the author, publisher, distributor nor retailer are engaged in rendering legal, accounting or other professional services. Accordingly, the publisher, author, distributor and retailer shall have neither liability nor responsibility to any party for any loss or damage caused or alleged to be caused by the use of this product.

# Copyright Notice

The purchaser of this guide is hereby authorized to reproduce in any form or by any means, electronic or mechanical, including photocopying, all forms and documents contained in this guide, provided it is for nonprofit, educational or private use. Such reproduction requires no further permission from the publisher and/or payment of any permission fee.

The reproduction of any form or document in any other publication intended for sale is prohibited without the written permission of the publisher. Publication for nonprofit use should provide proper attribution to E-Z Legal Forms.

# Money-back guarantee

E-Z Legal Forms offers you a limited guarantee. If you consider this product to be defective or in any way unsuitable you may return this product to us within 30 days from date of purchase for a full refund of the list or purchase price, whichever is lower. This return must be accompanied by a dated and itemized sales receipt. In no event shall our liability—or the liability of any retailer—exceed the purchase price of the product. Use of this product constitutes acceptance of these terms.

# Table of contents

How to use this guide ................................................................. 7

Introduction ................................................................................ 9

**1** Do you need a lawyer? ...................................................... 11

**2** Preparing for divorce ........................................................ 21

**3** What property is divided and who gets what .................... 33

**4** Alimony, custody and support ........................................... 45

**5** The Marital Settlement Agreement .................................... 55

**6** Preparing the paperwork for court .................................... 71

**7** Your day in court ............................................................. 101

**8** Getting on with your life ................................................. 107

The forms in this guide ........................................................... 121

Glossary of useful terms .......................................................... 151

Resources ................................................................................ 157

Divorce laws by state .............................................................. 171

How To Save On Attorney Fees ............................................... 199

Index ....................................................................................... 223

# How to use this guide

E-Z Legal's Made E-Z™ Guides can help you achieve an important legal objective conveniently, efficiently and economically. But it is important to properly use this guide if you are to avoid later difficulties.

- ◆ Carefully read all information, warnings and disclaimers concerning the legal forms in this guide. If after thorough examination you decide that you have circumstances that are not covered by the forms in this guide, or you do not feel confident about preparing your own documents, consult an attorney.

- ◆ Complete each blank on each legal form. Do not skip over inapplicable blanks or lines intended to be completed. If the blank is inapplicable, mark "N/A" or "None" or use a dash. This shows you have not overlooked the item.

- ◆ Always use pen or type on legal documents—never use pencil.

- ◆ Avoid erasures and "cross-outs" on final documents. Use photocopies of each document as worksheets, or as final copies. All documents submitted to the court must be printed on one side only.

- ◆ Correspondence forms may be reproduced on your own letterhead if you prefer.

- ◆ Whenever legal documents are to be executed by a partnership or corporation, the signatory should designate his or her title.

- ◆ It is important to remember that on legal contracts or agreements between parties all terms and conditions must be clearly stated. Provisions may not be enforceable unless in writing. All parties to the agreement should receive a copy.

- ◆ Instructions contained in this guide are for your benefit and protection, so follow them closely.

- ◆ You will find a glossary of useful terms at the end of this guide. Refer to this glossary if you encounter unfamiliar terms.

- ◆ Always keep legal documents in a safe place and in a location known to your spouse, family, personal representative or attorney.

# Introduction to Divorce Law Made E-Z™

Divorce doesn't have to be expensive and painful. Whether you are considering a divorce, or have already started a legal separation, there are ways to control the costs and emotions when partners agree to part. *Divorce Law Made E-Z* provides a step-by-step strategy for working through an uncontested divorce, even when children are involved.

By taking steps now, you can confidently resolve your divorce. An uncontested divorce enables you to customize your divorce settlement to best suit your family's needs without interference from expensive lawyers or legal professionals.

You will also find important information on how to divide and preserve your assets when you are both a marriage and business partner with your spouse. Discover how to come to an agreement on dividing assets, assigning debts, setting reasonable support amounts, and having achievable, post-divorce goals. This guide will help you prepare and survive an uncontested divorce without suffering a crushing financial defeat—the E-Z way!

# Do you need a lawyer?

# 1

# Chapter 1
## Do you need a lawyer?

### What you'll find in this chapter:
- The uncontested divorce
- What to do if you have minor children
- When to use an attorney
- Advantages to representing yourself
- How to find the right attorney for you

A divorce is one of the most important events in your life. It can affect you emotionally, financially and, of course, legally. Your divorce will legally resolve important rights and obligations concerning:

1) financial support

2) division of property

3) custody and visitation of your minor children

While these are certainly vital issues, the law on these points is not overly complicated and is reasonably uniform among the different states. Considerably more complex is the process for obtaining a divorce. But, this too can be simplified with the aid of this guide and perhaps some casual advice from the clerk of the divorce court.

# How should you handle your divorce?

Will you need a lawyer to handle your divorce? To answer that, ask yourself the following questions:

♦ *Is your divorce contested or uncontested?*

DEFINITION

If you and your spouse both agree that you should divorce, then you have an *uncontested divorce*. A contested divorce obviously requires the services of an attorney, as you must litigate whether you are entitled to a divorce as a matter of law.

You and your spouse may both agree about the divorce but not about other issues, such as how your property will be divided or who will have custody of your children. These disagreements mean the divorce is still contested, and you will most likely need an attorney to litigate these issues in court.

♦ *Do you have minor children?*

Unquestionably, the most important issues in a divorce concern the welfare of your minor children. These include child support, custody and visitation rights. Because these issues are so important, the court will be quite concerned with their resolution and that what has been decided is, in fact, in the best interest of your minor children. An experienced divorce lawyer can guide you to a settlement that a court will approve as fair and in the best interests of the children.

**E-Z TIP**: Because the rights of your children are paramount, it is wise to have an attorney review provisions concerning your children—even if you and your spouse are in complete agreement.

### ◆ *Do you have minimal and easily divided property?*

If your divorce is nothing more than deciding who gets the dog or some furniture, then you and your spouse can resolve these questions on your own without an attorney.

If you own considerable property, you will want an attorney to make certain you receive your fair share. You'll also want to make certain that the property is divided in a way that will protect you on existing liabilities as well as be most tax-favorable.

### ◆ *Do you need or expect future support from your spouse?*

> **note:** Alimony and spousal support are becoming less common as more wives pursue careers today.

If you will be financially dependent upon your spouse, you may need an attorney to help you negotiate equitable support as well as make the obligation binding through valid support agreements.

If you have questions about whether you are entitled to alimony—or what a proper support amount should be—then you'll need an attorney's advice.

You can see that you probably do not need an attorney if:

- You and your spouse both want the divorce and agree on the division of property.

- You have no minor children.

- Your marital or separately owned property is minimal.

- You are not seeking alimony or spousal support.

- You and your spouse are not in active military service.

If you meet these criteria you must still ask yourself whether you are comfortable handling your own divorce. If you are confident about your ability to handle matters, then why not try?

Other factors may also influence your decision on whether to hire a lawyer. If your situation has unusual complications, or if your spouse has an attorney, then you should consider representation.

> **E-Z TIP**
> Should you reach a point where you no longer feel comfortable representing yourself, you should always hire an attorney, or at least consult an attorney on a particular aspect of the divorce that may be causing you difficulty.

## Advantages of using an attorney

Whether or not you think you need an attorney, retaining an attorney does offer you several advantages:

> **note**
> A lawyer can be emotionally supportive during the divorce. It can be comforting to have an attorney to turn to for objectivity when your feelings cloud clear thinking.

- You can let your attorney handle all the details while you get on with your life with less concern over legal matters.

- An attorney will certainly provide you with added protection—particularly in areas where you may not now see the need for protection.

- Your attorney can be a buffer between you and your spouse and resolve some of the more emotionally charged issues.

- The judge and court clerk will prefer to work with your attorney. And, since your attorney knows the procedures, your case can be processed more efficiently

## Advantages of representing yourself

There are corresponding benefits to handling your own divorce without an attorney:

- You save legal fees. This can be considerable. A simple contested divorce can cost $1,000 or more, and fees can become astronomical in large, contested cases. Attorneys generally charge between $150 and $300 an hour for their time, so you can see how a fee can quickly climb on even the smallest case.

- Your divorce may be less adversarial. Attorneys can bring an adversarial atmosphere to a case that may be resolved more quickly and smoothly in an informal atmosphere involving only you and your spouse.

- Your case may move faster without an attorney. Your attorney may be too busy with other cases, causing needless delays that you can avoid by personally staying in charge of your case.

- Without an attorney the judge *may* give you more leeway—but this can't always be counted on.

Of course, you can compromise and hire an attorney, on an hourly basis, who will not formally represent you but will answer questions that may arise. You will save on legal fees but still have available to you the professional assistance you need. Many users of this *Divorce Law Made E-Z* Guide have discovered this is an ideal way to proceed.

# Finding an attorney

Many attorneys handle divorce cases and quite a few specialize in family law. It should be easy to find an attorney to handle your divorce, but you may have to interview several attorneys before you find one that makes you feel comfortable and can handle your divorce efficiently and economically. How can you find such an attorney?

- Seek referrals from friends or family members who have gone through a divorce.

- Call the lawyer referral service of your local bar association.

> **E-Z TIP:** Ask the clerk of your local divorce court for the names of the more active divorce lawyers in your area. Similarly, the various social service agencies may be excellent referral sources.

- Ask your family lawyer for a referral. You may have used a real estate lawyer or bankruptcy lawyer, for example, who may also know of a good divorce lawyer.

- Look through the *Yellow Pages* advertising, since divorce lawyers frequently advertise their divorce specialty in the *Yellow Pages.*

Once you have a number of names, set up interviews with four or five attorneys. When interviewing the attorney, seek answers to these specific questions:

◆ How long has the attorney been in practice?

◆ What percentage of his or her cases are divorce?

◆ Does the attorney generally represent the husband, the wife or both?

# Chapter 1

- Who will actually handle the case, and will associates be involved?

- What will be the general strategy for the case, and how long will it take?

- What approximate outcome might be expected?

- Approximately how much will it cost and how is the fee to be paid?

Since an important objective is to save money on legal fees, here are a few ways to keep legal fees to an absolute minimum:

- Use your time with the lawyer efficiently. Be concise on the phone and limit your phone calls. The same rule applies to office visits.

- Give information to your lawyer's secretary whenever possible. This is sure to save expensive time.

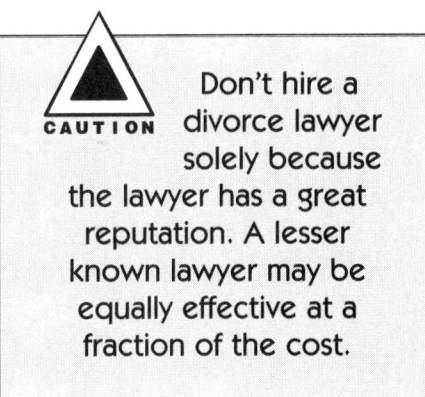

Don't hire a divorce lawyer solely because the lawyer has a great reputation. A lesser known lawyer may be equally effective at a fraction of the cost.

- Do the routine work (deliver papers, etc.) yourself.

It may be that after you talk to several lawyers—or even retain one—you will decide you can handle or complete the divorce on your own, or perhaps with an attorney as an occasional advisor.

As you can see, this guide is not intended to replace your attorney. It's designed to help you decide if you need one, and it will also help you work more effectively with your attorney should one be retained.

# Preparing for divorce

# Chapter 2
## Preparing for divorce

### What you'll find in this chapter:
- Is divorce the right answer?
- The grounds for divorce
- The residency requirement
- How to organize your divorce
- Safeguarding your assets

Divorce doesn't just happen. It requires a lot of thought not only about your relationship with your spouse, but also about your financial condition. Is our relationship really beyond repair? Can we regain the respect and love we once had for each other? Can I support myself? Who will pay the mortgage? The answers to these questions will help prepare you for your ultimate decision.

## Do you really want a divorce?

Before you start divorce proceedings make absolutely certain you want a divorce. No marriage is without its occasional problems. There are a number of things you can do to assure yourself that you are making the correct decision.

# Divorce Law Made E-Z

***Don't act hastily.*** Never rush into a divorce. Make certain you have given your problems adequate time to work themselves out. Anger and feelings do change over time and with patience you and your spouse may be able to resolve your difficulties and enjoy a happy marriage.

***Seek professional help.*** Can a psychologist or marriage counselor help you and your spouse improve your relationship? These professionals can oftentimes more clearly see the reasons for your conflict and offer valuable suggestions for overcoming your problem. Don't forget, these professionals have counseled many other couples who have shared precisely the same problems.

There are no particular advantages to a legal separation, and it's primarily used by people who cannot divorce for religious or other reasons.

***Try a separation.*** Rather than jump from marriage straight into divorce, why not try a trial (non-legal) separation? Living apart from your spouse allows you to realistically assess the importance of your spouse in your life. You can simply agree to live apart for a while or file for a legal separation.

# Grounds for divorce

You or your spouse may want a divorce, but that does not mean you can automatically obtain a divorce. You must satisfy the legal requirements of your state, as each state has "legal grounds" that it considers justification for the divorce. Years ago these laws were much more strict and it was much more difficult to obtain a divorce. Attitudes about divorce have changed and most of the states have liberalized their laws. Most states today recognize *no fault divorces*. This means neither party necessarily did anything wrong but that the couple simply has irreconcilable differences and no longer wish to remain married to each other. You can grounds for divorce in your state in the Appendix of this guide.

# Residency requirements

Of course, you or your spouse can always relocate to another state for purposes of obtaining a divorce. But to obtain a divorce in any state you must satisfy its residency requirements. That means you must have lived there with the intent to stay for a minimum period of time. Some states, such as Nevada, have exceptionally short residency requirements, whereas others may require residency for a year or more before you are eligible for divorce. The residency requirements for each state can be found in the Appendix.

# Organizing yourself for divorce

Divorce may be quite complicated financially and legally, particularly when couples share considerable wealth.

To fairly resolve your financial matters, you need your complete financial and legal picture. You then must organize and have ready:

- deeds and mortgages on real estate

- IRA, Keogh, pension and other retirement plans

- life insurance policies

- last will and testament, codicils and any testamentary trusts

- pre-nuptial or post-nuptial agreements

- prior divorce decrees and property agreements

- savings and checking accounts

- wills or trusts where you are a beneficiary or grantor

- ownership interests in any closely held business, including corporate or partnership documents and financial statements of each business

- notes or evidence of other obligations due you

- notes or evidence of other obligations you owe others

- tax returns for three prior years

- leases

- outstanding major contracts

> **E-Z TIP:** When filing for divorce, organize and have ready titles, registration and appraisals on any autos, boats, planes or other vehicles among the other items listed.

- inventory of valuable personal assets (antiques, jewelry, art)

- lawsuits or evidence concerning contemplated suits against third parties

- lawsuits, judgments or potential claims against you

- malpractice or liability insurance

- applications for credit or loans issued within the prior five years

You will, of course, want the same information about your spouse. If you or your spouse own a business, you'll also want to review:

- corporate books and records, if incorporated, or partnership agreements, if a partnership

- copies of any notes or loans between yourself and your business

- corporate obligations to which you are a guarantor

- life insurance policies maintained by the company

- financial statements of the business

- tax returns of the business

Make certain every important asset you and/or your spouse own is accounted for. It's remarkably easy to overlook valuable assets unless you regularly review this asset inventory:

- cash on hand

- checking and savings accounts

- cash value life insurance

- motor vehicles

- residential real estate

- investment real estate

- stocks or bonds in publicly owned corporations

- certificates of deposit

- money-market funds

- stocks or equities in any closed corporations, partnerships or other business entities

- notes or mortgages receivable

- savings bonds

- accounts receivable

- boats, airplanes or other recreational vehicles

- options to acquire property

- leases or leasehold interests

- beneficial interests in trusts

- revocable trusts to which you are a grantor

- licenses or franchise rights

- IRA, Keogh, 401K or other retirement accounts

- tax refunds due

- claims or potential claims against third parties

- inheritances and future interests

- safe deposit box inventory

- copyrights, trademarks or patents

Have you accounted for all art, jewelry and antiques owned by you and your spouse as well as all other assets?

Estimate the approximate value of each item as closely as possible. Indicate how each asset is titled (singly in your name, jointly with spouse, or in trust). Also specify your percentage of ownership in assets owned with others. Finally, list liens or encumbrances against each asset to determine the equity to be protected, and repeat this exercise for your liabilities:

- mortgages

- tax liabilities

- notes on car loans

- unsecured loans

- other secured installment loans

- charge account balances

- credit card balances

- alimony or child support from previous marriages

- business debts guaranteed

- other guaranteed debts

- outstanding judgments

- potential or threatened claims

> **note**: Compile your records so you fully understand every facet of your finances as well as your spouse's.

Finally, project ahead over the next year or two so you anticipate inheritances, other windfalls, or even financial problems that should be factored into the divorce agreement.

# Safeguarding assets

With approaching dissolution of the marriage, one or both spouses may try to hide assets from the other. Your spouse, for instance, may sell stocks or bonds, or withdraw savings and claim the proceeds were spent or lost. Divorce courts, of course, see such tactics daily and severely penalize the spouse suspected of such conduct. Don't let that be you. Play fair and you'll come out further ahead. That doesn't necessarily mean your spouse will be as honest. Your goal must be to protect marital assets until they can be equitably divided by the court or an agreement is reached:

- **Valuables**—Remove all the jewelry, artwork and other valuable but movable objects to a secure place beyond the reach of your spouse. However, give your spouse a complete inventory of what was taken so you can't be accused of concealing marital assets.

- **Insurance**—If both you and your spouse hold joint insurance policies, then draw down any cash value for safekeeping.

> **E-Z TIP**
> Place all cash, securities, stocks, bonds and notes or mortgages due you in a secure place. If these assets are in your joint names, notify your stock broker or transfer agent not to put through any transfers without your written consent.

- **Real Estate**—Does your spouse own real estate in his or her name only? You'll need your lawyer to file in court for a restraining order preventing transfer of the property. You may instead file a lis pendens against the property. This puts any prospective buyer on notice of your claim to the property. This effectively encumbers the property so you don't lose your rights to it even if it is sold.

- **Business interests**—Your business interests are best protected by a restraining order preventing your spouse from transferring his or her interest. You may also seek a restraining order against the corporate entity itself, thus preventing actions out of the ordinary course of business that may dissipate the value of the business.

- **Bank accounts**—Empty checking accounts and savings accounts that your spouse can sign on. Escrow these funds pending the divorce.

> **E-Z Tip:** When you prepare the list of assets that you and your spouse own, also record serial numbers and other means of identification.

Timing is the key to asset protection when a divorce looms on the horizon. Don't wait for your spouse to act first. There may then be very few assets left to protect. There are several ways one or both spouses in a divorce can play "hide and seek" with property:

1) *Relocate property to a safer locale.* This may mean transferring assets to offshore havens where privacy is assured.

2) *Camouflage ownership.* Did one spouse "sell" his or her interest in a business for cash or other consideration of little value? Fraudulent transfers of assets—particularly business interests—are notoriously common in a divorce. The defrauded spouse can attempt to prove it a fraudulent transfer, but such an effort can be quite difficult and expensive.

3) *Delay receiving income, inheritances or assets from other sources until the divorce is final.* Substantial income can also be secreted in defined-benefit pension plans. These hidden payments may be as much as 100 percent of income.

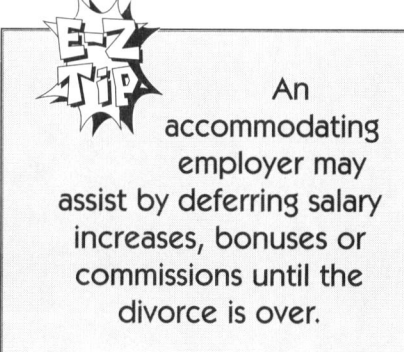

> **E-Z Tip:** An accommodating employer may assist by deferring salary increases, bonuses or commissions until the divorce is over.

Endless possibilities abound in a divorce for one or both parties to hide assets or income. Such actions may seem smart, but in practice you'll discover yourself to be in an even better position by remaining honest. For example, if your spouse can prove that you transferred cash to an offshore bank, the court may well award your spouse equal or greater amounts of other marital assets. As you can see, it matters little that courts can't attach some assets when they can divide others. For maximum protection read *Asset Protection Made E-Z*. It is must reading for people going through divorce and with assets to protect. You can order it through E-Z Legal Forms, Inc.

> **E-Z TIP** Divorce courts award a disproportionately large share of assets to the innocent spouse when the other spouse is believed to have secreted assets.

# What property is divided and who gets what

## 3

# Chapter 3
## What property is divided and who gets what

### What you'll find in this chapter:
- Marital vs. non-marital property
- Community vs. separate property
- Dividing property by agreement
- Dealing with specific assets
- Dividing debts and liabilities

A major part of most divorce cases is the division of marital property and marital obligations between spouses.

Even if you conclude you have no assets or debts to concern yourself with, review the checklist in the prior chapter. It may remind you of property or liabilities that are easily overlooked in a divorce agreement.

## How courts divide assets and obligations

How do courts divide property when the spouses cannot agree? They basically follow one of two approaches:

### 1) Equitable distribution states

In an equitable distribution state, the court "equitably divides" the marital property. The court normally considers the length of the marriage and the age, health, conduct, occupation, skills and employment of the parties.

With equitable distribution, all property acquired during the marriage is *marital property* and all property owned before the marriage is *non-marital property*. Gifts or inheritances to either spouse during the marriage are non-marital property. This doesn't mean non-marital property is safe in a divorce. The court may leave this property with the respective spouses, but courts in most equitable distribution states apportion these assets between spouses as they do with marital property. In fact, one purpose of a pre-marriage agreement is to keep separate the couple's pre-marriage assets.

> **note:** Equitable division does not mean equal division, and seldom is property equally divided.

The following are equitable distribution states, by either statute or common law:

| | | | | |
|---|---|---|---|---|
| Alabama | Alaska | Arkansas | Colorado | Connecticut |
| Delaware | District of Columbia | | Florida | Georgia |
| Hawaii | Illinois | Indiana | Iowa | Kansas |
| Kentucky | Maine | Maryland | Massachusetts | Michigan |
| Minnesota | Missouri | Montana | Nebraska | New Hampshire |
| New Jersey | New York | North Carolina | North Dakota | Oklahoma |
| Ohio | Oregon | Pennsylvania | Rhode Island | South Carolina |
| South Dakota | Tennessee | Utah | Vermont | Virginia |
| West Virginia | Wyoming | | | |

## 2) *Community property states*

Community property states, in contrast, require equal division of the community property in the event of divorce. This includes property acquired by each spouse prior to the marriage, as well as property acquired thereafter.

There are nine community property states:

| | | |
|---|---|---|
| Arizona | California | Idaho |
| Louisiana | Nevada | New Mexico |
| Texas | Washington | Wisconsin. |

To understand the theory of asset division in community property states, you must first understand that community property states view marriage as an equal business partnership. The law then divides property into two categories: community property and separate property. *Community property* is anything acquired jointly, or by either spouse, during the marriage. *Separate property* is from one of two sources:

DEFINITION

**note** Whether a state follows equitable distribution laws or is governed by community property statutes, upon marital dissolution the assets may be unfairly divided by the courts.

1) Property that each spouse owned individually before the marriage and retained in his or her name after the marriage.

2) Property that each spouse received as a gift or inheritance either before or during the marriage.

Each spouse's separate property remains separate property and is not subject to division upon divorce. If you exchange one item of separate property for another, the new property continues as separate property. So too if the proceeds of sale of separate property are used to acquire new property.

If you commingle separate property with joint property, the separate property becomes joint property subject to division. Separate property must always remain separate so it can always be distinguished from joint property.

> **note** As with assets, liabilities that either spouse has incurred prior to the marriage remain a separate obligation.

While the parties may agree to keep separate debts incurred during the marriage, these provisions do not bind creditors. Be certain that marital bills are discharged or indemnified against should you go through a divorce.

 How do you best protect your property in a community property state? Start by listing your property when you marry. Clearly stipulate that it is to remain separate property thereafter. Similarly, keep separate any gifts or inheritances you receive during your marriage. These assets will then always remain yours.

## Dividing property by agreement

This guide assumes that you and your spouse will reach agreement on the division of marital assets and liabilities and there will thus be no need for the court to divide the property.

> **note** Judges in uncontested divorces nearly always go along with the property agreement of the spouses if it is generally fair and the judge is convinced the agreement was freely entered into by both spouses with no fraud or coercion.

If you have minimal property, you and your spouse may simply go ahead and divide it up with no more formality. If you have more substantial assets, then you will want a written agreement.

In negotiating your agreement, be guided by how a court is likely to divide your property if you cannot reach agreement:

The court will order an approximately equal division of the assets and liabilities when:

- It was a marriage of long duration
- The spouses had near-equivalent wealth before the marriage
- Both spouses have adequate earning ability
- There are no minor children

The court will award more property (and fewer debts) to the spouse who has:

1) less earning ability

2) less financial contribution to the marriage if a short-term marriage

3) poorer health or other adverse circumstances

4) custody of the minor children

# How to deal with specific assets

## *The family home*

In a divorce with minor children, the family home is nearly always awarded to the spouse with custody. This is less disruptive than uprooting children from their community, friends and home.

This does not necessarily mean the custodial parent gets to permanently keep the home. The court, for example, may order the custodial spouse to have possession of the home until the youngest child is 18 or 21, or out of college.

At that point the home may be required to be sold with some determined portion of the equity going to each spouse.

Your agreement may be based along such lines. Obviously, you have other alternatives:

- sell the house now and split the proceeds

- have one spouse buy out the interest of the other

*note* It's important to remember that you are dealing with the equity in the house, not the fair market value of the home. If the home is worth $200,000 but has a $150,000 mortgage, then the equity shared by you and your spouse is only $50,000. It is that amount you must focus on when negotiating your settlement.

## Pension and profit-sharing plans

What happens in divorce to all the retirement funds you or your spouse accumulated? These include Social Security, IRAs, Keoghs, 401K Plans, Tax Sheltered Annuities, Employee Stock Options (ESOPs) and Self-Employed persons' Individual Retirement Accounts.

*note* You have a right to Social Security benefits that accumulated during your marriage if that marriage lasted for ten years or more.

There are some general guidelines to follow in determining which of these assets are subject to division in a divorce:

- Because Social Security benefits flow directly from the federal government, they are never considered to be either marital or community property. They are not subject to division by the court in divorce nor are they governed by state law. This is true even if you later become divorced.

- You are also entitled to Social Security survivor benefits if your marriage lasted at least ten years.

- Stock option profit-sharing plans and defined pension plans are normally considered marital property and are subject to division no matter which spouse accrued the benefits. The challenge is in determining the present value of these assets. This can best be accomplished with the aid of the plan administrator or some other qualified expert.

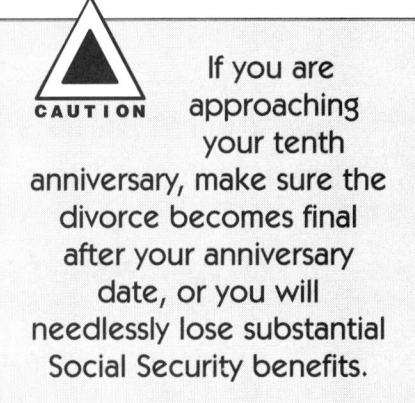

**CAUTION:** If you are approaching your tenth anniversary, make sure the divorce becomes final after your anniversary date, or you will needlessly lose substantial Social Security benefits.

- All military and federal pensions and benefits, like Social Security, are federally sponsored and administered, and they are usually divided upon divorce. Military disability benefits are not considered marital property subject to division. There is a requirement that the parties be married for at least ten years for spouses to share in any military retirement benefits that have accrued during the marriage.

Generally, all property owned by spouses—whether singly or jointly—can be divided by the divorce courts. This, however, does not extend to veteran's pensions and other veteran's benefits. While veteran's benefits cannot be given to the other spouse, a divorce court can take these benefits into account for purposes of making a fair and equitable division of other property or for establishing alimony.

## *Professional licensure*

Academic diplomas and professional licenses may be considered marital assets. This is particularly true when one spouse helped put the other through school to become a professional. Most valuable: licenses to practice the high-income professions—medicine, dentistry and law. Doctorates are also an asset the courts are likely to attach a value to.

A divorce court may easily determine that professional status is a marital asset worth $1 million or more. To balance outcomes, the court may leave the spouse with professional status very little in other marital assets.

## Other assets to consider

If you have prepared a thorough list of assets before you negotiated your agreement, you will be less likely to overlook some less visible assets.

- inheritances due
- options to acquire property
- claims or lawsuits against third parties

## Dividing debts and liabilities

If there are bills incurred by you and your spouse, they must be divided along with your assets. A bill may stand in the name of one spouse, but that doesn't mean the other spouse can't agree to pay it or share in its payment as part of the divorce agreement.

> **note** You must realize that orders of the court or your agreement concerning division of debts do not affect your creditors.

The spouse who was originally liable on a debt remains liable on the debt even if the other spouse agrees to pay it. The creditor's recourse is against the spouse who owes the money, not the spouse who agreed to assume the debt. If your spouse agrees to pay one of your debts and fails to, you can sue your spouse, but your creditor can still sue you.

Bear this in mind when dividing liabilities. Make certain your spouse has the financial responsibility to, in fact, pay the debts he or she agrees to pay. If you believe your spouse may default, then try to obtain security to ensure his or her payments. You may take a mortgage on any real estate or personal property (a car or boat) conveyed to your spouse. You may require your spouse to escrow funds to ensure payment. There are ways to protect yourself!

Unfortunately, you can easily lose your good credit, either because your spouse ran up big bills on your charge accounts and credit cards or through your own inability to cope with finances amidst the turmoil and expense of divorce.

Good credit is also an asset, and one certainly worth protecting during a divorce.

Three timely steps can protect you from whatever your spouse may do to injure your credit:

1) **Immediately notify everyone you have charge privileges with** that you will no longer be responsible for debts incurred by your spouse. Send the notice by certified mail so there can be no question of its receipt.

2) **Destroy all credit cards for which you and your spouse share liability.** Never assume you have no liability on credit cards that stand only in your spouse's name. You may have unwarily signed and guaranteed the credit application years earlier.

3) **Publish your disclaimer of liability** for your spouse's debts incurred after the notice. In many states publication is sufficient notice to third parties of your refusal to accept liability for debts incurred by your spouse after publication. Check the laws in your state and follow their procedures carefully.

> **CAUTION** Make certain you receive all bills that you may be liable for. If your spouse receives these bills it may be many, many months before you become aware of long overdue bills—only to also discover your now-ruined credit rating.

Next, turn your attention to your own credit responsibilities. If you cannot meet your credit obligations on a timely basis during the divorce, then communicate this to your creditors before they press for payment. Let creditors know why you are having financial problems, and explain that it is a temporary situation. Offer reasonable installment payments to show good faith.

Most importantly, ask your creditors not to issue a negative credit report to the credit bureau. Creditors usually will work with you if you cooperate with them.

# Alimony, custody and support

# Chapter 4
## Alimony, custody and support

### What you'll find in this chapter:
- The changing face of alimony
- The different types of custody
- Visitation rights
- Factors the court considers
- Child support

Knowing how courts typically respond to alimony and child custody matters can help you deal more rationally with these emotional issues. While the concept of alimony has changed dramatically over the years, no other aspect of divorce presents greater potential for conflict than that of child custody, visitation and support.

## Alimony

Laws and practices concerning alimony have changed enormously over the past two decades. Much of this change is because so many women are working or employable and are no longer viewed as financially dependent on their husbands.

Alimony is designed to provide the wife a reasonable standard of living and one as close as possible to the one she enjoyed during the marriage. Alimony, in some unusual cases, is paid by the wife to the husband. Most commonly there is no award of alimony.

### When will a court consider alimony?

- when it was a long marriage. A marriage of 2-3 years is not likely to require alimony.

- when the wife spent nearly all her marital years at home raising the family

- when the wife must continue to remain at home to properly care for the children

- when the wife is ill, unemployable, or has no special skills

- when the husband has high earnings or earnings potential

Even when alimony is awarded, it is usually an insignificant amount.

Obviously, alimony stops when the wife remarries. There may be other provisions for termination. For example, alimony may be provided for a specific number of years—usually until the youngest child reaches a certain age, or the wife can complete her education or a training program to make herself employable.

Related to alimony is the issue of continued health coverage for a spouse. This is a major problem for many divorcing couples, as a spouse may no longer be covered under the other spouse's insurance—although federal law now requires that employer-sponsored health plans must provide an employee's ex-spouse with continued health coverage at their group rates for three years following the divorce.

> **note** Fewer than 20 percent of today's divorces include alimony.

# Chapter 4

# Child custody

The most emotional part of your divorce will involve the custody decision. It is also the most important. In the past there was a strong presumption that the mother would make the best custodial parent. This is because the mother was the homemaker and caretaker of the children, while the husband was the breadwinner. This presumption was particularly true with younger children and daughters.

> **note** If you have children, the court will compel you and your ex-spouse to maintain as harmonious a relationship as possible, because your cooperation is vital to the well-being of your children.

Fathers, in the past, could only hope for custody by convincing the court that the mother was unfit to care for the children. This usually meant that the mother was an alcoholic, on drugs or otherwise unsuitable because of psychological or behavioral problems that would be injurious to the children.

In recent years the presumption that the mother is the best custodian of the children has weakened. Courts now consider what's in the best interests of the children when deciding upon the custodial parent.

DEFINITION

Before we proceed further it is important to understand the different types of custody. Historically, *sole custody* was the usual form of custody. That meant that the custodial parent had both *physical custody* or possession of the child and *legal custody* or sole authority to make all decisions concerning the child. This type of custody, with the non-custodial parent only having visitation rights, remains the most common arrangement.

DEFINITION

In recent years the concept of *shared* or *joint custody* has gained in popularity. This means that both parents have an equal say in the up-bringing of the child, that is, they share legal custody. One spouse may continue to have sole physical custody.

*Joint physical custody* of the children can also be provided for. Under this type of custody, each parent has exclusive physical custody for alternating periods—which may, for example, be certain days, weeks or months per year. This arrangement is also called *divided* or *alternating custody*.

> **note:** While it seems a fair arrangement, many courts and psychologists believe joint physical custody is harmful to the stability of the child, who loses his or her sense of "home."

Another possibility is *split custody*. Here each parent receives sole custody of at least one child with visitation rights to the other children. In essence, the family becomes divided. Courts understandably frown on split custody because it means not only separation from one's parent but also separation from siblings.

In deciding custody, more and more courts are looking to determine which parent is the more active caregiver. That is, who does the child most rely upon for day-to-day care? They believe continuing the primary caregiver as custodian provides the child the most stability.

## Visitation

Related to the issue of custody is the matter of visitation. The parent denied physical custody of the child has the right to reasonable visitation with the children. The only exception is if the parent is abusive or behaves in a way that can be harmful to the child.

The frequency and duration of your visitation is one major decision that must be carefully worked out with your spouse. The more frequent the visits, the closer is the relationship between child and non-custodial parent. Therefore, the most liberal and flexible visitation arrangement that is possible is encouraged.

While you and your spouse may agree on custody and visitation, this is always subject to review and modification by the court. What factors will the court consider when evaluating whether your agreement is in the best interests of your children?

- the age, sex and health of the child

- the physical capability and mental willingness of each parent to provide the child's needs on a day-to-day basis

- the bond between the child and each parent

- the desires of the child (if of sufficient age and capacity)

- the desires of the parents

- the health and age of the parents

- the effect on the child of moving

**E-Z TIP:** The court will generally favor a fixed or detailed visitation schedule rather than rely on vague terms such as "reasonable visitation," which can only invite disagreement when the spouses are not getting along.

Additionally, the court will more willingly grant joint custody when:

- the parents can cooperate and harmoniously make decisions together

- the relationship between the child and each parent is reasonably balanced

- both parents enthusiastically welcome joint custody

You can, however, build some flexibility into your agreement as long as you stay close to the standard of what a court may consider reasonable.

# Child support

The obligation of the parent to support a child is basic and one strongly enforced by the courts. Most judges look closest at this issue realizing it is here where the agreement may be inequitable and not adequately provide for the minor child.

Some states have guidelines for support. Obviously, the goal is to provide the children with as much support as possible and at the same time leave the obligated parent with sufficient income to live in reasonable style. Achieving these two objectives is seldom easy. Most often the obligated spouse (usually the husband) does not have sufficient income to adequately support both himself and his children.

*What does a court consider in awarding support?*

> **note:** When considering child support, a court will consider all other financial responsibilities of the obligated spouse, including support obligations from a prior marriage.

- the number of children and their ages. Courts may award less support when you have teenage children with some earning power of their own.

- whether the custodial spouse has any earning capabilities and can contribute to the support of the children

- the health or special needs of the children

- the income of the obligated spouse, as well as the earnings potential

- the assets or wealth of the obligated spouse

# Chapter 4

Child support, like custody and visitation, is never permanent. Either party can seek modification of the terms for good cause. For example, the husband may lose his job or become ill—events that may, at least temporarily, justify a reduction in support. Conversely, the husband may become wealthy, prompting the ex-wife to have the court increase the support payments.

In addition to support, a parent may become obligated to provide for the child's medical care (including maintenance of health insurance) and for the child's daycare costs or college education. Support may continue until the child is 18 or "emancipated"—which means that he or she is self-supporting. This is typically when the child leaves college, and may thus extend the support obligation until the child is about 22 years old.

*note* For tax purposes, child support payments are not deductible as an expense, or considered income to the receiving spouse. On the other hand, alimony is tax deductible to the obligor and counted as income to the recipient.

# The Marital Settlement Agreement

5

# Chapter 5
## The Marital Settlement Agreement

### What you'll find in this chapter:
- About your Marital Settlement Agreement
- Sample Marital Settlement Agreement
- Other factors to consider
- Provisions you may add to your Agreement
- The Financial Affidavit

This is an easier step in the divorce process because the hard negotiations are behind you. The Marital Settlement Agreement simply reduces to writing what you and your spouse have agreed upon.

It must be remembered that for the agreement to be approved by the court, the court must agree the interests of the minor children are properly protected in terms of custody, visitation and support. The court must also believe the agreement is basically fair and neither party used fraud, coercion or threat in reaching agreement.

No two agreements are identical, of course, nor does the agreement have to be complex.

A sample Marital Settlement Agreement follows.

Sample Marital Settlement Agreement

## MARITAL SETTLEMENT AGREEMENT

THIS AGREEMENT made and entered into this __15th__ day of __May__, __1992__ (year), between __Jane Public__ (Wife) residing at __1300 Somewhere St, Anytown, SomeState 00001__ and __Richard Public__ (Husband) residing at __200 Elsewhere Ave, Somewhere, SomeState 00002__.

WHEREAS, Husband and Wife were married to each other on __July 15__, __1980__ (year) at __Happytown__, __SomeState__.
                    (City)          (State)

WHEREAS, a permanent breakdown of the marriage has arisen between us and we are now living separate and apart from each other; and

[Use if there are children involved.]

WHEREAS, children were born into our marriage as follows:

| Child's Name | Child's Birth Date | Child's Sex |
|---|---|---|
| Carl Public | 4/22/84 | Male |
| | | |
| | | |

(hereinafter "children") and it is the further purpose of this Agreement to provide for the future custody, control and support of said children, and

# Chapter 5

## Sample Marital Settlement Agreement

WHEREAS, it is the desire and intentions of the parties to settle by agreement all of their marital affairs with respect to property, financial matters, [spousal support or maintenance (use if applicable)] [and all issues relating to their children, including custody, visitation, and child support (use if applicable)].

NOW, THEREFORE, in consideration of the premises and the mutual promises and undertakings herein contained, and for other good and valuable consideration, the parties agree to the following:

I. SEPARATION:

The parties agree to permanently live separate and apart from the other party, free from any control, restraint, or interference, direct or indirect, by the other party, and in all respects to live as if he or she were sole and unmarried.

II. DIVISION OF PROPERTY:

1. Husband transfers to Wife as her sole and separate property the following:

    ```
    1.   1990 Mustang LX
    2.   All furniture, furnishings, household goods located at:
         1300 Somewhere St, Anytown, SomeState 00001.
    3.   $3,000 of the total value of $7,000 of the parties' bank
         account located at:
         1st National Bank, 123 Gold Ave, Anytown, SomeState 00001
         Account No. 1234
    ```

2. Wife transfers to Husband as his sole and separate property the following:

    ```
    1.   Husband's IRA which is valued at $10,000.
    2.   Husband's pension which is valued at $25,000.
    3.   $4,000 of the total value of $7,000 of the parties' bank
         account located at:
         1st National Bank, 123 Gold Ave, Anytown, SomeState 00001
         Account No. 1234
    ```

## Sample Marital Settlement Agreement

III. DIVISION OF DEBTS:

1. Husband shall pay the following debts and will not at any time hold Wife responsible for them, and shall indemnify Wife from any liability on same:
    1. Citibank VISA account No. 67356677
    2. Ford Motor Credit account No. 90562

2. Wife shall pay the following debts and will not at any time hold Husband responsible for them, and shall indemnify Husband from any liability on same:
    1. Citibank MasterCard account No. 33627812

IV. ALIMONY - [Choose one of the following]:

1. Both parties hereby agree to waive any rights or claims that either may now have or in the future to receive alimony, maintenance, or spousal support from each other. Both parties understand the full import of this provision.

2. Monthly payments - The __husband__ shall pay to __wife__ for his/her support and maintenance the sum of $ __600__ per month/week. This sum shall be payable on the __first__ day of each and every __month__, commencing on __July 1__, __1992__ (year). Said sum will continue until [choose any or all of the following]: (a) the date that either party dies; (b) the date that the receiving spouse remarries; or (c) any other specific date that both of you agree on. Both parties intend that the amount and duration of the payments __may not__ (may or may not) be modified by a court in the future.

3. Lump sum payment - The parties hereby agree that in full payment of any claims or rights to alimony, spousal support, or maintenance the _____ shall pay to _____ the sum of $_____, which shall be payable on _____, _____(year).

## Sample Marital Settlement Agreement

V. CHILD CUSTODY AND VISITATION - [Choose one of the following]:

1. The parties agree that it is in the best interest of the child(ren) that the _____ have sole physical and legal custody of the child(ren). We further agree that the custodial parent will make the major decisions regarding the care and upbringing of said child(ren). However, the other parent has the right to be notified of any major decisions. The parties also agree to share in an equitable fashion the child(ren)'s birthday, holidays, and all vacations. Furthermore, the parties agree to allow the other parent to have a frequent and liberal visitation with the child(ren).

[Optional] - If the parties cannot agree on future visitation, then the _____ will have the right to be with the child(ren) as follows: (Draft a schedule i.e., vacation periods which the child(ren) will spend with the non-custodial parent.)

2. The Husband and Wife shall share joint legal custody for the minor child(ren). Both parents shall retain full parental rights and responsibilities. Both parents shall confer with one another so that major decisions affecting the best interests and welfare of the child(ren) may be determined jointly, where reasonably possible. We further agree that ___wife___ shall have sole physical custody of the child(ren).

Each party shall have full access to the child(ren)'s medical, dental, or school records. The parties shall consult with one another with regards to all medical and educational matters including religious education and training.

The parties also agree to share in an equitable fashion the child(ren)'s birthday, holidays and all vacations. Furthermore, the parties agree to allow the other parent to have a frequent and liberal visitation with the child(ren). The non-custodial parent will have the right to be with the child(ren) at least, but not limited to, as follows: (Note: make a detailed schedule).

VI. CHILD SUPPORT:

Subject to the power of the court to modify these terms, ___husband___ shall pay to ___wife___ as and for child support, the sum of $800 per month/week. This sum shall be payable on the first day of each and every ___month___, commencing on ___July 1___, ___1992___ (year). Said sum shall continue until the child(ren)

## Sample Marital Settlement Agreement

shall have married, died, become self-supporting, or reach the age of eighteen. [Furthermore, if the parent obligated to pay said support receives an increase in salary or income in the future, the amount of child support shall increase proportionately.] Said sum shall be reduced by $\_\_\_800\_\_\_ (or shall be reduced proportionately) for each child to reach the age of eighteen or otherwise emancipated.

The parties agree that the \_\_\_husband\_\_\_ will carry and maintain life insurance naming the child(ren) as irrevocable beneficiary(ies). Said life insurance is in the amount of $\_40,000\_\_\_.

Furthermore, it is agreed that \_husband\_\_ will carry and maintain adequate health, dental, and hospitalization insurance for the child(ren)'s benefit. The \_\_husband\_\_ shall each year transmit to the \_\_\_wife\_\_\_ evidence of payment showing that such dues, premiums and assessments have been paid.

VII. NECESSARY DOCUMENTS

The parties agree to execute and deliver to the other party any documents that may be reasonably required to accomplish the intention of this instrument and shall do all other necessary things to this end.

VIII. INCOME TAX:

For the year _____ the parties hereto shall file separate income tax returns. Each party hereto shall receive the refund or pay additional taxes based on his or her separate income.

[Or] The parties agree to file a joint income tax return for the year _____. In the event that there is a credit of any tax payment the \_\_\_husband\_\_\_ shall pay the \_\_\_wife\_\_\_ (1/2, 1/3) of any tax payments.

[Use if child(ren) are involved.] The parties agree that the \_\_husband\_\_ may claim the federal dependency tax exemption for the child(ren).

## Sample Marital Settlement Agreement

IX. SUBSEQUENT DISSOLUTION OF MARRIAGE:

It is agreed that this Agreement may be offered into evidence by either party in any dissolution of marriage proceeding, and if acceptable to the Court, this Agreement shall be incorporated by reference in any Final Judgment that may be rendered. However, notwithstanding incorporation in the Final Judgment, this Agreement shall not be merged in it but shall survive the Final Judgment and be binding on the parties for all times.

X. REPRESENTATION:

The parties represent to each other:
(a) Each had the right to independent counsel. Each party fully understands their legal rights and each is signing this Agreement freely and voluntarily, intending to be bound by it.
(b) Each has made a full disclosure to the other of his or her current financial condition.
(c) Each understands and agrees that this Agreement is intended to be the full and entire contract of the parties.
(d) Each agrees that this Agreement and each provision of it is expressly made binding upon the heirs, assigns, executors, administrators, successors in interest and representatives of each party.

XI. CHANGE OF NAME:

The parties agree that the Wife may have her name changed or restored to:
_____Jane Single_____.

XII. WAIVER OF BREACH:
No waiver of any breach by any party of the terms of this Agreement shall be deemed a waiver of any subsequent breach.

XIII. ENFORCEMENT OF AGREEMENT:
Both parties agree that the Court granting the divorce, at the request of either party, insert in the Final Judgment a reservation of jurisdiction for the purpose of compelling either party to perform this Agreement, or any part thereof. The prevailing party shall be entitled to attorney's fees in connection with such proceedings.

## Sample Marital Settlement Agreement

XIV. GOVERNING LAW:

This Agreement shall be interpreted and governed by the laws of the State of <u>SomeState</u>.

Signed in the presence of:

_____*Joe Witness*_____          _____*Jane Public*_____
_____*Wilma Witness*____                Wife's Signature
Witnesses for Wife

Signed in the presence of:

_____*Wally Witness*_____         _____*Richard Public*_____
_____*Jim Witness*_____               Husband's Signature
Witnesses for Husband


State of ___SomeState___ )
County of ___SomeCounty___ )

On <u>May 15, 1992</u> before me, _____Nick Notary_____, personally appeared ___Richard Public___ and ___Jane Public___, personally known to me (or proved to me on the basis of satisfactory evidence) to be the person(s) whose name(s) is/are subscribed to the within instrument and acknowledged to me that he/she/they executed the same in his/her/their authorized capacity(ies), and that by his/her/their signature(s) on the instrument the person(s), or the entity upon behalf of which the person(s) acted, executed the instrument.

WITNESS my hand and official seal.

Signature ___*Nick Notary*___          Affiant  √ Known    ___ Produced ID
            Signature of Notary              Type of ID _____

(Seal)

## Sample Marital Settlement Agreement

Signed in the presence of:

___*Wally Witness*___        ___*Richard Public*___
                              Husband's Signature
___*Jim Witness*___
Witnesses for Husband


State of ___SomeState___ )
County of ___SomeCounty___ )

On ___May 15, 1992___ before me, ___Nick Notary___, personally appeared ___Richard Public___ and ___Jane Public___, personally known to me (or proved to me on the basis of satisfactory evidence) to be the person(s) whose name(s) is/are subscribed to the within instrument and acknowledged to me that he/she/they executed the same in his/her/their authorized capacity(ies), and that by his/her/their signature(s) on the instrument the person(s), or the entity upon behalf of which the person(s) acted, executed the instrument.

WITNESS my hand and official seal.

Signature ___*Nick Notary*___        Affiant __√__ Known  _____ Produced ID
          Signature of Notary         Type of ID _____
                                                        (Seal)


**IF A NONLAWYER HELPED YOU FILL OUT THIS FORM THEY MUST FILL IN THE BLANKS BELOW** (fill in **all** blanks):

I (*name of nonlawyer*) ___Joe Friend___, nonlawyer located at (*street*) ___20 Main Street___ (*city*) ___AnyCity___ (*state*) ___AnyState___, (*phone*) ___666-5555___ helped (*name*) ___Richard Public___ who is the [✔ **one** only] __petitioner or √ respondent, fill out this form.

# Additional terms

You'll note there are several additional marital settlement provisions that may be included in the Agreement:

- how you and your spouse will handle the filing of tax returns for the current year (singly, jointly)

- whether support will include camp or college

- whether the wife wishes to—and can—resume her maiden name

- what the children's surname shall be

- which spouse may claim the federal dependency tax exemption for the minor children

- that the agreement shall survive the divorce and be enforceable in any court of jurisdiction

- that both spouses agree to the terms of the agreement

- that the financial statements are accurate

- that both spouses acknowledge rights to independent counsel

- that both spouses will sign all documents and undertake all acts contemplated under the agreement

- that the agreement shall be binding upon personal representatives

> **E-Z TIP**
> If you have considerable property or lack confidence that you can adequately prepare your own agreement, then you may want to have a lawyer handle this part of the divorce.

# Chapter 5

# The Financial Affidavit

*note* — Some states require both spouses to file a Financial Affidavit as part of the agreement. Its purpose is to allow the court to determine the reasonableness of the agreement and whether child support is fair and equitable given the financial circumstances of the parties.

*note* — Some states mandate use of their specific Financial Affidavit forms which are available from the clerk of the divorce court. Many other states allow you to submit the information using any format—provided the information is reasonably detailed and understandable. It is your responsibility in either instance to make sure your Financial Affidavit is as accurate as you can reasonably make it.

A sample of the Financial Affidavit found in this guide follows.

## Sample Financial Affidavit

**FINANCIAL AFFIDAVIT**

State of ___SomeState___ )
County of ___SomeCounty___ )

On _May 15, 1992_ before me, ___Nick Notary___, personally appeared ___Richard Public___, personally known to me (or proved to me on the basis of satisfactory evidence) to be the person(s) whose name(s) is/are subscribed to the within instrument and acknowledged to me that he/she/they executed the same in his/her/their authorized capacity(ies), and that by his/her/their signature(s) on the instrument the person(s), or the entity upon behalf of which the person(s) acted, executed the instrument and was sworn and says that the following statement of affiant's income, assets and liabilities is true:

Occupation ___Accountant___
Employed By ___ABC Corp.___
Business Address ___1234 Evergreen Blvd, Anytown, SomeState 00002___
Pay Period ___Weekly___
Rate of Pay ___650/week___
Social Security # ___123-45-6789___

ITEM 1: INCOME (Averaged on ___Weekly___ basis):
   Average GROSS Wage     $___650___
     Less Deductions
       Federal Income Tax     $___150___

# Sample Financial Affidavit

|  |  |  |
|---|---|---|
| Social Security | $  50 | |
| Other | $  30 | |
| Total Deductions | $  230 | |
| Minus Total Deductions | | $  230 |
| Average NET Wage | | $  420 |
| Plus Other Income | | |
| _____ | | $_____ |
| _____ | | $_____ |
| TOTAL NET INCOME | | $  420 |

ITEM 2: ASSETS (Ownership: If joint, allocate equally):

| | |
|---|---|
| Cash on hand or in banks | $  4,000 |
| Stocks, bonds, notes | $  1,000 |
| Real estate | |
|    Home | $ 60,000 |
|    Other | $  5,000 |
| Automobiles | $_____ |
| Other personal property | $_____ |
| Other assets  _____ | $_____ |
| TOTAL ASSETS | $ 70,000 |

ITEM 3: LIABILITIES

| Creditor | Balance Due | Monthly Payments |
|---|---|---|
| Citibank VISA | $  600 | $  75 |
| _____ | $_____ | $_____ |
| _____ | $_____ | $_____ |
| TOTAL LIABILITIES | | $  75 |

## Sample Financial Affidavit

ITEM 4: AVERAGE MONTHLY EXPENSES

Household:

 Mortgage or rent payments    $ 325/month

 Food and grocery items    $_____

 Utilities    $_____

Automobile:

 Gasoline and oil    $ 60/month

 Repairs    $_____

 Insurance    $ 55/month

Children's Expenses:

 Clothing    $100/month

 Medical, dental, prescriptions    $ 50/month

 School supplies    $150/school yr

Other expenses:

 _____    $_____

TOTAL AVERAGE MONTHLY EXPENSES    $ 740/month

*Richard Public*
Affiant's Signature

Affiant   √ Known   ___ Produced ID

WITNESS my hand and official seal.   Type of ID _____

Signature *Nick Notary*
Signature of Notary

(Seal)

# Preparing the paperwork for court

6

# Chapter 6
## Preparing the paperwork for court

### What you'll find in this chapter:
- General filing requirements
- Specific state requirements
- The documents you will need
- The nature of the hearing
- The Judgement of Divorce

With your Marital Settlement Agreement completed, you and your spouse can next prepare the divorce papers that must be filed in court.

Each state sets its own procedures for processing divorce cases. Counties within a state may also adopt slightly different procedures than those followed in other counties. The process described in this book follows the more common procedures found in an overwhelming number of states.

Accordingly, while this guide gives you the information needed to prepare your divorce papers in compliance with the rules in most states, there may be specific requirements you must follow in your state. Most of the specific requirements for your state can be found in the Appendix. *It is advisable to check with the clerk of your local divorce court for the requirements of that court.*

# General requirements

Legal documents must be prepared following certain rather uniform procedures and standards. These instructions apply to all documents in your divorce whether filed in court or not.

- Use 8-1/2" x 11" white typing paper. Some states still use 8-1/2" x 14" legal bond paper, and this document size should be used in these states. Some courts also require a "blue backer."  Check with the clerk of your court for specific requirements. All documents should be neatly typed double-spaced on one side only. Be sure to number each page. Photocopies of the forms in the back of this guide may be submitted to the court, but should be printed on one side only.

- Make certain that all documents are properly completed, signed and notarized, where required. Do not leave any blanks.

- Keep all documents in one file, and bring it with you to court.

# Specific state requirements

 In the Appendix you will find specific document preparation instructions for your state. Each state has a slightly different format and verbiage that it uses on its court papers and to caption documents. Unless you comply with local rules, the court clerk will not accept your documents for filing. *Be sure to check with the clerk of the court regarding caption requirements in your area before filing any documents.*

# Chapter 6

Every caption includes:

- the name of the court
- the name of the parties
- title or heading of the document
- the case number

The Appendix contains the information on how to properly caption documents in your state. You may also examine documents from other court cases to become more familiar with the format.

Below is a sample caption:

```
In the _____ Court for _____ County, State of _____
         [Insert Name of Court as shown in Appendix]
                                              )
In re: The Marriage of:                       )
                                              ) Case No: [Given by Court Clerk]
    [Your Name],                              )
    Petitioner or Plaintiff                   )
    and                                       )
    [Your Spouse's Name],                     )
    Respondent or Defendant                   )
                                              )
And in the interest of:                       )
                                              )
    [Name(s) of minor children, if any]
```

# The documents you will need

Besides your Marital Settlement Agreement and Financial Statements, the various documents needed to actually process the divorce are the following:

- Divorce Complaint or Petition
- Appearance, Consent and Waiver
- Child Custody Jurisdiction Form
- Final Judgment of Divorce/Decree of Dissolution of Marriage
- Certificate of Corroborating Witness
- Certificate of Divorce or Marriage Dissolution

> **note:** Each additional required form should be available from the clerk of the divorce court or other local sources.

Other forms may be required under local rules. Several states, for instance, require supplemental financial information concerning child support. California courts routinely require couples to sign marriage counseling waivers. Still other states have special forms for the assignment of wages to pay child support.

In addition, some states still require a summons or citation to formally serve the divorce papers upon the respondent spouse. The Divorce Complaint or Petition would be served together with the citation after the original complaint has been filed with the court.

> **note:** Because you and your spouse are proceeding cooperatively with an uncontested divorce, it should not be necessary to actually serve your spouse, and therefore there should be no need for the citation or summons.

Chapter 6

In an uncontested divorce, the respondent spouse (or both spouses) may sign and file an *Appearance, Consent and Waiver*, which is explained more fully in this chapter, rather than employing a summons or citation.

# The Divorce Complaint or Petition

The principal divorce document is the Verified Divorce Complaint or Petition. The Appendix will show you how to properly caption the Complaint/Petition. The contents of your Complaint will, at the least, include:

- the full names and social security numbers of both spouses

- your address and the length of time you and your spouse resided in the county and state where the divorce is filed

- the date and place of your marriage

- the date you and your spouse separated

- the age, occupation and employment of both spouses

- the names and birth dates of any children

- the grounds for divorce

> **note**: The Divorce Complaint or Petition is your formal request to the court to dissolve and end your marriage.

A sample Divorce Complaint/Petition follows.

## Sample Divorce Complaint or Petition

In the  Circuit  Court for SomeCounty County, State of SomeState

In re: The Marriage of:  )
    Jane Public  )
    Petitioner  )
      )
and  )   Case No:   [Given by Court Clerk]
    Richard Public  )
    Respondent  )
    and in the interest of:  )
    Carl Public  )

### Verified  PETITION FOR DISSOLUTION

1. This is a petition of dissolution from the bonds of matrimony between  Jane Public , Petitioner , and  Richard Public , Respondent .

2. The  Petitioner  is a resident of  SomeState  and has been for more than  6 months  immediately prior to filing this  Petition  and has resided in the County of  SomeCounty  for at least  1 year .

3. The  Respondent  has agreed to file an Answer and Affidavit in Support of  Final Judgment . No service of process is necessary at this time.

4. Neither party is currently an active member of any branch of the Armed Services.

5. The parties were married to each other on  July 15, 1980  in the state of  SomeState  and have been separated since  April 1, 1992 .

# Chapter 6

## Sample Divorce Complaint or Petition

6. Choose one of the following:

a. No children were born to or adopted by the parties of the marriage and none are expected.

b. There was/were __1__ child(ren) born as issue to this marriage, to wit: (name and date of birth)

1. __Carl Public, 4/22/84__
2. _____
3. _____
7. _____

The __Petitioner__ seeks a Final __Judgment__ on the grounds of: __Irreconcilable differences__

8. The parties have made provisions for the division of their property and payment of their joint obligations, they have signed a Marital Settlement Agreement and they are satisfied with those provisions. Their signed Financial Statements are attached and incorporated by reference. Each party certifies that the Marital Settlement Agreement and Financial Statements were signed without duress, force or collusion. (The Marital Settlement Agreement is attached and marked as Exhibit A.)

9. The __Respondent__ hereby waives any rights to findings of fact and conclusions of law, a record of testimony, motion for a new trial, notice of entry of Final Judgment or Decree, and the right to appeal, but does not waive any rights to the future modification of any judgment or decree in this cause.

10. The marriage is irretrievably broken and any continuance of these proceedings will not result in a reconciliation.

Wherefore, the __Petitioner__ respectfully asks and prays that the court:

1. Take jurisdiction of the parties and subject matter.

2. That a Final __Judgment__ be granted by the court dissolving the marriage between the parties.

3. That all of the terms and conditions of the parties' Marital Settlement Agreement, which is attached, be approved and be incorporated, and made part of a Final __Judgment__,

## Sample Divorce Complaint or Petition

and that the court enforce the Marital Settlement Agreement. Regardless, the Marital Settlement Agreement shall survive.

4. That the court award the parties any other further relief as may be just and equitable.

Dated this __15th__ day of __May__, 19__92__.

_____*Jane Public*_____
Wife's Signature

VERIFICATION

Address: __1300 Somewhere St__
__Anytown, SomeState 00001__

Phone: __(123)456-7890__

State of __SomeState__ )
County of __SomeCounty__ )

I, __Jane Public__, being duly sworn, depose and say that: I am the Petitioner/~~Respondent~~ in the within action for divorce; I have read the foregoing ~~Complaint~~/Petition and know the contents thereof; the contents of the ~~Complaint~~/Petition are true to my knowledge, except as to those matters therein stated to be alleged upon information and belief, and as to those matters, I believe them to be true.

_____*Jane Public*_____
Wife's Signature

On __May 20, 1992,__ before me, __Nick Notary__, personally appeared __Jane Public__, personally known to me (or proved to me on the basis of satisfactory evidence) to be the person(s) whose name(s) is/are subscribed to the within instrument and acknowledged to me that he/she/they executed the same in his/her/their authorized capacity(ies), and that by his/her/their signature(s) on the instrument the person(s), or the entity upon behalf of which the person(s) acted, executed the instrument.
WITNESS my hand and official seal.

Signature __*Nick Notary*__          Affiant __√__ Known ____ Produced ID
Signature of Notary                   Type of ID _____

## Sample Divorce Complaint or Petition

___Richard Public___
Husband's Signature

Address: __200 Elsewhere Ave__

__Somewhere, SomeState 00002__

Phone: __(987) 654-3210__

VERIFICATION

State of ___SomeState___ )

County of ___SomeCounty___ )

I, ___Richard Public___, being duly sworn, depose and say that: I am the ~~Petitioner~~/Respondent in the within action for divorce; I have read the foregoing ~~Complaint~~/Petition and know the contents thereof; the contents of the ~~Complaint~~/Petition are true to my knowledge, except as to those matters therein stated to be alleged upon information and belief, and as to those matters, I believe them to be true.

___Richard Public___
Husband's signature

On __May 20, 1992__ before me, ___Nick Notary___, personally appeared ___Richard Public___ personally known to me (or proved to me on the basis of satisfactory evidence) to be the person(s) whose name(s) is/are subscribed to the within instrument and acknowledged to me that he/she/they executed the same in his/her/their authorized capacity(ies), and that by his/her/their signature(s) on the instrument the person(s), or the entity upon behalf of which the person(s) acted, executed the instrument.

WITNESS my hand and official seal.

Signature ___Nick Notary___     Affiant _√_ Known ___ Produced ID
Signature of Notary

Type of ID _____
(Seal)

**IF A NONLAWYER HELPED YOU FILL OUT THIS FORM THEY MUST FILL IN THE BLANKS BELOW** (fill in **all** blanks):

I (*name of nonlawyer*) ___Joe Friend___, nonlawyer located at (*street*) __20 Main Street__ (*city*) ___AnyCity___ (*state*) __AnyState__, (*phone*) ___666-5555___ helped (*name*) ___Jane Public___ who is the [✔ **one** only] √ petitioner or __respondent, fill out this form.)

# Answer and Affidavit in Support of Final Judgment or Decree

As indicated earlier, this form can be used by both you and your spouse to avoid formal service by summons. Ask the clerk of court if a summons will be required even though your spouse files a written waiver in the Answer and Affidavit. The summons may be available from the clerk's office. If not, you may usually obtain a summons form at your local stationery store. Some states allow joint divorce petitions, and no Answer and Affidavit need be filed if both spouses file together.

> **note:** In some states formal service by summons is still required, even though your spouse has filed an Answer and Affidavit to your Petition or Complaint.

With the Answer and Affidavit, the signing spouse formally submits himself/herself to the jurisdiction of the court and thus acknowledges the validity of the divorce or any other order issued by the court.

In an uncontested divorce, this document will make it easier to process. Once the respondent spouse signs this document, he or she need not participate further in the divorce.

A sample Answer and Affidavit in Support of Final Judgment or Decree follows.

## Sample Answer and Affidavit in Support of Final Judgment

In the __Circuit__ Court for __SomeCounty__ County, State of __SomeState__

In re: The Marriage of: )
       Jane Public )
       Petitioner )
and )   Case No:
       Richard Public )       [Given by Court
       Respondent )            Clerk]
and in the interest of: )
       Carl Public )

### ANSWER AND AFFIDAVIT IN SUPPORT OF
### FINAL __Judgment__

The undersigned, __Respondent__, files this answer and states under oath the following:

1. I have received a copy of the __Petition__ and acknowledge all the allegations contained therein.

2. I further state that I am not on active duty in the armed services of the United States or of any foreign country.

3. I waive the __20__ days required for setting the above-captioned matter for trial and waive notice of the final hearing, requesting a copy of the Final __Judgment__ be mailed to me.

4. I have been a resident of and domiciled in the State of __SomeState__ for the preceding __12 years__ and the County of __SomeCounty__ for the preceding __8 years__.

## Sample Answer and Affidavit in Support of Final Judgment

5. The parties have made provisions for the division of their property and payment of their joint obligations. They are satisfied with those provisions. I have freely and voluntarily entered into a Marital Settlement Agreement. The Marital Settlement Agreement entered into by the parties attached marked as Exhibit A to the __Petition__ is a true copy.

6. I further waive my rights to notice of trial, findings of fact and conclusions of law, a record of testimony, motion for a new trial, notice of entry of final judgment or decree, and right to appeal; however, I do not waive any rights to the future modification of any judgment or decree in this cause.

**AFFIDAVIT IN SUPPORT OF FINAL __Judgment__**

The undersigned files this Affidavit in Support of the Final __Judgment__ containing the following:

1. The Court has jurisdiction of the parties and subject matter.

2. The Court finds the marriage to be irretrievably broken and grants a Final __Dissolution__.

3. The Marital Settlement Agreement filed in this proceeding as Exhibit A be approved and incorporated in the Final __Judgment__ by reference, and that the parties be ordered to comply with said agreement.

## Sample Answer and Affidavit in Support of Final Judgment

Further your Affiant Sayeth Naught.

Dated this __20th__ day of _____May_____, 19__92__.

___*Richard Public*___
Signature of Respondent/Defendant

Address: __200 Elsewhere Ave__

__Somewhere, SomeState 00002__

Phone: __(987)654-3210__

State of _____SomeState_____ )
County of _____SomeCounty_____ )

On __May 20, 1992__ before me, _____Nick Notary_____, personally appeared _____Richard Public_____, personally known to me (or proved to me on the basis of satisfactory evidence) to be the person(s) whose name(s) is/are subscribed to the within instrument and acknowledged to me that he/she/they executed the same in his/her/their authorized capacity(ies), and that by his/her/their signature(s) on the instrument the person(s), or the entity upon behalf of which the person(s) acted, executed the instrument.
WITNESS my hand and official seal.

Signature ___*Nick Notary*___     Affiant __√__ Known  ____ Produced ID
Signature of Notary

Type of ID _____

(Seal)

**IF A NONLAWYER HELPED YOU FILL OUT THIS FORM THEY MUST FILL IN THE BLANKS BELOW** (fill in **all** blanks):

I (*name of nonlawyer*) __Joe Friend__, nonlawyer located at (*street*) __20 Main Street__ (*city*) __AnyCity__ (*state*) __AnyState__, (*phone*) __666-5555__ helped (*name*) __Richard Public__ who is the [✔ **one** only] __petitioner or √ respondent, fill out this form.

# Child Custody Jurisdiction form

The Uniform Child Custody Jurisdiction Act, followed in all states, requires use of this declaration if you have minor children. Both spouses must make a formal declaration under oath stating:

> **note:** The Child Custody Jurisdiction form applies only if you have minor children. Its purpose is to give the court information by which the court can determine whether it has proper jurisdiction to issue orders pertaining to the children.

- the number of minor children subject to custody orders

- their sex, social security numbers, dates and places of birth

- that the child(ren) are not involved in prior divorce proceedings or subject to other custody orders

- that neither spouse knows of any pending custody action or claim for custody by any third party

A sample Declaration Under the Uniform Child Custody Jurisdiction Act follows.

# Chapter 6

## Sample Declaration Under the Uniform Child Custody Jurisdiction Act

In the  Circuit  Court for SomeCounty County, State of SomeState

In re: The Marriage of:  )
    Jane Public  )
    Petitioner  )
and  )  Case No: [Given by Court Clerk]
    Richard Public  )
    Respondent  )
and in the interest of  )
    Carl Public  )

### DECLARATION UNDER THE UNIFORM CHILD CUSTODY JURISDICTION ACT

We, the undersigned, Jane Public and Richard Public, are both parties to this proceeding to determine the custody of a minor child, and under oath state:

1. There is/are  one  minor child(ren) subject to this proceeding. For each child, the name, sex, Social Security number, date and place of birth, and time and place of residence and name and relationship of person child lived with for the past 5 years, is as follows: (Attach additional sheet if necessary.)

Child's Name:  Carl Public  Sex: Male  Date of Birth: 4/22/84
Place of Birth:  Anytown, SomeState  Social Security Number: _____
Present Residence: 1300 Somewhere St, Anytown, SomeState 00001
Person Child Lives With:  Jane Public  Relationship:  Mother
Dates of Residence: From:  4/84  To: Present
Previous Residence: _____
Person Child Lived With: _____ Relationship: _____
Dates of Residence: From: _____ To: _____

## Sample Declaration Under the Uniform Child Custody Jurisdiction Act

Child's Name: _____ Sex: _____ Date of Birth: _____

Place of Birth: _____ Social Security Number: _____

Present Residence: _____

Person Child Lives With: _____ Relationship: _____

Dates of Residence: From: _____ To: Present

Previous Residence: _____

Person Child Lived With: _____ Relationship: _____

Dates of Residence: From: _____ To: _____

2. Neither party has participated as a party, witness or any other capacity in any other court decision, order, or custody proceeding in this state or any other state, concerning the custody of a child subject to this proceeding.

3. Neither party has any information concerning any other court decision, order, or custody proceeding in this state or any other state, concerning the custody of a child subject to this proceeding.

4. Neither party knows of any other person who is not already a party to this proceeding who has physical custody of, or who claims to have custody or visitation rights with, any child subject to this proceeding.

Sample Declaration Under the Uniform Child Custody Jurisdiction Act

Dated this  20th  day of      May      ,  1992   (year).

__*Jane Public*__
Wife's Signature

Address:  1300 Somewhere St

  Anytown, SomeState 00001

Phone:    (123)456-7890

State of     SomeState       )
County of    SomeCounty      )

On  May 20, 1992,  before me,       Nick Notary       , personally appeared     Jane Public     , personally known to me (or proved to me on the basis of satisfactory evidence) to be the person(s) whose name(s) is/are subscribed to the within instrument and acknowledged to me that he/she/they executed the same in his/her/their authorized capacity(ies), and that by his/her/their signature(s) on the instrument the person(s), or the entity upon behalf of which the person(s) acted, executed the instrument.
WITNESS my hand and official seal.

Signature  *Nick Notary*          Affiant   √  Known    ___ Produced ID
     Signature of Notary          Type of ID _____
                                                              (Seal)

## Sample Declaration Under the Uniform Child Custody Jurisdiction Act

___*Richard Public*___
Husband's Signature

Address: __200 Elsewhere Ave__

__Somewhere, SomeState 00002__

Phone: __(987) 654-3210__

State of __SomeState__ )
County of __SomeCounty__ )

On __May 20, 1992__, before me, __Nick Notary__, personally appeared __Richard Public__, personally known to me (or proved to me on the basis of satisfactory evidence) to be the person(s) whose name(s) is/are subscribed to the within instrument and acknowledged to me that he/she/they executed the same in his/her/their authorized capacity(ies), and that by his/her/their signature(s) on the instrument the person(s), or the entity upon behalf of which the person(s) acted, executed the instrument.
WITNESS my hand and official seal.

Signature __*Nick Notary*__
Signature of Notary

Affiant  √ Known  ___ Produced ID
Type of ID _____
(Seal)

# Notice of Hearing

When the date of your court hearing is set, some states require that both parties receive official notification of the time, date and place of the hearing. This can be accomplished by mailing your spouse a Notice of Hearing. A Notice of Hearing with your original signature should be submitted to the Court. A copy can be sent to your spouse, and you should retain a copy for your records.

A sample Notice of Hearing follows.

Sample Notice of Hearing

In the ___Circuit___ Court for __SomeCounty__ County, State of __SomeState__

In re: The Marriage of: )

Jane Public )

Petitioner )

)

and ) Case No: [Given by Court Clerk]

Richard Public )

Respondent )

and in the interest of: )

Carl Public )

)

**NOTICE OF HEARING**

TO: Richard Public
200 Elsewhere Ave
Somewhere, SomeState 00002

You are hereby notified that a hearing has been scheduled in this cause as indicated below. In the absence or disqualification of the Judge, this cause will be brought on for hearing before another Judge who is available and qualified to act thereon.

Date: ___June 25, 1992___ Time: ___9 a.m.___

Judge: The Honorable ___Henry Honor___

Place: Room ___222,___ ___SomeCounty___ County Courthouse

Address: ___1500 Justice Ave___

___Somewhere, SomeState 00002___

Matter: ___Jane Public's Petition for Dissolution of Marriage___

I hereby certify that on ___June 1, 1992___ a true and correct copy of this Notice of Hearing was furnished by mail to the parties indicated above.

___Jane Public___
Plaintiff

Chapter 6

# Final divorce judgment or decree

Once the court decides you qualify for divorce, the judge will sign the document most often called *Decree of Divorce, Judgment of Divorce,* or *Decree of Dissolution of Marriage*. Each state has a specific title for the final divorce papers, and it is this document that formalizes the divorce.

 Prepare this document carefully. It must coincide with what you and your spouse have agreed to in your Marital Settlement Agreement as well as what you requested from the court in your Petition/Complaint.

You will need this document at your court hearing, as it is then that the judge usually signs it. Of course, if the judge changes terms (such as custody or child support) he or she may alter your documents with these changes or ask you to prepare new documents reflecting these changes.

A sample Final Judgment/Decree of Divorce follows.

## Sample Judgment of Divorce

In the _Circuit_ Court for _SomeCounty_ County, State of _SomeState_

In re: The Marriage of:　　　　　　　　　　)

　　Jane Public　　　　　　　　　　　　　　)

　　Petitioner　　　　　　　　　　　　　　)

　　　　　　　　　　　　　　　　　　　　　)

　　and　　　　　　　　　　　　　　　　　　)　　Case No:　　[Given by Court Clerk]

　　Richard Public　　　　　　　　　　　　)

　　Respondent　　　　　　　　　　　　　　)

　　and in the interest of:　　　　　　　)

　　Carl Public　　　　　　　　　　　　　　)

_Judgment of Divorce_

This Cause came to be heard on _petitioner's petition for Dissolution of marriage_ on _June 25_, _1992_ (year), and the Court hearing testimony in support of the _petition for Dissolution of marriage_.

THE COURT FINDS:

1.　That the Court has jurisdiction of the parties and subject matter of this cause.

2.　That the parties have voluntarily waived findings of fact, conclusions of law, a record of testimony, motion for a new trial, notice of entry of final judgment, and right of appeal, but have not waived their rights to future modification of this judgment.

IT IS ORDERED AND ADJUDGED:

1.　That the marriage of the _Petitioner_ and _Respondent_ is hereby dissolved.

## Sample Judgment of Divorce

2. The separation agreement between the parties, filed in this proceeding as Exhibit A, was executed voluntarily after full disclosure, and is in the best interests of the parties, and is approved and incorporated in this judgment by reference and the parties are ordered to comply with it.

3. That the ___husband___ shall pay $__150__ per _week_ beginning ___July 1___, __1992__ (year), to ___wife___ as alimony and shall terminate: January 1, 1993.

4. That the ___husband___ shall pay $__200__ per _week_ beginning ___July 1___, __1992__ (year), to ___wife___ as child support per child, said support shall terminate for each child when the child reaches 18 years of age, becomes self-supporting, marries or dies, whichever comes first.

5. ___Jane Public's___ former name is restored and shall be known as ___Jane Single___ hereafter.

*Henry Honor*
_____
Judge

# Certificate of Corroborating Witness

Some states require a Certificate of Corroborating Witness. In some instances this must be filed with the Divorce Petition, and in others it may be presented to the judge when he or she awards the divorce. You should check with the clerk on this. The role of the corroborating witness is to affirm under oath that you, in fact, resided within the state sufficiently long enough to qualify for a divorce in that state.

A sample Certificate of Corroborating Witness follows.

Sample Certificate of Corroborating Witness

In the <u>Circuit</u> Court for <u>SomeCounty</u> County, State of <u>SomeState</u>

In re: The Marriage of:  )
    Jane Public  )
    Petitioner  )
and  )  Case No:
    Richard Public  )
    Respondent  )  [Given by Court Clerk]
and in the interest of:  )
    Carl Public  )

**CERTIFICATE OF CORROBORATING WITNESS**

UNDER PENALTY OF PERJURY I CERTIFY that I am a resident of the State of <u>SomeState</u>; I have known <u>Jane Public</u> for more than <u>7 years</u> preceding the date of the filing of the above cause on <u>May 20, 1992</u> and I know of my own personal knowledge that such person has resided in the State of <u>SomeState</u> for at least that period of time.

## Sample Certificate of Corroborating Witness

_____*Wilma Witness*_____          _____123 Place St_____
Witness' Signature

_____Wilma Witness_____          _____Anytown, SomeState 00001_____
Witness' Name Typed                    Witness' Residence Address

State of ____SomeState____ )

County of ____SomeCounty____ )

On __May 20, 1992__, before me, _____Nick Notary_____, personally appeared _____Wilma Witness_____, personally known to me (or proved to me on the basis of satisfactory evidence) to be the person(s) whose name(s) is/are subscribed to the within instrument and acknowledged to me that he/she/they executed the same in his/her/their authorized capacity(ies), and that by his/her/their signature(s) on the instrument the person(s), or the entity upon behalf of which the person(s) acted, executed the instrument.
WITNESS my hand and official seal.

Signature __*Nick Notary*__          Affiant __✓__ Known   ____ Produced ID
          Signature of Notary

                                       Type of ID _____
                                                                    (Seal)

**IF A NONLAWYER HELPED YOU FILL OUT THIS FORM THEY MUST FILL IN THE BLANKS BELOW** (fill in **all** blanks):
I (*name of nonlawyer*) ____Joe Friend____, nonlawyer located at (*street*) 20 Main Street (*city*)____AnyCity____ (*state*) ____AnyState__, (*phone*) ____666-5555____ helped (*name*) __Wilma Witness__ who is the [✓ **one** only] __petitioner or __respondent, fill out this form.

# Certificate of Divorce or Marriage Dissolution

Most states require this document when a final divorce is granted. The specific form used in your state will normally be available from the clerk of the divorce court, and because it is state specific, it is not included in this guide.

# Your day in court

# Chapter 7
## Your day in court

### What you'll find in this chapter:
- Preparing for your court appearance
- Witnesses and hearings
- Documents you will need
- Tips for a smooth day in court
- How to handle difficulties in court

Appearing in court to obtain your divorce may be the most stressful part of the entire divorce process. This is natural. You are unfamiliar with court proceedings, and the courtroom atmosphere can be imposing.

In actuality there is little to fear. If you are unrepresented, the judge will take this into account and assist you through the procedure.

Procedures do, of course, vary from state to state and often from county to county. Most states follow simplified divorce procedures to relieve the caseload and because there are so many no-fault "do-it-yourself" divorces today. Some states have even eliminated court appearances in uncontested cases; others delegate the hearing to a court clerk or special hearing officer. In any case, your uncontested divorce should take no more than a few minutes and will require you only to answer a few questions honestly.

Here are some steps you can take to prepare for your day in court:

1) ***Schedule the hearing date.*** Some courts automatically set the hearing date, but in most others you must formally request a hearing. The court clerk can advise you on the exact procedure to follow in your state.

2) ***Check on any witnesses.*** Witnesses may be required to testify concerning your residency in the state, or that the defendant has been served the divorce papers. You should check witness requirements with the court clerk.

It is also wise to have the court clerk review the file to make certain all necessary papers are on file for the judge.

3) ***Attend several other uncontested divorce hearings before the day of your hearing.*** Write down the questions that are asked and the documents the court asks to see. Once you observe the process you will know what you can expect and can better prepare. You will also be more confident and less anxious.

4) ***Bring all documents to court.*** Unless it is already filed with the court, this will include:

- Marital Settlement Agreement

- Verified Petition or Complaint

- Answer and Affidavit in Support of Final Judgment

- Financial Affidavits

- Notice of Hearing

- Child Custody Jurisdiction Form

- Final Judgment or Final Decree

- Certificate of Corroborating Witness

Again, it is a good idea to review with the clerk any special documents the court is likely to want. Also bring copies of all documents previously filed with the court.

5) ***Arrive early on the hearing date.*** This will give you the opportunity to observe several additional hearings. Also, you will need to check in with the clerk in advance of the hearing.

6) ***Be respectful.*** Make certain your courtroom behavior is deferential and courteous. Dress appropriately. Avoid arguments or hostility with your spouse. Address the judge as "Your Honor." Carefully listen to the judge's questions and then answer firmly but in a respectful manner. Most of these questions will simply attempt to corroborate the truthfulness of the statements made in the various documents.

> **note** Questioning may become more vigorous if you have children. The court is most concerned that your children's welfare is protected. Understandably, courts are less concerned about your property once you and your spouse have reached agreement on its division.

7) ***Know how to handle difficulties.*** Things can go wrong in any court hearing. If you don't understand the judge, politely ask the judge to restate the question. If matters go very wrong or you find yourself in a situation you cannot handle, then simply ask the court for a continuance so you can better prepare the case for presentation. Possibly the judge will see you in chambers if a

continued courtroom hearing is embarrassing or perplexing you. In any case, try to find out precisely what the problem is so you can correct it. Did you overlook a procedural step? Are you missing an essential document? Must one or more of your documents be re-drafted? And if so, in what manner? The point is to leave the courtroom with confidence that you can correct the problem and gain your divorce at the continued hearing.

**note:** Very often judges will want changes made in the agreement or final divorce decree. If these changes are minor, the court may accept handwritten modifications made in the courtroom. More substantive changes will require re-draft and presentation again to the judge. This should be re-scheduled as quickly as possible.

# Getting on with your life

# Chapter 8
## Getting on with your life

---

**What you'll find in this chapter:**
- The post-divorce checklist
- Protecting both parties' rights
- Problems with child support
- Child support and bankruptcy
- What to do when you re-marry

---

Your divorce decree makes you a single person once again, and you are free to live your own life free of interference from your spouse except for those obligations in your divorce agreement or court decree. Several states require you to wait a period of time before you can marry again. This gives you the opportunity to nullify the divorce should you and your ex-spouse desire to get together again and continue the marriage.

## Post-divorce checklist

Once divorced, there are some basic steps you and your spouse must take so you can separate as cleanly as possible financially and legally:

1) *Obtain from the court certified copies of your final divorce decree.* You'll need this to transfer property, divide bank accounts, etc.

2) *Exchange personal and household property* as soon as possible after the divorce. Electronics, jewelry, art, furniture, etc. that are due you may otherwise disappear no matter what your agreement says.

3) *Close any remaining joint checking accounts and savings accounts.* But first verify balances and insist upon bank checks so you are certain the check representing your share is, in fact, a good check.

4) *Joint credit accounts should be formally closed.* However, this action should have been taken earlier, when you first decided upon the divorce. Estimate and pro-rate utility bills if you don't have a final balance. Destroy all joint charge cards or return them to the issuing company. Also notify them that you no longer have responsibility for your ex-spouse's debts. Finally, establish a new account solely in your name, and with a change of address, if applicable.

5) *Similarly, notify lenders owed joint loans.* If your spouse is responsible for paying the entire loan under the divorce agreement, then request a release from the obligation. This is generally not granted unless the lender is comfortable with the collateral or your spouse's creditworthiness alone. If you do remain bound on the loan, and your spouse indemnified you for losses under the loan, then ask the lender for immediate notice should your spouse default in payments. You can then take timely legal action against your spouse, as well as intervene with the lender, before the lender looks to your assets for satisfaction of the debt.

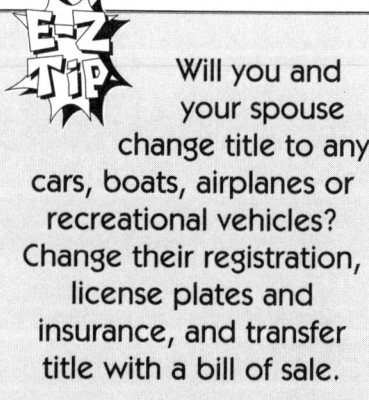

E-Z TIP: Will you and your spouse change title to any cars, boats, airplanes or recreational vehicles? Change their registration, license plates and insurance, and transfer title with a bill of sale.

# Chapter 8

6) *Review your insurance policies.* Direct changes of beneficiary to your insurance company or to the agent who administers your policies. Review all policies, including accident and health, disability, homeowners, and insurance on children.

7) *If real estate is to change hands*, you'll need your attorney to convey the property. If the real estate has a mortgage against it, you may need to notify the mortgage holder. But if the property is simply being transferred mortgage-free from you and your spouse as joint owners to one of you singly, no consent by the lender is normally required.

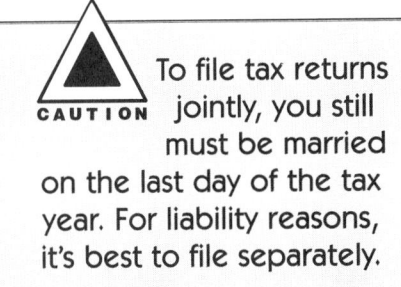
To file tax returns jointly, you still must be married on the last day of the tax year. For liability reasons, it's best to file separately.

8) *Decide on joint or separate tax returns.* Will you and your spouse file a joint tax return for the year or will you file separately? If you do file jointly, decide beforehand who will pay the taxes due or be entitled to the refund.

9) *Check what needs to be done with your last will and testament.* Some states automatically revoke wills upon divorce, others only upon remarriage, and in still other states neither divorce nor remarriage have an affect upon a prior will. It's safest to prepare a new will. Preparing your own will is not difficult. *Last Wills Made E-Z* is ideal for that purpose.

## Protecting both parties' rights

No matter how smoothly your divorce proceeds, a number of legal problems can arise after the divorce. This is particularly true when children are involved or there are alimony obligations.

# Child support problems

One of the most common problems is that the non-custodial parent (usually the father) fails or refuses to pay child support as ordered in the divorce decree. What, then, are the rights of the ex-spouse to collect?

There are many ways for an ex-spouse, or even a state, to compel payments for child support. The number of remedies for non-payment have substantially increased in recent years as the states have attempted to shift the burden of support from taxpayers to the non-custodial parent. This is almost always the father, who may, for a variety of reasons, have stopped support. The five most prevalent ways of enforcing support include:

1) **Levy of income tax refunds.** If you are in arrears and your ex-spouse collects welfare, he or she can request the state prosecutor charged with enforcing child support payments to notify the IRS and issue an "intercept" on any refunds due you. You would receive a notice of the intercept, and you do have the opportunity to challenge it, but you will be successful only if you can establish you don't owe the amount claimed. Other reasons for non-payment are not considered, no matter how compelling they may be.

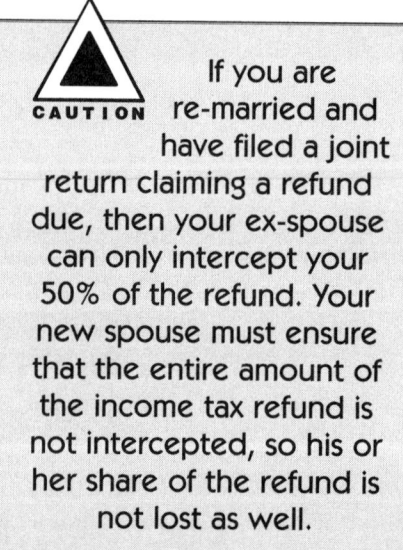

CAUTION: If you are re-married and have filed a joint return claiming a refund due, then your ex-spouse can only intercept your 50% of the refund. Your new spouse must ensure that the entire amount of the income tax refund is not intercepted, so his or her share of the refund is not lost as well.

2) **Posting bond to ensure payment.** Courts in certain states require parents under a support order default to guarantee future payments by posting bond. This may, for example, take the form of a pledge of stocks or bonds, or even delivery in escrow of a deed to real estate.

3) **Property liens.** Property liens can be placed on real or personal property of an ex-spouse who has fallen behind on child support payments. The custodial parent can then foreclose on the lien to collect the arrears.

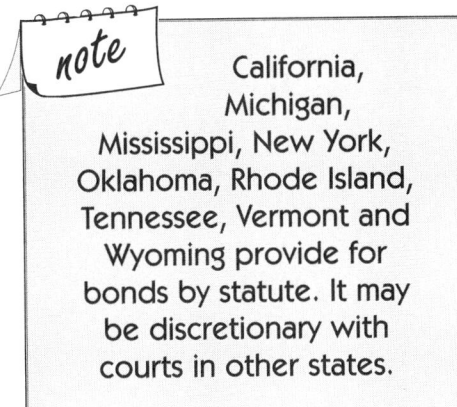

note: California, Michigan, Mississippi, New York, Oklahoma, Rhode Island, Tennessee, Vermont and Wyoming provide for bonds by statute. It may be discretionary with courts in other states.

Most states require that the past due support be reduced to a court judgment before the lien can be imposed. In any case, you will have ample opportunity to defend yourself and explain why support payments have not been made.

4) **Contempt of court proceedings.** Since child support orders are court orders, failure to support technically constitutes contempt of court. Your ex-spouse can petition the court to schedule a contempt hearing, at which time you would be given the opportunity to explain why payments had not been made and why you should not be held in contempt.

Unless you offer a reasonable explanation for non-payment, the court can find you in contempt. You may then be jailed, and/or fined. As a practical matter, the court's objective is to throw its weight behind the child support obligation so that the errant parent will choose to pay rather than incur criminal sanctions.

5) **Wage garnishment.** A child support judgment is enforced the same way as are other judgments. One popular method is *wage garnishment*. The court authorizes garnishment once a judgment is issued. The sheriff serves this upon your employer, who must then send a portion of your net wages each payroll period to satisfy the judgment.

**note:** An important point: In most states a creditor garnishment cannot attach more than 25 percent of your net wages. This is not true of child support garnishments. Courts can set the garnishment for any amount, and frequently compel garnishment for 50 percent or more of the paycheck.

If you cannot satisfy the judgment from a wage garnishment, your spouse may attach and sell any other property you have in the same manner as can any other judgment creditor. Seizure of a car, boat, savings or checking account, or even your home or business interests are all possibilities.

In addition to the more direct path to your assets to enforce child support, your ex-spouse can also indirectly pressure you for payments in four lesser-known ways:

1) *Reporting you to the credit bureau.* Did you know your ex-spouse can ruin your credit if you fall behind on your support payments? If you owe $1,000 or more in child support, the support enforcement agencies must report it to the credit bureaus in accordance with the Child Support Enforcement Amendments of 1984. But the credit bureau can reflect your default on child support even if you owe less than $1,000 if it is reported by anyone, including your ex-spouse.

2) *"Most Wanted" lists.* A recent and even more embarrassing tactic is for certain states to publish in newspapers the names of parents who have defaulted on their child support payments.

**note:** Delaware, Florida, Virginia, Maryland and Pennsylvania are five states that publish the names of parents who have defaulted on their child support payments.

Other states are strongly considering this procedure as the child support default rate continues to climb. While the other states simply use newspapers to list the defaulting fathers, Pennsylvania also publicizes them on cable TV. Controversial as it is, the strategy nevertheless encourages many more fathers to pay child support after all other efforts fail.

3) *Criminal prosecution.* Your ex-spouse may seek criminal prosecution, or a district attorney may independently commence criminal proceedings if you default on child support. This seldom happens unless your default is continual and flagrant. Criminal prosecution results in court-ordered support restitution, plus possible fines, court costs and even incarceration, particularly if you are a chronic repeater.

4) *Automatic wage withholding.* Wage withholding occurs when your ex-spouse, or the court, forwards the child support order to your employer. Thereafter, with each payroll, your employer must withhold for your ex-spouse the proper amount from your paycheck. If you are not a wage-earner but still have regular income from Social Security, pensions, unemployment compensation or annuities, the court can direct the withholding order to your source of funds. An alternative: If you and your ex-spouse agree, payments can be made through a third-party escrow that you both select as intermediary. In Arizona, Kansas and Idaho, payments must go through the court clerks.

> **note** The automatic wage withholding program, under the federal Family Support Act of 1988, now applies if your ex-spouse is collecting Aid to Dependent Children. Each state was required to include automatic wage withholding procedures in all new or modified child support orders by 1994.

# Child support and bankruptcy

Child support and alimony obligations cannot be discharged in either Chapter 7 or Chapter 13 bankruptcy. Chapter 13, however, can protect you from collection efforts on past due alimony or child support. Under a Chapter 13, you can arrange to pay arrears over a three-to-five-year period as part of your repayment plan. Your ex-spouse cannot coerce faster collection during this period. She would have the right, however, to proceed against you for late support or alimony payments due after you file Chapter 13.

There are three exceptions to the rule that bankruptcy—whether a Chapter 7 or Chapter 13—does not discharge child support or alimony obligations:

1) ***Support between unmarried persons.*** If there's merely an agreement to provide for support, but no court order, the obligation is dischargeable in bankruptcy as between parties who never married.

2) ***Support assigned to a third party.*** If your ex-spouse assigns and transfers her right to receive income support to a third party, that obligation is no longer enforceable in a bankruptcy. There is one exception: Support payments assigned to a state welfare agency are not discharged.

3) ***Support payments not pursuant to a court order.*** Support and alimony are dischargeable unless there is actually a court order in effect. Stated another way, only court-ordered support and alimony obligations are not dischargeable.

# Visitation rights

Divorce never completely ends the relationship between spouses with children. Just as the non-custodial parent typically has the obligation to pay child support, the non-custodial parent also has the right to reasonable visitation with his or her children. And, just as child support may not be honored by the non-custodial parent, visitation may be denied or frustrated by the custodial parent.

Should one ex-spouse deny visitation to the other in violation of the court decree, the ex-spouse in violation of the court decree can be held in contempt and the court can even order the suspension of support until visitation is duly restored.

> **note:** The custodial parent cannot deny visitation simply because he or she is upset or even because the ex-spouse failed to make child support payments

The Child's Bill of Rights, observed in most states, reminds parents that their children also have certain rights in a divorce—and one of these rights is the opportunity to maintain as close a relationship as possible with each parent.

# When you marry again

You may eventually re-marry. Most divorced people do. You can avoid considerable grief should that marriage fail if you resolve certain matters before you marry. You achieve this with a pre-marriage (pre-nuptial or antenuptial) agreement.

Pre-marriage agreements are popular because they so effectively resolve the many complex issues not easily reconciled by divorce courts. Here's an example: One spouse has accumulated substantial assets before marriage and has children targeted to inherit the wealth. A pre-marriage agreement can make this wish secure. A pre-marriage agreement can also guarantee a spouse a pre-determined amount of money or property upon separation, divorce or death. Both parties can then be confident their respective needs will be met should the marriage end.

> **note** You may think of pre-marriage agreements only in connection with the wealthy or famous. But people of ordinary means increasingly find pre-marriage agreements an efficient and equitable way to settle matters should they later divorce.

Pre-marriage agreements are particularly helpful to spouses who are both wealthy and need not rely upon each other for financial support. These couples often marry for companionship. If one or both spouses has significant wealth, or has children from a prior marriage, a pre-marriage agreement is vital. Here, the couple may agree to share assets accumulated during the marriage, but keep separate and apart those assets accumulated prior to the marriage.

There are, of course, many other situations where a pre-marriage agreement is advisable. Example: A couple in an interfaith marriage may want a clear understanding beforehand concerning the religion to be followed in the upbringing of their children. Contemplating marriage? Consider the many ways a pre-marriage agreement can help you:

- ***Avoids hostility.*** Divorces are usually hostile because spouses fight over property and their children at the worst possible time—when angry emotions are at their peak. A pre-marriage agreement allows you to resolve these matters in advance, when both parties are friendly, rational and obliging. With a comprehensive pre-marriage agreement, the dissolution of your marriage involves little more than filing the necessary papers in court. Costly, time consuming and emotionally turbulent legal battles are avoided.

# Chapter 8

- ***Promotes fairness.*** You can't always rely upon the divorce courts to divide your property equitably. Courts are often unfair because they don't always hear all the relevant facts. Nevertheless, without a pre-marriage agreement the court decides how your property is to be divided. The judgment of a court is necessarily substituted for what the parties themselves may have considered equitable and fair. Seldom are both parties satisfied with a court decree.

- ***Saves money.*** Contested divorces are costly. A couple with modest assets may easily pay their attorneys many thousands of dollars to do battle for them. Lawyers often end up with one-third of the family assets, or even more. This costly conflict is avoided with a pre-marriage agreement. Your attorney need only file the appropriate divorce papers in court and obtain court confirmation of your pre-marriage agreement so it becomes a part of your divorce decree.

- ***Speeds up the divorce.*** A contested divorce is nearly always a long, drawn out matter. In many states a two or three year wait for a divorce is not unusual. This delay is because the court must decide disputes that could have been effectively resolved before marriage through a pre-marriage agreement.

> **E-Z TIP:** A couple planning marriage would be wise to discuss how large a family, if any, each envisions. Do they anticipate pursuing lifelong careers, or does one want to stay home and raise a family or follow other pursuits? If so, which one? An agreement brings these issues to the forefront.

- ***Aids planning.*** Perhaps the greatest value of a pre-marriage agreement is that it encourages both parties to consider what they really desire from the marriage. The agreement has you express what you want from the relationship, both in terms of what you expect to give and what you expect in return from your partner. Remember: If you cannot agree on such basic issues before you marry, it's unlikely you'll reach an amicable agreement afterward.

Seriously consider these important benefits of a pre-marriage agreement. You'll better appreciate why a pre-marriage agreement is one of your most important asset protection documents.

# The forms in this guide

Marital Settlement Agreement ......................................................123

Financial Affidavit ...........................................................................131

Verified Complaint or Petition .....................................................134

Answer and Affidavit in Support of Final Judgment....................138

Notice of Hearing...........................................................................141

Declaration Under the Uniform Child Custody Jurisdiction Act..142

Decree of Divorce* ........................................................................146

Certificate of Corroborating Witness............................................148

*This form is most often titled *Decree of Divorce*. It may also be titled *Final Decree of Divorce, Final Judgment of Divorce, Decree of Dissolution of Marriage,* or something similar. See the Appendix of divorce laws by state in this guide for the exact wording required by your state.

About These E-Z Legal Forms:
While the legal forms and documents in this product generally conform to the requirements of courts nationwide, certain courts may have additional requirements. Before completing and filing the forms in this product, check with the clerk of the court concerning these requirements.

# NOTICE

This product is sold for informational purposes only. The forms included are samples of divorce forms commonly used by courts throughout the nation. State-specific forms may be required but are not supplied by this kit nor are they available from E-Z Legal. The purchaser of this product is responsible for obtaining any additional or modified documents necessary to pursue his/her own divorce as is required by local courts. Please check with the clerk of the Divorce court concerning specific forms required in your area.

*NOTE: Some states provide assistance in obtaining supplemental forms and more are likely to do so in the future. Call the Clerk of your Court to find out if the court will assist you in obtaining additional documents.*

# MARITAL SETTLEMENT AGREEMENT

THIS AGREEMENT made and entered into this _____ day of _____, _____(year), between _____ (Wife) residing at _____ and _____ (Husband) residing at _____.

WHEREAS, Husband and Wife were married to each other on _____, _____(year) at _____, _____.
                                                                (City)                (State)

WHEREAS, a permanent breakdown of the marriage has arisen between us and we are now living separate and apart from each other; and

[Use if there are children involved.]

WHEREAS, children were born into our marriage as follows:

| Child's Name | Child's Birth Date | Child's Sex |
|---|---|---|
| _____ | _____ | _____ |
| _____ | _____ | _____ |
| _____ | _____ | _____ |

(hereinafter "children") and it is the further purpose of this Agreement to provide for the future custody, control and support of the said children, and

WHEREAS, it is the desire and intentions of the parties to settle by agreement all of their marital affairs with respect to property, financial matters, [spousal support or maintenance (use if applicable)] [and all issues relating to their children, including custody, visitation, and child support (use if applicable)].

NOW, THEREFORE, in consideration of the premises and the mutual promises and undertakings herein contained, and for other good and valuable consideration, the parties agree to the following:

I.  SEPARATION:

The parties agree to permanently live separate and apart from the other party, free from any control, restraint, or interference, direct or indirect, by the other party, and in all respects to live as if he or she were sole and unmarried.

II.  DIVISION OF PROPERTY:

1.  Husband transfers to Wife as her sole and separate property the following:

2.  Wife transfers to Husband as his sole and separate property the following:

III. DIVISION OF DEBTS:

1. Husband shall pay the following debts and will not at any time hold Wife responsible for them, and shall indemnify Wife from any liability on same:

2. Wife shall pay the following debts and will not at any time hold Husband responsible for them, and shall indemnify Husband from any liability on same:

IV. ALIMONY - [Choose one of the following]:

1. Both parties hereby agree to waive any rights or claims that either may now have or in the future to receive alimony, maintenance, or spousal support from each other. Both parties understand the full import of this provision.

2. Monthly payments - The _____ shall pay to _____ for his/her support and maintenance the sum of $_____ per month/week. This sum shall be payable on the _____ day of each and every _____, commencing on _____, _____(year). Said sum will continue until [choose any or all of the following]: (a) the date that either party dies; (b) the date that the receiving spouse remarries; or (c) any other specific date that both of you agree on. Both parties intend that the amount and duration of the payments _____ (may or may not) be modified by a court in the future.

3. Lump sum payment - The parties hereby agree that in full payment of any claims or rights to alimony, spousal support, or maintenance the _____ shall pay to _____ the sum of $_____, which shall be payable on _____, _____(year).

V.   CHILD CUSTODY AND VISITATION - [Choose one of the following]:

1.   The parties agree that it is in the best interest of the child(ren) that the _____ have sole physical and legal custody of the child(ren). We further agree that the custodial parent will make the major decisions regarding the care and upbringing of said child(ren). However, the other parent has the right to be notified of any major decisions. The parties also agree to share in an equitable fashion the child(ren)'s birthday, holidays, and all vacations. Furthermore, the parties agree to allow the other parent to have a frequent and liberal visitation with the child(ren).

[Optional] - If the parties cannot agree on future visitation, then the _____ will have the right to be with the child(ren) as follows: (Draft a schedule i.e., vacation periods which the child(ren) will spend with the non-custodial parent.)

2.   The Husband and Wife shall share joint legal custody for the minor child(ren). Both parents shall retain full parental rights and responsibilities. Both parents shall confer with one another so that major decisions affecting the best interests and welfare of the child(ren) may be determined jointly, where reasonably possible. We further agree that _____ shall have sole physical custody of the child(ren).

Each party shall have full access to the child(ren)'s medical, dental, or school records. The parties shall consult with one another with regards to all medical and educational matters including religious education and training.

The parties also agree to share in an equitable fashion the child(ren)'s birthday, holidays and all vacations. Furthermore, the parties agree to allow the other parent to have a frequent and liberal visitation with the child(ren). The non-custodial parent will have the right to be with the child(ren) at least, but not limited to, as follows: (Note: make a detailed schedule).

VI.   CHILD SUPPORT

Subject to the power of the court to modify these terms, _____ shall pay to _____ as and for child support, the sum of $_____ per month/week. This sum shall be payable on the first day of each and every _____, commencing on _____, _____(year). Said sum shall continue until the child(ren) shall have married, died, become self-supporting, or reach the age of eighteen (or, if in Alabama, nineteen). [Furthermore, if the parent obligated to pay said support receives an increase in salary or income in the future, the amount of child support shall increase proportionately.] Said sum shall be reduced by $_____ (or shall be reduced proportionately) for each child to reach the age of eighteen (or, if in Alabama, nineteen) or otherwise emancipated.

The parties agree that the _____ will carry and maintain life insurance naming the child(ren) as irrevocable beneficiary(ies). Said life insurance is in the amount of $_____.

Furthermore, it is agreed that _____ will carry and maintain adequate health, dental, and hospitalization insurance for the child(ren)'s benefit. The _____ shall each year transmit to the _____ evidence of payment showing that such dues, premiums and assessments have been paid.

VII. NECESSARY DOCUMENTS

The parties agree to execute and deliver to the other party any documents that may be reasonably required to accomplish the intention of this instrument and shall do all other necessary things to this end.

VIII. INCOME TAX:

For the year _____ the parties hereto shall file separate income tax returns. Each party hereto shall receive the refund or pay additional taxes based on his or her separate income.

[Or] The parties agree to file a joint income tax return for the year _____. In the event that there is a credit of any tax payment the _____ shall pay the _____ (1/2, 1/3) of any tax payments.

[Use if child(ren) are involved.] The parties agree that the _____ may claim the federal dependency tax exemption for the child(ren).

IX. SUBSEQUENT DISSOLUTION OF MARRIAGE:

It is agreed that this Agreement may be offered into evidence by either party in any dissolution of marriage proceeding, and if acceptable to the Court, this Agreement shall be incorporated by reference in any Final Judgment that may be rendered. However, notwithstanding incorporation in the Final Judgment, this Agreement shall not be merged in it but shall survive the Final Judgment and be binding on the parties for all times.

X. REPRESENTATION:

The parties represent to each other:

(a) Each had the right to independent counsel. Each party fully understands their legal rights and each is signing this Agreement freely and voluntarily, intending to be bound by it.

(b) Each has made a full disclosure to the other of his or her current financial condition.

(c) Each understands and agrees that this Agreement is intended to be the full and entire contract of the parties.

(d) Each agrees that this Agreement and each provision of it is expressly made binding upon the heirs, assigns, executors, administrators, successors in interest and representatives of each party.

XI. CHANGE OF NAME:

The parties agree that the Wife may have her name changed or restored to: _____.

XII. WAIVER OF BREACH:

No waiver of any breach by any party of the terms of this Agreement shall be deemed a waiver of any subsequent breach.

XIII. ENFORCEMENT OF AGREEMENT:

Both parties agree that the Court granting the divorce, at the request of either party, insert in the Final Judgment a reservation of jurisdiction for the purpose of compelling either party to perform this Agreement, or any part thereof. The prevailing party shall be entitled to attorney's fees in connection with such proceedings.

XIV. GOVERNING LAW:

This Agreement shall be interpreted and governed by the laws of the State of _____ _____.

Signed in the presence of:

_____          _____
                                                                          Wife's Signature

_____
Witnesses for Wife

State of _____ )
County of _____ )

On _____ before me, _____, personally appeared _____ and _____, personally known to me (or proved to me on the basis of satisfactory evidence) to be the person(s) whose name(s) is/are subscribed to the within instrument and acknowledged to me that
he/she/they executed the same in his/her/their authorized capacity(ies), and that by his/her/their signature(s) on the instrument the person(s), or the entity upon behalf of which the person(s) acted, executed the instrument.
WITNESS my hand and official seal.

Signature_____          Affiant _____ Known      _____ Produced ID
                Signature of Notary                              Type of ID _____

Signed in the presence of:

_____          _____
                                          Husband's Signature

_____
Witnesses for Husband


State of _____ )
County of _____ )

On _____ before me, _____, personally appeared _____ and _____, personally known to me (or proved to me on the basis of satisfactory evidence) to be the person(s) whose name(s) is/are subscribed to the within instrument and acknowledged to me that
he/she/they executed the same in his/her/their authorized capacity(ies), and that by his/her/their signature(s) on the instrument the person(s), or the entity upon behalf of which the person(s) acted, executed the instrument.

WITNESS my hand and official seal.

Signature_____     Affiant _____ Known      _____Produced ID
         Signature of Notary                 Type of ID _____
                                                                        (Seal)


**IF A NONLAWYER HELPED YOU FILL OUT THIS FORM THEY MUST FILL IN THE BLANKS BELOW** (fill in **all** blanks):

I (*name of nonlawyer*) _____, nonlawyer located at (*street*) _____ (*city*)_____ (*state*) _____, (*phone*) _____ helped (*name*) _____ who is the [✔ **one** only] __petitioner **or** __respondent, fill out this form.

# FINANCIAL AFFIDAVIT

State of _____ )

County of _____ )

On _____ before me, _____, personally appeared _____, personally known to me (or proved to me on the basis of satisfactory evidence) to be the person(s) whose name(s) is/are subscribed to the within instrument and acknowledged to me that he/she/they executed the same in his/her/their authorized capacity(ies), and that by his/her/their signature(s) on the instrument the person(s), or the entity upon behalf of which the person(s) acted, executed the instrument and was sworn and says that the following statement of affiant's income, assets and liabilities is true:

Occupation _____

Employed By _____

Business Address _____

Pay Period _____

Rate of Pay _____

Social Security # _____

ITEM 1: INCOME (Averaged on _____ basis):

  Average GROSS Wage                                        $_____

    Less Deductions

      Federal Income Tax              $_____

| | | |
|---|---|---|
| Social Security | $_____ | |
| Other | $_____ | |
| Total Deductions | $_____ | |
| Minus Total Deductions | | $_____ |
| Average NET Wage | | $_____ |
| Plus Other Income | | |
| _____ | | $_____ |
| _____ | | $_____ |
| TOTAL NET INCOME | | $_____ |

ITEM 2: ASSETS (Ownership: If joint, allocate equally):

| | |
|---|---|
| Cash on hand or in banks | $_____ |
| Stocks, bonds, notes | $_____ |
| Real estate | |
|    Home | $_____ |
|    Other | $_____ |
| Automobiles | $_____ |
| Other personal property | $_____ |
| Other assets _____ | $_____ |
| TOTAL ASSETS | $_____ |

ITEM 3: LIABILITIES

| Creditor | Balance Due | Monthly Payments |
|---|---|---|
| _____ | $_____ | $_____ |
| _____ | $_____ | $_____ |
| _____ | $_____ | $_____ |
| TOTAL LIABILITIES | | $_____ |

ITEM 4: AVERAGE MONTHLY EXPENSES

    Household:

        Mortgage or rent payments     $_____

        Food and grocery items     $_____

        Utilities     $_____

    Automobile:

        Gasoline and oil     $_____

        Repairs     $_____

        Insurance     $_____

    Children's Expenses:

        Clothing     $_____

        Medical, dental, prescriptions     $_____

        School supplies     $_____

        Other expenses: _____     $_____

    TOTAL AVERAGE MONTHLY EXPENSES     $_____

_____
Affiant's Signature

State of _____ )
County of _____ )

On _____ before me, _____, personally appeared _____ and _____, personally known to me (or proved to me on the basis of satisfactory evidence) to be the person(s) whose name(s) is/are subscribed to the within instrument and acknowledged to me that he/she/they executed the same in his/her/their authorized capacity(ies), and that by his/her/their signature(s) on the instrument the person(s), or the entity upon behalf of which the person(s) acted, executed the instrument.

WITNESS my hand and official seal.

Signature_____     Affiant _____ Known _____ Produced ID
        Signature of Notary     Type of ID _____
                                                                                                                            (Seal)

**IF A NONLAWYER HELPED YOU FILL OUT THIS FORM THEY MUST FILL IN THE BLANKS BELOW** (fill in **all** blanks):

I (*name of nonlawyer*) _____, nonlawyer located at (*street*) _____ (*city*)_____ (*state*) _____, (*phone*) _____ helped (*name*) _____ who is the [✔ **one** only] __petitioner **or** __respondent, fill out this form.

In the _____ Court for _____ County, State of _____

In re: The Marriage of:        )
                               )
                               )
                               )
        and                    )    Case No:
                               )
                               )
                               )
                               )

**VERIFIED**_____

1. This is a _____ between _____, _____, and _____ _____, _____.

2. The _____ is a resident of _____ and has been for more than _____ immediately prior to filing this _____ and has resided in the County of _____ for at least _____.

3. The _____ has agreed to file an Answer and Affidavit in Support of _____. No service of process is necessary at this time.

4. Neither party is currently on active duty in any branch of the Armed Services.

5. The parties were married to each other on _____ in the state of _____ and have been separated since _____.

6. Choose one of the following:

a. No children were born to or adopted by the parties of the marriage and none are expected.

b. There was/were _____ child(ren) born as issue to this marriage, to wit: (name and date of birth)

1._____
2._____
3._____

7. The _____ seeks a Final _____ on the grounds of:


8. The parties have made provisions for the division of their property and payment of their joint obligations, they have signed a Marital Settlement Agreement and they are satisfied with those provisions. Their signed Financial Statements are attached and incorporated by reference. Each party certifies that the Marital Settlement Agreement and Financial Statements were signed without duress, force or collusion. (The Marital Settlement Agreement is attached and marked as Exhibit A.)

9. The _____ hereby waives any rights to findings of fact and conclusions of law, a record of testimony, motion for a new trial, notice of entry of Final Judgment or Decree, and the right to appeal, but does not waive any rights to the future modification of any judgment or decree in this cause.

10. The marriage is irretrievably broken and any continuance of these proceedings will not result in a reconciliation.

Wherefore, the _____ respectfully asks and prays that the court:

1. Take jurisdiction of the parties and subject matter.

2. That a Final_____ be granted by the court dissolving the marriage between the parties.

3. That all of the terms and conditions of the parties' Marital Settlement Agreement, which is attached, be approved and be incorporated, and made part of a Final _____, and that the court enforce the Marital Settlement Agreement. Regardless, the Marital Settlement Agreement shall survive.

4. That the court award the parties any other further relief as may be just and equitable.

Dated this _____ day of _____, _____(year).

_____
Wife's Signature

Address:_____

_____

Phone: _____

VERIFICATION

State of _____ )

County of _____ )

I,_____, being duly sworn, depose and say that: I am the Petitioner/Respondent in the within action for divorce; I have read the foregoing Complaint/Petition and know the contents thereof; the contents of the Complaint/Petition are true to my knowledge, except as to those matters therein stated to be alleged upon information and belief, and as to those matters, I believe them to be true.

_____
Wife's signature

On _____ before me, _____, personally appeared _____, personally known to me (or proved to me on the basis of satisfactory evidence) to be the person(s) whose name(s) is/are subscribed to the within instrument and acknowledged to me that he/she/they executed the same in his/her/their authorized capacity(ies), and that by his/her/their signature(s) on the instrument the person(s), or the entity upon behalf of which the person(s) acted, executed the instrument.
WITNESS my hand and official seal.

Signature_____     Affiant____ Known ____ Produced
ID            Signature of Notary

Type of ID _____

(Seal)

_____
Husband's Signature

Address:_____

_____

Phone: _____

VERIFICATION

State of _____ )

County of _____ )

I,_____, being duly sworn, depose and say that: I am the Petitioner/Respondent in the within action for divorce; I have read the foregoing Complaint/Petition and know the contents thereof; the contents of the Complaint/Petition are true to my knowledge, except as to those matters therein stated to be alleged upon information and belief, and as to those matters, I believe them to be true.

_____
Husband's signature

On _____ before me, _____, personally appeared _____, personally known to me (or proved to me on the basis of satisfactory evidence) to be the person(s) whose name(s) is/are subscribed to the within instrument and acknowledged to me that he/she/they executed the same in his/her/their authorized capacity(ies), and that by his/her/their signature(s) on the instrument the person(s), or the entity upon behalf of which the person(s) acted, executed the instrument.

WITNESS my hand and official seal.

Signature_____    Affiant ____ Known ____ Produced
ID            Signature of Notary

Type of ID _____
(Seal)

**IF A NONLAWYER HELPED YOU FILL OUT THIS FORM THEY MUST FILL IN THE BLANKS BELOW** (fill in **all** blanks):

I (*name of nonlawyer*) _____, nonlawyer located at (*street*) _____ (*city*)_____ (*state*) _____, (*phone*) _____ helped (*name*) _____ who is the [✔ **one** only] __petitioner **or** __respondent, fill out this form.

In the _____ Court for _____ County, State of _____

In re: The Marriage of:        )
                               )
                               )
                               )
                               )  Case No:
and                            )
                               )
                               )
                               )

## ANSWER AND AFFIDAVIT IN SUPPORT OF

## FINAL _____

The undersigned, _____, files this answer and states under oath the following:

1. I have received a copy of the _____ and acknowledge all the allegations contained therein.

2. I further state that I am not on active duty in the armed services of the United States or of any foreign country.

3. I waive the _____ days required for setting the above-captioned matter for trial and waive notice of the final hearing, requesting a copy of the Final _____ be mailed to me.

4. I have been a resident of and domiciled in the State of _____ for the preceding _____ and the County of _____ for the preceding _____.

5. The parties have made provisions for the division of their property and payment of their joint obligations. They are satisfied with those provisions. I have freely and voluntarily entered into a Marital Settlement Agreement. The Marital Settlement Agreement entered into by the parties attached marked as Exhibit A to the _____ is a true copy.

6. I further waive my rights to notice of trial, findings of fact and conclusions of law, a record of testimony, motion for a new trial, notice of entry of final judgment or decree, and right to appeal; however, I do not waive any rights to the future modification of any judgment or decree in this cause.

## AFFIDAVIT IN SUPPORT OF FINAL _____

The undersigned files this Affidavit in Support of the Final _____ containing the following:

1. The Court has jurisdiction of the parties and subject matter.

2. The Court finds the marriage to be irretrievably broken and grants a Final _____.

3. The Marital Settlement Agreement filed in this proceeding as Exhibit A be approved and incorporated in the Final _____ by reference, and that the parties be ordered to comply with said agreement.

Further your Affiant Sayeth Naught.

Dated this _____ day of _____, _____(year).


_____
Signature of Respondent/Defendant

Address:_____

_____

Phone: _____

State of _____ )
County of _____ )

On _____before me, _____, personally appeared _____, personally known to me (or proved to me on the basis of satisfactory evidence) to be the person(s) whose name(s) is/are subscribed to the within instrument and acknowledged to me that he/she/they executed the same in his/her/their authorized capacity(ies), and that by his/her/their signature(s) on the instrument the person(s), or the entity upon behalf of which the person(s) acted, executed the instrument.
WITNESS my hand and official seal.

Signature_____     Affiant ____ Known     ____ Produced
ID
       Signature of Notary
                                      Type of ID _____
                                                                                 (Seal)


**IF A NONLAWYER HELPED YOU FILL OUT THIS FORM THEY MUST FILL IN THE BLANKS BELOW** (fill in **all** blanks):
I (*name of nonlawyer*) _____, nonlawyer located at (*street*) _____ (*city*)_____ (*state*) _____, (*phone*) _____ helped (*name*) _____ who is the [✔ **one** only] __petitioner **or** __respondent, fill out this form.

In the _____ Court for _____ County, State of _____

In re: The Marriage of:            )
                                   )
                                   )
                                   )
and                                )      Case No:
                                   )
                                   )
                                   )

**NOTICE OF HEARING**

TO:

You are hereby notified that a hearing has been scheduled in this cause as indicated below. In the absence or disqualification of the Judge, this cause will be brought on for hearing before another Judge who is available and qualified to act thereon.

Date: _____ Time: _____

Judge: The Honorable _____

Place: Room _____ County Courthouse

Address: _____
_____

Matter: _____

I hereby certify that, on _____, a true and correct copy of this Notice of Hearing was furnished by mail to the parties indicated above.

_____
Plaintiff

**IF A NONLAWYER HELPED YOU FILL OUT THIS FORM THEY MUST FILL IN THE BLANKS BELOW** (fill in **all** blanks):

I (*name of nonlawyer*) _____, nonlawyer located at (*street*) _____ (*city*)_____ (*state*) _____, (*phone*) _____ helped (*name*) _____ who is the [✔ **one** only] __petitioner **or** __respondent, fill out this form.

In the _____ Court for _____ County, State of _____

In re: The Marriage of:  )
                                                    )
                                                    )
                                                    )
and                                        )    Case No:
                                                    )
                                                    )
                                                    )

## DECLARATION UNDER THE UNIFORM CHILD CUSTODY JURISDICTION ACT

We, the undersigned, _____ and _____, are both parties to this proceeding to determine the custody of a minor child, and under oath state:

1.      There is/are _____ minor child(ren) subject to this proceeding. For each child, the name, sex, Social Security number, date and place of birth, and time and place of residence and name and relationship of person child lived with for the past 5 years, is as follows: (Attach additional sheet if necessary.)

Child's Name: _____ Sex : _____ Date of Birth: _____

Place of Birth: _____ Social Security Number: _____

Present Residence: _____

Person Child Lives With: _____ Relationship: _____

Dates of Residence: From: _____ To: Present

Previous Residence: _____

Person Child Lived With: _____ Relationship: _____

Dates of Residence: From: _____ To: _____

Child's Name: _____ Sex: _____ Date of Birth: _____

Place of Birth: _____ Social Security Number: _____

Present Residence: _____

Person Child Lives With: _____ Relationship: _____

Dates of Residence: From: _____ To: Present

Previous Residence: _____

Person Child Lived With: _____ Relationship: _____

Dates of Residence: From: _____ To: _____

2. Neither party has participated as a party, witness or any other capacity in any other court decision, order, or custody proceeding in this state or any other state, concerning the custody of a child subject to this proceeding.

3. Neither party has and information concerning any other court decision, order, or custody proceeding in this state or any other state concerning the custody of a child subject to this proceeding.

4. Neither party knows of any other person who is not already a party to this proceeding who has physical custody of, or who claims to have custody or visitation rights with, any child subject to this proceeding.

Dated this _____ day of _____, _____(year).

_____
Wife's Signature

Address:_____

_____

Phone: _____

State of _____ )

County of _____ )

On _____ before me, _____, personally appeared _____, personally known to me (or proved to me on the basis of satisfactory evidence) to be the person(s) whose name(s) is/are subscribed to the within instrument and acknowledged to me that he/she/they executed the same in his/her/their authorized capacity(ies), and that by his/her/their signature(s) on the instrument the person(s), or the entity upon behalf of which the person(s) acted, executed the instrument.
WITNESS my hand and official seal.

Signature_____     Affiant ____ Known      ____ Produced
ID
        Signature of Notary
                                    Type of ID _____
                                                                                                  (Seal)

_____
Husband's Signature

Address:_____

_____

Phone: _____

State of _____ )

County of _____ )

On _____ before me, _____, personally appeared _____, personally known to me (or proved to me on the basis of satisfactory evidence) to be the person(s) whose name(s) is/are subscribed to the within instrument and acknowledged to me that he/she/they executed the same in his/her/their authorized capacity(ies), and that by his/her/their signature(s) on the instrument the person(s), or the entity upon behalf of which the person(s) acted, executed the instrument.

WITNESS my hand and official seal.

Signature_____   Affiant ____ Known   ____ Produced ID
        Signature of Notary

Type of ID _____

(Seal)

**IF A NONLAWYER HELPED YOU FILL OUT THIS FORM THEY MUST FILL IN THE BLANKS BELOW** (fill in **all** blanks):

I (*name of nonlawyer*) _____, nonlawyer located at (*street*) _____ (*city*)_____ (*state*) _____, (*phone*) _____ helped (*name*) _____ who is the [✔ **one** only] __petitioner **or** __respondent, fill out this form.

In the _____ Court for _____ County, State of _____

In re: The Marriage of: )
)
)
)
)
and )  Case No:
)
)
)

_____

This Cause came to be heard on _____

_____on _____, _____(year), and the Court hearing testimony in

support of the _____

THE COURT FINDS:

1. That the Court has jurisdiction of the parties and subject matter of this cause.

2. That the parties have voluntarily waived findings of fact, conclusions of law, a record of testimony, motion for a new trial, notice of entry of final judgment, and right of appeal, but have not waived their rights to future modification of this judgment.

IT IS ORDERED AND ADJUDGED:

1. That the marriage of the _____ and _____ is hereby dissolved.

2. The separation agreement between the parties, filed in this proceeding as Exhibit A, was executed voluntarily after full disclosure, and is in the best interests of the parties, and is approved and incorporated in this judgment by reference and the parties are ordered to comply with it.

3. That the _____ shall pay $_____ per ____ beginning _____, _____(year), to _____ as alimony and shall terminate:

4. That the _____ shall pay $_____ per ____ beginning _____, _____(year), to _____ as child support per child, said support shall terminate for each child when the child reaches eighteen years of age (or, if in Alabama, nineteen years of age), becomes self-supporting, marries or dies, whichever comes first.

5. _____ former name is restored and shall be known as _____ hereafter.

 

_____
Judge

In the _____ Court for _____ County, State of _____

In re: The Marriage of:                    )
                                           )
                                           )
                                           )
     and                                   )    Case No:
                                           )
                                           )
                                           )

## CERTIFICATE OF CORROBORATING WITNESS

UNDER PENALTY OF PERJURY I CERTIFY that I am a resident of the State of _____; I have known _____ for more than _____ preceding the date of the filing of the above cause on _____ and I know of my own personal knowledge that such person has resided in the State of _____ for at least that period of time.

_____  _____
Witness' Signature

_____  _____
Witness' Name Typed                   Witness' Residence Address

State of _____ )

County of _____ )

On _____ before me, _____, personally appeared _____, personally known to me (or proved to me on the basis of satisfactory evidence) to be the person(s) whose name(s) is/are subscribed to the within instrument and acknowledged to me that he/she/they executed the same in his/her/their authorized capacity(ies), and that by his/her/their signature(s) on the instrument the person(s), or the entity upon behalf of which the person(s) acted, executed the instrument.

WITNESS my hand and official seal.

Signature_____   Affiant____ Known  ____ Produced ID
           Signature of Notary
                                                  Type of ID _____
                                                                                                                        (Seal)

**IF A NONLAWYER HELPED YOU FILL OUT THIS FORM THEY MUST FILL IN THE BLANKS BELOW** (fill in **all** blanks):

I (*name of nonlawyer*) _____, nonlawyer located at (*street*) _____ (*city*)_____ (*state*) _____, (*phone*) _____ helped (*name*) _____ who is the [✔ **one** only] __petitioner **or** __respondent, fill out this form.

# Glossary of useful terms

## Ac-An

### Action
A court proceeding or lawsuit.

### Affidavit
A written statement of facts, sworn to be true under oath before a notary public.

### Agreement
An understanding and intention between the parties with respect to their relative rights and duties.

### Allegations
The assertions or claims made in a pleading against the other party in a lawsuit.

### Alimony
A lump sum or periodic payments made to a divorced spouse by a former spouse for maintenance or support. Alimony (Maintenance or Spousal Support) may be temporary or permanent.

### Annulment
A court procedure that dissolves a marriage and declares that a valid marriage never existed.

# An-D

### Answer (Response)

The defendant's legal response to a complaint or petition.

### Appearance

The voluntary submission by a defendant to a court's jurisdiction. The appearance can be made in person or by filing an answer, response or an appearance and waiver.

### Award

A formal order by the court giving a party the right to compensation.

### Cause of Action

The grounds upon which a suit is maintained.

### Community Property Distribution

A system of property ownership. In most community property states, both spouses are considered to own equal shares of the community property.

### Complaint (Petition)

The first document filed in court by one party (plaintiff, petitioner) stating the grievance against the other party.

### Contested Divorce

When the court decides issues which have not been resolved by the parties.

### Custodial Parent

The parent with whom the child(ren) resides.

### Decree (Final Judgment)

The final court order dissolving the marriage.

# D-J

### Default Judgment

Where the defendant (respondent) fails to answer an allegation or make an appearance in the case; the court will give judgment to plaintiff (petitioner) based on the relief sought.

### Defendant (Respondent)

The person defending against or denying the claim.

### Divorce (Dissolution of Marriage)

The termination of a marriage by the courts through the powers given to them by the state.

### Domicile (Residence)

Where a person lives and intends to reside.

### Equitable Distribution

The equitable, but not necessarily equal, division of property acquired during the marriage. This is defined according to state law.

### Fault-Based Divorce

A divorce granted because of marital wrongs.

### Grounds

The legal reasons for the granting of a divorce.

### Hold Harmless

An agreement whereby one party assumes the liability and agrees to relieve the other party of responsibility on the obligation.

### Joint Legal Custody

Where the parents share the responsibilities and major decisions of the child(ren). Usually one parent is awarded physical custody.

# J-P

### Joint Physical Custody

Both parents share the physical custody of the child over alternating periods of time (also called shared parenting or co-parenting).

### Jointly Owned Property

Property owned together.

### Joint Tenancy

Property held by two or more persons equally. When one dies, the other owns the property without its passing through probate.

### Jurisdiction

The legal right by which judges exercise their authority. The court must have subject matter jurisdiction and personal jurisdiction to grant a divorce.

### Legal Separation

A court order used as the basis for support, allowing the parties to live separate and apart even though they are still married to each other.

### Marital Property

Property acquired by persons while married and divided by the court upon divorce (dissolution of marriage).

### No-Fault Divorce

A divorce in which the plaintiff does not have to accuse the other spouse of marital wrongdoings.

### Pleading

Any document filed with the court which seeks action by the court.

### Pre-nuptial Agreement

A contract entered into by people about to enter marriage. This agreement helps resolve issues of support, property distribution, or inheritance upon divorce. This is also called a pre-marriage agreement.

# P-W

### Primary Caregiver

The parent who has provided most of the daily care to a child; a determination often used in awarding custody.

### Separate Property

The property that is not owned by both of the parties but owned individually. This may, nevertheless, be divided by the court.

### Service of Process

The delivery of a summons informing the defendant (respondent) of a lawsuit.

### Sole Custody

One parent is given physical custody of the child, along with the right to make all major decisions regarding the child.

### Subject Matter Jurisdiction

The authority of a court to deal with the general subject involved in the action.

### Subpoena

A document which commands a person to appear to give testimony upon a certain matter.

### Summons

A document which informs that a lawsuit has been filed against you.

### Uncontested Divorce (Friendly Divorce)

A divorce that is agreed upon by both parties and where there are no legal issues in dispute.

### Waiver

A document which intentionally or voluntarily relinquishes a person's right.

# Resources

## Where you'll find these Resources:

- Online resources .................. 157
- Legal search engines ............. 160
- State Bar Associations ........... 163

## ••• Online resources •••

◆ **ABA Law Practice Management Section—Estate Planning and Probate Interest Group**

URL:  http://www.abanet.org/lpm/lpdiv/estate.html

◆ **Adult Children of Divorce**

URL:  http://www.mindspring.com/~blittle/odosbucket/adoc
home.html

◆ **American Academy of Matrimonial Lawyers**

URL:  http://www.aaml.org

◆ **American Divorce Information Network**

URL:  http://www.divorceonline.com

- **American Assoc. for Marriage and Family Therapy**
  *URL: http://www.aamft.org*

- **Divorce+Plus**
  *URL: http://pages.prodigy.com/divorceplus*

- **Divorce Central**
  *URL: http://www.divorcecentral.com*

- **Divorce Helpline Webworks**
  *URL: http://www.divorcehelp.com*

- **DivorceInfo.com**
  *URL: http://www.divorceinfo.com*

- **DivorceNet**
  *URL: http://www.divorcenet.com*

- **Divorce Source**
  *URL: http://www.divorcesource.com*

- **Divorcing.com**
  *URL: http://www.divorcing.com*

- **Flying Solo**
  *URL: http://www.flyingsolo.com*

- **Divorce Support**
  *URL: http://divorcesupport.miningco.com*

- **Internet Imagers**
  *URL: http://www.iimagers.com/divorce-resources.html*

- **Legal Information Institute**
  *URL: http://www.divorcesource.com/search/general
  /divorcelaws.html*

- **Men's Defense Association**
  *URL: http://www.mensdefense.org*

- **MoneyCentral Family**
  *URL: http://moneycentral.msn.com/quickref
  /quickref.asp?Cat=1&Topic=3#h*

- **National Council for the Divorced and Separated**
  *URL: http://www.ncds.org.uk*

- **Talkway**
  *URL: http://decaf.talkway.com/cgi-bin/
  cgi?request=enter&group=alt.support.divorce*

- **Yahoo Business and Economics**

    URL: http://dir.yahoo.com/Business_and_Economy/Companies/Law/Family/Divorce

- **Yahoo Society and Culture — Relationships**

    URL: http://dir.yahoo.com/Society_and_Culture/Relationships/Divorce

## ••• Legal Search Engines •••

- **All Law**

    http://www.alllaw.com

- **American Law Sources On Line**

    http://www.lawsource.com/also/searchfm.htm

- **Catalaw**

    http://www.catalaw.com

- **FindLaw**

    URL: http://www.findlaw.com

- **Hieros Gamos**

    http://www.hg.org/hg.html

# Resources

- **InternetOracle**

    *http://www.internetoracle.com/legal.htm*

- **LawAid**

    *http://www.lawaid.com/search.html*

- **LawCrawler**

    *http://www.lawcrawler.com*

- **LawEngine, The**

    *http://www.fastsearch.com/law*

- **LawRunner**

    *http://www.lawrunner.com*

- **'Lectric Law Library™**

    *http://www.lectlaw.com*

- **Legal Search Engines**

    *http://www.dreamscape.com/frankvad/search.legal.html*

- **LEXIS/NEXIS Communications Center**

    *http://www.lexis-nexis.com/lncc/general/search.html*

- **Meta-Index for U.S. Legal Research**

    *http://gsulaw.gsu.edu/metaindex*

- **Seamless Website, The**

    *http://seamless.com*

- **USALaw**

    *http://www.usalaw.com/linksrch.cfm*

- **WestLaw**

    *http://westdoc.com* (Registered users only. Fee paid service.)

# ··· State Bar Associations ···

## ALABAMA

Alabama State Bar
415 Dexter Avenue
Montgomery, AL 36104

**mailing address:**
PO Box 671
Montgomery, AL 36101
(205) 269-1515

*http://www.alabar.org*

## ALASKA

Alaska Bar Association
510 L Street No. 602
Anchorage, AK 99501

**mailing address**
PO Box 100279
Anchorage, AK 99510

## ARIZONA

State Bar of Arizona
111 West Monroe
Phoenix, AZ 85003-1742
(602) 252-4804

## ARKANSAS

Arkansas Bar Association
400 West Markham
Little Rock, AR 72201
(501) 375-4605

## CALIFORNIA

State Bar of California
555 Franklin Street
San Francisco, CA 94102
(415) 561-8200

*http://www.calbar.org*

Alameda County Bar Association

*http://www.acbanet.org*

## COLORADO

Colorado Bar Association
No. 950, 1900 Grant Street
Denver, CO 80203
(303) 860-1115

*http://www.cobar.org*

## CONNECTICUT

Connecticut Bar Association
101 Corporate Place
Rocky Hill, CT 06067-1894
(203) 721-0025

## DELAWARE

Delaware State Bar Association
1225 King Street, 10th floor
Wilmington, DE 19801
(302) 658-5279
(302) 658-5278 (lawyer referral service)

## DISTRICT OF COLUMBIA

District of Columbia Bar
1250 H Street, NW, 6th Floor
Washington, DC 20005
(202) 737-4700

Bar Association of the District of Columbia
1819 H Street, NW, 12th floor
Washington, DC 20006-3690
(202) 223-6600

## FLORIDA

The Florida Bar
The Florida Bar Center
650 Apalachee Parkway
Tallahassee, FL 32399-2300
(904) 561-5600

## GEORGIA

State Bar of Georgia
800 The Hurt Building
50 Hurt Plaza
Atlanta, GA 30303
(404) 527-8700

*http://www.gabar.org*

## HAWAII

Hawaii State Bar Association
1136 Union Mall
Penthouse 1
Honolulu, HI 96813
(808) 537-1868

*http://www.hsba.org*

## IDAHO

Idaho State Bar
PO Box 895
Boise, ID 83701
(208) 334-4500

## ILLINOIS

Illinois State Bar Association
424 South Second Street
Springfield, IL 62701
(217) 525-1760

## INDIANA

Indiana State Bar Association
230 East Ohio Street
Indianapolis, IN 46204
(317) 639-5465

*http://www.iquest.net/isba*

## IOWA

Iowa State Bar Association
521 East Locust
Des Moines, IA 50309
(515) 243-3179

*http://www.iowabar.org*

## KANSAS

Kansas Bar Association
1200 Harrison Street
Topeka, KS 66601
(913) 234-5696

*http://www.ink.org/public/cybar*

## KENTUCKY

Kentucky Bar Association
514 West Main Street
Frankfort, KY 40601-1883
(502) 564-3795

*http://www.kybar.org*

## LOUISIANA

Louisiana State Bar Association
601 St. Charles Avenue
New Orleans, LA 70130
(504) 566-1600

## MAINE

Maine State Bar Association
124 State Street
PO Box 788
Augusta, ME 04330
(207) 622-7523

*http://www.mainebar.org*

## MARYLAND

Maryland State Bar Association
520 West Fayette Street
Baltimore, MD 21201
(410) 685-7878

*http://www.msba.org/msba*

## MASSACHUSETTS

Massachusetts Bar Association
20 West Street
Boston, MA 02111
(617) 542-3602
(617) 542-9103 (lawyer referral service)

## MICHIGAN

State Bar of Michigan
306 Townsend Street
Lansing, MI 48933-2083
(517) 372-9030

*http://www.michbar.org*

## MINNESOTA

Minnesota State Bar Association
514 Nicollet Mall
Minneapolis, MN 55402
(612) 333-1183

## MISSISSIPPI

The Mississippi Bar
643 No. State Street
Jackson, Mississippi 39202
(601) 948-4471

## MISSOURI

The Missouri Bar
P.O. Box 119, 326 Monroe
Jefferson City, Missouri 65102
(314) 635-4128

*http://www.mobar.org*

## MONTANA

State Bar of Montana
46 North Main
PO Box 577
Helena, MT 59624
(406) 442-7660

## NEBRASKA

Nebraska State Bar Association
635 South 14th Street, 2nd floor
Lincoln, NE 68508
(402) 475-7091

*http://www.nebar.com*

## NEVADA

State Bar of Nevada
201 Las Vegas Blvd.
Las Vegas, NV 89101
(702) 382-2200

*http://www.nvbar.org*

## NEW HAMPSHIRE

New Hampshire Bar Association
112 Pleasant Street
Concord, NH 03301
(603) 224-6942

## NEW JERSEY

New Jersey State Bar Association
One Constitution Square
New Brunswuck, NJ 08901-1500
(908) 249-5000

## NEW MEXICO

State Bar of New Mexico
121 Tijeras Street N.E.
Albuquerque, NM 87102

mailing address:
PO Box 25883
Albuquerque, NM 87125
(505) 843-6132

## NEW YORK

New York State Bar Association
One Elk Street
Albany, NY 12207
(518) 463-3200

*http://www.nysba.org*

## NORTH CAROLINA

North Carolina State Bar
208 Fayetteville Street Mall
Raleigh, NC 27601

mailing address:
PO Box 25908
Raleigh, NC 27611
(919) 828-4620

North Carolina Bar Association
1312 Annapolis Drive
Raleigh, NC 27608

mailing address:
PO Box 12806
Raleigh, NC 27605
(919) 828-0561

*http://www.barlinc.org*

## NORTH DAKOTA

State Bar Association of North Dakota
515 1/2 East Broadway, suite 101
Bismarck, ND 58501

**mailing address:**
PO Box 2136
Bismarck, ND 58502
(701) 255-1404

## OHIO

Ohio State Bar Association
1700 Lake Shore Drive
Columbus, OH 43204

**mailing address:**
PO Box 16562
Columbus, OH 43216-6562
(614) 487-2050

## OKLAHOMA

Oklahoma Bar Association
1901 North Lincoln
Oklahoma City, OK 73105
(405) 524-2365

## OREGON

Oregon State Bar
5200 S.W. Meadows Road
PO Box 1689
Lake Oswego, OR 97035-0889
(503) 620-0222

## PENNSYLVANIA

Pennsylvannia Bar Association
100 South Street
PO Box 186
Harrisburg, PA 17108
(717) 238-6715

Pennsylvania Bar Institute
*http://www.pbi.org*

## PUERTO RICO

Puerto Rico Bar Association
PO Box 1900
San Juan, Puerto Rico 00903
(787) 721-3358

## RHODE ISLAND

Rhode Island Bar Association
115 Cedar Street
Providence, RI 02903
(401) 421-5740

## SOUTH CAROLINA

South Carolina Bar
950 Taylor Street
PO Box 608
Columbia, SC 29202
(803) 799-6653

*http://www.scbar.org*

## SOUTH DAKOTA

State Bar of South Dakota
222 East Capitol
Pierre, SD 57501
(605) 224-7554

## TENNESSEE

Tennessee Bar Assn
3622 West End Avenue
Nashville, TN 37205
(615) 383-7421

*http://www.tba.org*

## TEXAS

State Bar of Texas
1414 Colorado
PO Box 12487
Austin, TX 78711
(512) 463-1463

## UTAH

Utah State Bar
645 South 200 East, Suite 310
Salt Lake City, UT 84111
(801) 531-9077

## VERMONT

Vermont Bar Association
PO Box 100
Montpelier, VT 05601
(802) 223-2020

## VIRGINIA

Virginia State Bar
707 East Main Street, suite 1500
Richmond, VA 23219-0501
(804) 775-0500

Virginia Bar Association
701 East Franklin St., Suite 1120
Richmond, VA 23219
(804) 644-0041

## VIRGIN ISLANDS

Virgin Islands Bar Association
P.O. Box 4108
Christiansted, Virgin Islands 00822
(809) 778-7497

## WASHINGTON

Washington State Bar Association
500 Westin Street
2001 Sixth Avenue
Seattle, WA 98121-2599
(206) 727-8200

*http://www.wsba.org*

## WEST VIRGINIA

West Virginia State Bar
2006 Kanawha Blvd. East
Charleston, WV 25311
(304) 558-2456

*http://www.wvbar.org*

West Virginia Bar Association
904 Security Building
100 Capitol Street
Charleston, WV 25301
(304) 342-1474

## WISCONSIN

State Bar of Wisconsin
402 West Wilson Street
Madison, WI 53703
(608) 257-3838

*http://www.wisbar.org/home.htm*

## WYOMING

Wyoming State Bar
500 Randall Avenue
Cheyenne, WY 82001
PO Box 109
Cheyenne, WY 82003
(307) 632-9061

# Appendix: Divorce laws by state

| | | | |
|---|---|---|---|
| Alabama | 172 | Montana | 185 |
| Alaska | 172 | Nebraska | 185 |
| Arizona | 173 | Nevada | 186 |
| Arkansas | 173 | New Hampshire | 186 |
| California | 174 | New Jersey | 187 |
| Colorado | 174 | New Mexico | 187 |
| Connecticut | 175 | New York | 188 |
| Delaware | 175 | North Carolina | 188 |
| District of Columbia | 176 | North Dakota | 189 |
| Florida | 176 | Ohio | 189 |
| Georgia | 177 | Oklahoma | 190 |
| Hawaii | 177 | Oregon | 190 |
| Idaho | 178 | Pennsylvania | 191 |
| Illinois | 178 | Rhode Island | 191 |
| Indiana | 179 | South Carolina | 192 |
| Iowa | 179 | South Dakota | 192 |
| Kansas | 180 | Tennessee | 193 |
| Kentucky | 180 | Texas | 193 |
| Louisiana | 181 | Utah | 194 |
| Maine | 181 | Vermont | 194 |
| Maryland | 182 | Virginia | 195 |
| Massachusetts | 182 | Washington | 195 |
| Michigan | 183 | West Virginia | 196 |
| Minnesota | 183 | Wisconsin | 196 |
| Mississippi | 184 | Wyoming | 197 |
| Missouri | 184 | | |

You will find the divorce laws for all 50 states and the District of Columbia in this Appendix. The information is believed to be accurate and complete, but in the event that laws have changed, check with an attorney or the clerk of the divorce court, or review your state laws in a large public library or any law library.

# ALABAMA

Residence Requirements:

A spouse filing for divorce must be a resident of the state for at least 6 months if the other spouse is a non-resident of Alabama.

| Where to File: | Name of Court: | Title of Divorce Action: |
|---|---|---|
| Circuit Court in: county where defendant lives, county where parties lived when separated* | Circuit Court. "In the Circuit Court for ____________County, Alabama." | Complaint for Divorce |

| Party Filing: | Other Party: | Title of Final Papers: |
|---|---|---|
| Plaintiff | Defendant | Final Judgment of Divorce |

Approved Grounds for Divorce:

No-Fault: (1) irretrievable breakdown of the marriage; (2) voluntary separation for over 1 year; (3) complete incompatibility of temperament, as a result the parties cannot live together. Fault-based: (1) adultery; (2) no cohabitation for over 2 years without husband supporting wife (divorce must be filed by wife); (3) imprisonment for over 2 years if the total sentence is 7 years; (4) alcoholism; (5) substance abuse; (6) confinement for mental disease for over 5 years; (7) wife pregnant by another at the time of the marriage without the husband's knowledge; (8) physical abuse or reasonable fear of physical abuse; (9) marriage is not consummated; or (10) unnatural sexual behavior before or after the marriage.

General Divorce Procedures:

Default judgment may be granted but only if evidence is presented to support your motion. However, acceptance and waiver of service is allowed if signed by both the defendant and a witness. Effective January 1, 1997, there is a 30-day waiting period after the filing of the summons and complaint before a judge may issue a final judgment of divorce. Testimony in uncontested divorces may be taken before a court clerk, by sworn statements, or by transcripts of oral depositions. If child support is requested, a standardized child support guideline form and child support income statement/affidavit must be filed.

Mediation or Counseling Requirements:

There is no legal provision in Alabama for mediation or counseling.

Legal Separation Provisions:

If the filing spouse wants the divorce limited to a divorce "from bed and board," it may be granted for cruelty or for any of the same grounds for which a standard divorce is granted.

Property Distribution:

Alabama is an "equitable distribution" state; therefore the judge has full discretion when dividing jointly owned real estate or personal property. However, the judge does not have authority to award the wife's separate property to the husband, regardless of whether it was obtained before or after the marriage. Gifts and inheritances are considered separate property and cannot be divided unless the real estate or personal property has been used to benefit both spouses.

Alimony/Spousal Support/Maintenance:

The judge has full discretion in awarding maintenance to either spouse if such spouse does not have sufficient property to provide for his or her maintenance. This award may be made out of the other spouse's property, unless it is separate property and it was never used for the benefit of both spouses. The court looks at the following: (1) the value of the estate of both spouses; and (2) the condition of the spouse's family. Up to 50% of a spouse's retirement benefits may be used for alimony if the retirement was accumulated during a marriage of 10 years or more. Misconduct by either spouse may be considered by the court in determining any award, if any, of allowance for maintenance. The spouse's right in receiving an allowance for maintenance will terminate if such spouse is living openly with a member of the opposite sex or re-married.

Child Custody and Visitation:

Custody may be granted to either parent after considering the following factors: (1) the age and sex of the child; (2) the safety and well-being of the child; and (3) the moral character of the parents. In addition, the desires of the child will also be considered. Joint custody may be awarded. There is a legal presumption against giving custody to any person who has inflicted any violence against either a spouse or a child. In abuse cases, the judge is required to consider any history of domestic abuse and may not consider the fact that a parent or spouse has relocated to avoid abuse.

As of January 1, 1997, Alabama officially favors joint custody (but not equal physical custody) if in the best interests of the child and the parents agree.Factors to be considered are (1) parental custody agreement; (2) parental cooperation; (3)parental ability to encourage love and sharing; (4) any history of abuse; (5) geographic proximity of parents. Joint custody may be awarded. However, if the wife abandons the husband and the children are over 7 years old, the husband is granted custody if he is suitable. Grandparents may be given visitation rights.

Child Support:

A standardized child support guidelines form and child support income statement/affidavit must be filed if child support is requested. The court may order either parent to provide support. There are official child support guidelines contained in the Alabama Rules of Judicial Administration, Rule 32. These guidelines are deemed correct unless the amount is shown to be unjust or inappropriate in a particular case. A standardized Child Support Guidelines form and Child Support Income Statement/Affidavit must be filed in every case in which child support is requested. In addition, a written agreement between the parents for a different amount with an explanation for the deviation will be allowed.

Rights to Maiden Name:

Wife may resume her maiden or former name upon divorce. Ex-husband may prevent his ex-wife from using his last name.

# ALASKA

Residence Requirements:

Filing spouse must be a resident of the state. There is no residency time limit.

| Where to File: | Name of Court: | Title of Divorce Action: |
|---|---|---|
| Superior Court | "Superior Court for the State of Alaska; #____________ Judicial District." | Petition for Dissolution of Marriage (No-fault based) Complaint for Divorce (Fault-based) |

| Party Filing: | Other Party: | Title of Final Papers: |
|---|---|---|
| Petitioner (No-fault) Plaintiff (Fault-based) | Respondent (No-fault) Defendant (Fault-based) | Decree of Dissolution of Marriage (No-fault based) Judgment of Divorce (Fault-based) |

Approved Grounds for Divorce:

No-fault: Incompatibility of temperament which results in the irremediable breakdown of the marriage. Fault-based: (1) adultery; (2) incurable mental disease and confinement for 18 months; (3) substance abuse; (4) marriage not consummated; (5) conviction of a felony; (6) abandonment for over 1 year; (7) cruel and/or inhuman treatment; (8) habitual drunkenness; and (9) personal indignities.

General Divorce Procedures:

The spouses may jointly petition the court for a dissolution of marriage on the grounds of incompatibility of temperament under the following conditions: (1) if there are no minor children or the wife is pregnant, the parties have agreed on custody, visitation, and support for the child. The parties must also agree on whether support payments will be made through the state child support enforcement agency, and/or the tax consequences of such support payments; (2) the spouses have agreed to divide jointly owned property in a fair and just manner (including retirement pensions), to the payment of maintenance, if any, and to the tax consequences of such payments; (3) lastly, the spouses have agreed on the payment of all debts incurred by either or both of them, and to the payment of obligations incurred jointly by them in the future.
The petition for dissolution of marriage may be made by one spouse individually if: (1) the grounds for the dissolution of marriage is the incompatibility of temperament, evidenced by extended separation of the spouses, which has caused the irremediable breakdown of the marriage; (2) the petitioning spouse has been unable to ascertain the other spouse's position regarding the dissolution of their marriage, the division of their property, and the division of their obligations, custody, support and visitation of any child or children, because the whereabouts of the other spouse is unknown to the petitioning spouse, after reasonable efforts to locate the absent spouse; (3) the other spouse cannot be personally served with process inside or outside the state. Filing for a dissolution of marriage does not preclude filing for a divorce. Official state forms for obtaining a dissolution of marriage under these provisions may be obtained from the clerk of any Superior Court, or from the Division of Social Services of the Alaska Department of Health and Social Services.

Mediation or Counseling Requirements:

At the request of either spouse, mediation may be granted. If no request for mediation is made by either spouse, the court may order the spouses to submit to mediation by a court-appointed mediator.

Legal Separation Provisions:

There is no legal provision which directly addresses this issue in Alaska.

Property Distribution:Property Distribution:

Alaska is an "equitable distribution" state. All property acquired either jointly or separately during the marriage will be divided in a "just" manner. In a dissolution of marriage action (no-fault), any property acquired prior to the marriage will not be divided unless it is in the best interest of the child or the spouses have agreed to do so. The contribution of each spouse as homemaker is considered in the contribution to the acquisition of marital property.
Gifts and inheritances are also subject to division by the court. Factors considered are: (1) length of marriage, (2) position in life of the parties during marriage, (3) the age and health of the parties, (4) the earning capacity of each spouse, (5) the financial condition of each spouse, (6) the parties' conduct regarding their assets, (7) the desirability of awarding the family home to the spouse with primary physical custody of children, (8) the time and manner of acquisition of their property, (9) the income producing capacity of the property and its value, and (10) all other relevant factors. Non-monetary contributions to the marriage (for example: home-making) are also considered.

Alimony/Spousal Support/Maintenance:

Spousal support may be awarded to either spouse. The award may be made in a lump sum or paid by installments. The contribution of each spouse as homemaker is considered.

Child Custody and Visitation:

Custody is determined according to the best interest of the child and is based on the following factors: (1) the ability and desire of each parent to meet the child's needs; (2) the physical, emotional, mental, religious and social needs of the child; (3) the preference of the child if of sufficient age and capacity; (4) the bond between the child and each parent; (5) the length of time the child has lived in a particular environment and the desirability of maintaining continuity; (6) the desire and ability of the custodial parent to allow a frequent relationship both open and loving between the child and the other parent; (7) any evidence of domestic violence; (8) child abuse or neglect; (9) any evidence of substance abuse that affects the emotional or physical well-being of the child; (10) distance between each parent as it relates to where the child will live and go to school; and (11) the advantage of keeping the child where he or she lives; or (12) any other relevant factors. Neither parent is considered to be entitled to custody. Joint/shared custody may be awarded, if it is in the best interests of the child.

Child Support:

The judge may order either parent to pay child support. There are official child support guidelines contained in Alaska Rules of Civil Procedure, Rule 903. These guidelines are presumed correct unless there is evidence that the amount would be unjust and inappropriate in a particular case. Child support payments may be ordered paid to a court-appointed trustee or through the state child support enforcement agency. Each parent must file a verified statement of income.

Rights to Maiden Name:

Either spouse may change their name in the decree for dissolution of marriage or final judgment for divorce (fault-based grounds).

 This product does not constitute the rendering of legal advice or services. This product is intended for informational use only and is not a substitute for legal advice. State laws vary, so consult an attorney on all legal matters. This product was not prepared by a person licensed to practice law in this state.

# ARIZONA

**Residence Requirements:**
Either spouse must have lived in the state for at least 90 days. There is a 60-day waiting period after the respondent has been served with service of process.

**Where to File:**
In the county in which the petitioner resides.

**Name of Court:**
Superior Court. "In the Superior Court in and for the County of_____, Arizona."

**Title of Divorce Action:**
Petition for Dissolution of Marriage

**Party Filing:**
Petitioner

**Other Party:**
Respondent

**Title of Final Papers:**
Decree of Dissolution of Marriage

**Important Note:**
Additional forms may be required. Call or visit your clerk of the court.

**Approved Grounds for Divorce:**
No-fault: Irretrievable breakdown of the marriage. Fault-based: The only ground for dissolution of marriage is irretrievable breakdown of the marriage.

**General Divorce Procedures:**
Acceptance and waiver of service by the respondent is allowed. The petition for dissolution of marriage may be heard before a court commissioner if an appearance and waiver is filed. Separation agreements are encouraged.

**Mediation or Counseling Requirements:**
Either spouse prior to filing for a dissolution of marriage may request the court to order mediation to save the marriage or help in a settlement. After filing for a dissolution of marriage the action may be transferred at the request of either spouse to the conciliation court for mediation. Official forms from the clerk of any Superior Court must be used when requesting this transfer. In addition, if one spouse denies that the marriage is irretrievably broken, the court may delay the case for up to 60 days and order the spouses to attend a conciliation conference.

**Legal Separation Provisions:**
There is no residency time limit, however, one spouse must live in Arizona when the action for legal separation is filed. The only ground for legal separation is that one spouse desires to live separate or the irretrievable breakdown of the marriage. However, if one party objects to legal separation, the case will be amended to an action for dissolution of marriage.

**Property Distribution:**
Arizona is a "community property" state. Community property is any property acquired during the marriage, and, therefore, it is divided and awarded equitably. Separate property will be retained by the owner of the property. Marital misconduct will not be considered in the division of community property. However, the court may consider the following factors in dividing the property: (1) excessive or abnormal use or expenditure; or, (2) any destruction, concealment, or fraudulent disposition of community property. The court may place a lien on the spouse's separate property to secure payment of child or spousal support.

**Alimony/Spousal Support/Maintenance:**
Either spouse may be awarded maintenance. The court will award maintenance if such spouse: (1) lacks sufficient property to provide for his or her maintenance; (2) cannot support him or herself through appropriate employment; (3) is the custodian of a child whose age and condition is such that the custodian should not be employed outside of the home; (4) lacks marketable skills in the labor market to support him or herself; (5) contributed to the education of the other spouse; or (6) had a marriage of long duration; or (7) is of an age which precludes the ability of gaining employment to adequately support him or herself.

Marital misconduct is not a factor to be considered. The factors to be considered are: (1) if it is appropriate for the spouse who is custodian of a child to seek outside employment; (2) the time for the spouse to acquire education and training for suitable employment; (3) the spouse's future earning capacity; (4) the spouse's standard of living during their marriage; (5) the duration of the marriage; (6)the ability of the spouse providing maintenance to meet his or her needs while providing the maintenance to the other; (7) the financial resources of the spouse seeking maintenance (including marital property awarded and the spouse's ability to meet his or her needs independently); (8) any destruction, concealment, fraudulent disposition, or excessive expenditures of jointly-held property; (9) the comparative financial resources of the spouses including their comparative earning capacities; (10) the age of the spouses; (11) the physical and emotional condition of the spouses; (12) the usual occupations of the spouses during the marriage; (13) the vocational skills of the spouse seeking maintenance; and (14) any other factors the court may deem just and equitable. Awards of maintenance are to be paid through the court unless the spouses agree otherwise. Maintenance agreements may be made non-modifiable by agreement of both spouses.

**Child Custody and Visitation:**
Custody is determined according to the best interest of the child and the following factors: (1) preference of the child; (2) the desire and ability of the custodial parent to allow a frequent relationship both open and loving between the child and other parent; (3) desire of each parent; (4) child's adjustment to his or her home, school, and community; (5) the mental and physical health of the child and parents; (6) bond between child and parents and any siblings; (7) evidence of domestic violence; (8) any coercion or duress in obtaining a custody agreement; and (9) which parent(s) have provided primary care of the child. No preference is to be given on the basis of the parent's sex. Joint/shared custody is not favored, however, if the parents can submit a written agreement on joint/shared custody, and have satisfied the above factors, and the following additional factors: (1) that neither parent was coerced or influenced by duress into withholding or granting his or her agreement to joint custody; (2) that the parents can sustain an ongoing commitment to the child; and (3) that the joint custody agreement is logistically possible. Grandparents and great-grandparents may be awarded visitation rights. The court may consider awarding joint/shared custody.

**Child Support:**
The court may order either parent to pay child support without regard to marital misconduct. Awards of child support are paid through the court unless the parents agree otherwise. Official Arizona Supreme Court child support guidelines are available from the clerk of any Superior Court. The guidelines set the required amount for child support unless the amount is shown to be unjust and inappropriate. Every child support order will assign one or both parents the responsibility of getting medical insurance for the child and for payment of any medical expenses not covered by insurance.

**Rights to Maiden Name:**
The wife may restore her former or maiden name upon request.

# ARKANSAS

**Residence Requirements:**
A spouse filing for a divorce must live in the state for 60 days and for 3 months before a divorce will be finalized.

**Where to File:**
In plaintiff's county; non-resident plaintiffs should file in the county of the defendant.

**Name of Court:**
Chancery Court. "In the Chancery Court of _____ Arkansas."

**Title of Divorce Action:**
Complaint for Divorce

**Party Filing:**
Plaintiff

**Other Party:**
Defendant

**Title of Final Papers:**
Decree of Divorce

**Approved Grounds for Divorce:**
No-fault: 3 years or more of voluntarily living separate without cohabitation. Fault-based: (1) impotence; (2) adultery; (3) confinement for incurable insanity or separation caused by mental illness for a period of 3 years; (4) convicted felon; (5) personal indignities; (6) cruel and inhuman treatment which imminently endangers the life of the spouse; (7) drunkenness for 1 year; (8) commission and/or conviction of an infamous crime; and (9) non-support to complaining spouse when other spouse is able to provide such support.

**General Divorce Procedures:**
In an uncontested divorce action, proof of a spouse's residency, separation, and no cohabitation may be evidenced by a signed affidavit from a third party. However, proof of the grounds for a divorce does not need to be corroborated by a third party.

**Mediation or Counseling Requirements:**
There is no legal provision which directly addresses this issue in Arkansas.

**Legal Separation Provisions:**
Legal separation may be granted for the same reasons as the fault-based grounds, plus (1) willful desertion for 1 year, and (2) voluntary separation for 18 months.

**Property Distribution:**
Arkansas is an "equitable distribution" state. All property acquired during the marriage, both jointly or separately, will be divided equally between the spouses. However, if the court finds that the division of property will be unfair, the court may then re-distribute the property with the following factors in mind: (1) each spouse's contribution to the acquisition of the marital property, including non-monetary contributions to the marriage, i.e. homemaking; (2) duration of the marriage; (3) age and health of each spouse; (4) the occupation of each spouse; (5) any and all sources of income to each spouse; (6) the vocational skill of each spouse; (7) earning ability in the job market; (8) the financial position of each spouse and ability to acquire more capital assets and income; and (9) the federal income tax consequence of dividing the property. All property acquired by the spouses prior to marriage, including gifts and inheritances, is retained unless the court finds it necessary to divide such property to achieve an equitable distribution. Fault may be considered in dividing the property if the grounds for divorce are voluntary separation for 3 years.

**Alimony/Spousal Support/Maintenance:**
Either spouse may be awarded alimony for a specific duration and subject to contingencies, such as the death or re-marriage of the receiving spouse. All awards of alimony to a spouse must be reasonable based on the particular circumstances of each case. Alimony payments may be ordered paid through the court.

**Child Custody and Visitation:**
Child custody may be awarded to either parent and is based on the best interest of the child. The court will base its decision on the following factors: (1) the circumstances of the parents and child, (2) the nature of the case; (3) which parent is most likely to allow frequent and continuing contact with the other parent; and (4) any acts of domestic violence. Joint/shared custody is only awarded in the best interest of the child. The sex of the parent is not a factor for decisions relating to child custody.

**Child Support:**
A reasonable amount will be awarded based on the following factors: (1) the circumstances of the parent and the child, and (2) the nature of the case. Child support payments may be ordered paid through the court and the court may also order that a bond be posted to secure the child support payment. In addition, official child support guidelines from the Arkansas Supreme Court are presumed to be correct unless the amount is shown to be unjust, considering the following factors: (1) any necessary medical, dental, or psychological care or insurance; (2) the creation or maintenance of trust fund for the child; (3) day care expenses; (4) extraordinary time spent with the non-custodial parent; and (5) any additional support provided by the parent obligated to pay support.

**Rights to Maiden Name:**
The wife may restore her former or maiden name upon request.

## CALIFORNIA

Residence Requirements:

The spouse filing for dissolution of marriage must be a resident for 6 months and a resident for 3 months in the county in which he or she is filing. There is a 6-month waiting period after the service of process or the appearance by the other spouse before the court finalizes the dissolution of marriage.

| Where to File: | Name of Court: | Title of Divorce Action: |
|---|---|---|
| In the county of the filing spouse; the spouse must have resided in the county for 3 months. | Superior Court. "Superior Court of California, County of_____________." | Petition for Dissolution of Marriage |

| Party Filing: | Other Party: | Title of Final Papers: |
|---|---|---|
| Petitioner | Respondent | Final Judgment of Dissolution of Marriage |

Important Note:

Additional forms may be required. Call or visit your clerk of the court.

Approved Grounds for Divorce:

No-fault: Irreconcilable differences which have caused the irremediable breakdown of the marriage. Fault-based: Incurable insanity.

General Divorce Procedures:

A joint petition for summary dissolution of marriage may be filed if: (1) the marriage is of 5 years or less; (2) one spouse meets the residency requirements; (3) there are no children born or adopted during the marriage and the wife is not pregnant; (4) neither spouse owns any real estate; (5) there are no unpaid obligations incurred during the marriage which exceed $4,000; (6) the community property has a total value of less than $25,000, including any and all deferred compensation or retirement but excluding cars and loans; (7) neither spouse has separate property which is greater than $25,000 (cars and loans excluded). [Note: This amount is subject to change in every odd-numbered year; (8) the spouses have a written and signed agreement regarding the division of property and payment of all debts and submit any documents or proof which gives legal effect to the agreement; (9) both spouses waive their right to spousal support; (10) the spouses waive their right to a new trial or to appeal the dissolution of marriage; (11) the spouses have read and understand the brochure on summary dissolution of marriage which is available in the county clerk's office; and (12) both spouses want the marriage dissolved. Unlike a "regular" dissolution, there is a 6-month waiting period before a summary divorce is final.

Mediation or Counseling Requirements:

If the court determines there is a reasonable possibility of reconciliation in a no-fault case, the proceedings will be delayed for 30 days. If there is no reconciliation, either spouse may request a dissolution of marriage or legal separation. A confidential counseling statement must be filed with the county clerk if there is a Conciliation Court. Forms are available at the clerk's office. If custody is a dispute, the court will order mediation.

Legal Separation Provisions:

To obtain a legal separation in California, the legal separation must be grounded on: (1) irreconcilable differences and (2) incurable insanity.

Property Distribution:

California is a "community property" state. All property acquired jointly during the marriage will be divided equally, unless it is clearly stated in a deed or written agreement that the property is "separate" property. However, the court may divide the property unequally if economic circumstances warrant it or if one of the spouses has willfully misappropriated the property. If one of the spouses has helped the other with education and training which will increase that spouse's earning abilities, then this contribution is reimbursable to the community property. Each spouse will be responsible for: (1) his or her debts acquired prior to the marriage; (2) debts acquired during the marriage which did not benefit the marriage; (3) any debts for non-necessities acquired after the separation but before the dissolution of the marriage (debts for necessities will be equally divided); (4) an equitable share of community debt incurred during the marriage.

Alimony/Spousal Support/Maintenance:

Either spouse may be awarded spousal support. In doing so the court will look at the following factors: (1) whether the spouse seeking support has custody of the child(ren) and is unable to work because the child requires care; (2) the earning capacity of each spouse; (3) the standard of living during the marriage; (4) the length of the marriage; (5) the contribution of each spouse to the marriage, including non-monetary contributions, i.e. homemaking; (6) each spouse's assets and ability to increase assets; (7) the needs and obligations of each spouse; (8) each spouse's age and physical and emotional health; (9) the time necessary to acquire sufficient education and training to enable the spouse to find appropriate employment, and that spouse's future earning capacity; (10) the tax consequences to each spouse; (11) the supporting spouse's ability to pay; (12) the balance of hardships to each party; (13) and any other factor the court considers relevant. However, marital misconduct will not be considered by the court.

Child Custody and Visitation:

Child custody may be awarded to either spouse. However, joint/shared custody may also be awarded. The court will consider the following factors: (1) preference of the child if of sufficient age and capacity; (2) the desire and ability of each parent to allow a frequent relationship, both open and loving, between the child and other parent; (3) the child's health, safety and welfare; (4) any history of child or spouse abuse by anyone seeking custody or who has had any caretaking relationship with the child, including anyone dating the parent; (5) the bond between the child and each parent; (6) any continued use of of alcohol or controlled substances; (7) marital misconduct, if any, may be considered. The court may order that a parent give the other parent 30 days' notice before changing the residence of the child.

Child Support:

Either parent may be ordered to pay an amount necessary for the support, maintenance and education of the child. Child support payments may be awarded on a temporary basis during custody of child support proceeding. There is a mandatory minimum amount of child support which is determined by official forms which are available from the county clerk of any county. These minimum payment amounts will apply unless there is a reasonable agreement between the parents providing otherwise that states that (1) the parents state that they are fully informed of their rights regarding child support under California law, (2) that the child support amount is being agreed to without coercion or duress, (3) that both parents declare that their children's needs will be adequately met, and (4) that the right to child support has not been assigned to the county and that no public assistance is pending. A parent may be required to provide medical insurance coverage for a child if such coverage is available at a reasonable cost. The parent required to pay may be required to give reasonable security for the support payments.

Rights to Maiden Name:

The former or maiden name of the wife will be restored upon request, regardless of the last name of any custodial child.

## COLORADO

Residence Requirements:

Either spouse must have lived in the state for at least 90 days before filing.

| Where to File: | Name of Court: | Title of Divorce Action: |
|---|---|---|
| Respondent's county or county in which the petitioner lives if respondent is a non-resident of Colorado. | District Court. "In the District Court in and for the County of__________ and State of Colorado." | Petition for Dissolution of Marriage |

| Party Filing: | Other Party: | Title of Final Papers: |
|---|---|---|
| Petitioner | Respondent | Decree of Dissolution of Marriage |

Important Note:

Additional forms may be required. Call or visit your clerk of the court.

Approved Grounds for Divorce:

Irretrievable breakdown of the marriage is the only grounds for a dissolution of marriage.

General Divorce Procedures:

Either or both spouses may obtain a dissolution of marriage by affidavit if: (1) there are no minor children and the wife is not pregnant or the spouses are represented by counsel and have a separation agreement granting custody and support; (2) there is no marital property or the spouses have agreed on how to divide the marital property; (3) there are no disputes; (4) the respondent has been served with the dissolution of marriage papers. In addition, a signed affidavit stating the facts of the case must be filed with the petition for dissolution of marriage.

Mediation or Counseling Requirements:

At the court's discretion or at the request of either party, the court may appoint a marriage counselor and stay the action for 30 to 60 days. A court may appoint an arbitrator to resolve disputes between parents concerning child support and custody.

Legal Separation Provisions:

The spouses may file for legal separation if there has been an irretrievable breakdown of the marriage.

Property Distribution:

Colorado is an "equitable distribution" state. All property acquired during the marriage will be divided without regard to any fault. The court will consider the following: (1) each spouse's contribution to the acquisition of marital property, including non-monetary contribution; (2) the value of each spouse's separate property; (3) the financial status of each spouse and the desirability to award the family home to the custodial parent or allow that parent to live in the home until the child(ren) is grown; (4) whether separate property has increased or decreased in value due to its use for the benefit of the marriage. Separate property acquired prior to the marriage is retained by that spouse.

Alimony/Spousal Support/Maintenance:

The court may award spousal support to either and will consider: (1) the property the spouse has; (2) the inability of the spouse to support himself or herself even with employment or the inability to work because of retaining custody of a child who requires special care; (3) the earning capability of the spouse; (4) the length of the marriage; and (5) the age and physical and emotional health of the spouse. Additionally, the court will consider: (1) the time necessary to acquire sufficient education and training to enable the spouse to find appropriate employment, and that spouse's future earning capacity; (2) the standard of living established during the marriage; (3) the ability of the spouse from whom support is sought to meet his or her needs while meeting those of the spouse seeking support; (4) the financial resources of the spouse seeking maintenance, including marital property apportioned to such spouse and such spouse's ability to meet his or her needs independently; and (6) any custodial and child support responsibilities. Maintenance payments may be ordered to be paid directly to the court for distribution to the spouse.

Child Custody and Visitation:

Child custody is determined according to the best interest of the child; therefore sole or joint custody may be awarded. The court will consider the following: (1) the parents' wishes; (2) the child's wishes; (3) the bond between the child and each parent and any siblings; (4) the length of time the child has lived in a particular environment; (5) the mental and physical health of all individuals involved; and (6) any child abuse or spouse abuse by either parent. Visitation may be restricted if there is a danger to the child.

Child Support:

Either spouse may be ordered to pay child support. The court will consider the following: (1) the financial assets of the child; (2) the financial assets of the parents; (3) the standard of living the child would have if the marriage had not been dissolved; (4) the physical and emotional conditions and educational needs of the child; and (5) the financial resources, needs, and obligations of both the non-custodial and the custodial parent. Provisions for medical insurance and medical care for any children may be ordered to be provided. There are official child support guidelines available at the county clerk's office in any county.

Rights to Maiden Name:

There is no legal provision in Colorado for restoration of the spouse's name upon divorce. However, there is a general statute which allows for the change of a person's name upon petition to the court.

# CONNECTICUT

**Residence Requirements:**
Either spouse must be a resident of the state for 1 year for the dissolution of marriage to be finalized, unless one spouse was a resident when he or she entered into the marriage and then returned with the intention of permanent residence, or if the grounds for dissolution of marriage arose in Connecticut.

**Where to File:**
If support sought, plaintiff must file in county where he/she resides, otherwise file where convenient for both spouses.

**Name of Court:**
Superior Court

**Title of Divorce Action:**
Complaint for Dissolution of Marriage

**Party Filing:**
Plaintiff

**Other Party:**
Defendant

**Title of Final Papers:**
Decree of Dissolution of Marriage

**Approved Grounds for Divorce:**
No-fault: (1) irretrievable breakdown of the marriage, or (2) incompatibility and voluntary separation for 18 months with no reasonable prospect for reconciliation. Fault-based: (1) adultery; (2) life imprisonment; (3) 7 years' absence; (4) fraud; (5) habitual drunkenness; (6) confinement for incurable insanity for 5 years; (7) cruel and inhuman treatment; (8) willful desertion and non-support for 1 year; or (9) commission and/or conviction of an infamous crime involving a violation of conjugal duty and imprisonment for at least one year.

**General Divorce Procedures:**
A dissolution of marriage will be granted if proof is submitted by: (1) an agreement signed by both spouses or affidavit stating that the marriage is irretrievably broken; or (2) an agreement signed by both spouses concerning custody, care, education, support or visitation of children, if any, applicable alimony and the division of property. In addition, the spouses must state in court that the marriage is irretrievably broken.

**Mediation or Counseling Requirements:**
Within 90 days after filing for a divorce, either spouse may ask the clerk of the court for conciliation. Two mandatory counseling sessions will be ordered. In addition, mediation is also available to settle property, support, custody, and visitation disputes.

**Legal Separation Provisions:**
A legal separation must be grounded on the same reasons as above (no-fault or fault-based).

**Property Distribution:**
Connecticut is an "equitable distribution" state. The court may award to either spouse all or part of the property of the other spouse, including gifts and inheritances, with the following factors in mind: (1) each spouse's contribution to the acquisition of the marital property, including non-monetary contributions, i.e. homemaking; (2) age and health of each spouse; (3) the occupation of each spouse; (4) the amount and sources of income of the spouses; (6) the vocational skills of the spouses; (7) the employability of the spouses; (8) the estate, liabilities, and needs of each spouse and the opportunity of each for further acquisition of capital assets and income; and (9) the causes that led to the breakdown of the marriage.

**Alimony/Spousal Support/Maintenance:**
Spousal support may be awarded to either spouse based on the following factors: (1) the cause for the divorce with regard to fault; (2) age and physical and emotional health of each spouse; (3) whether the spouse seeking support is the custodian of a child whose condition or circumstances make it appropriate for that spouse not to seek outside employment; (4) distribution of the marital property; (5) occupation of each spouse; (6) marketable skills, if any; and (7) the needs of each spouse.

**Child Custody and Visitation:**
Child custody may be awarded to either parent based on the best interest of the child. The court will consider the following factors: (1) the causes for the divorce and how it relates to the best interests of the child; and (2) the preference of the child if such child is of sufficient age and capacity. Joint custody will be awarded if both parents agree to it.

**Child Support:**
The court may order either parent to pay support based on the following: (1) earning ability of each parent; (2) age and health of the child and parents; (3) financial resources of the child and parents; (4) occupation, if any, of the child; (5) the occupation of each parent; (6) the vocational skills and employability of each parent; (7) the vocational skills of the child; (8) the employability of the child; (9) the estate and needs of the child; and (10) the relative financial means of the parents.

**Rights to Maiden Name:**
Either spouse's former name will be restored upon request.

# DELAWARE

**Residence Requirements:**
Either spouse must have been a resident for 6 months before filing.

**Where to File:**
In the county where either spouse lives.

**Name of Court:**
Family Court. "In the Family Court for the State of Delaware, In and For_____County."

**Title of Divorce Action:**
Petition for Divorce

**Party Filing:**
Petitioner

**Other Party:**
Respondent

**Title of Final Papers:**
Decree of Divorce

**Approved Grounds for Divorce:**
No-fault: Irretrievable breakdown of the marriage. Fault-based: Separation caused by mental illness.

**General Divorce Procedures:**
The requirement for service of process may be satisfied by the respondent by filing an appearance.

**Mediation or Counseling Requirements:**
The court may order mediation, in which case the proceedings for a dissolution of marriage will be delayed for 60 days.

**Legal Separation Provisions:**
There is no legal provision that directly addresses this issue in the state of Delaware.

**Property Distribution:**
Delaware is an "equitable distribution" state. Property acquired before the marriage will be retained by that spouse. All property acquired during the marriage will be divided equally based upon the following: (1) age and health of each spouse; (2) occupation of each spouse; (3) each spouse's contribution to the acquisition of the marital property, including non-monetary contributions to the marriage, i.e. homemaking; (4) duration of the marriage; (5) the value of each spouse's separate property; (6) earning ability of each spouse; (7) the tax consequence of dividing the property; (8) any and all sources of income of each spouse; (9) the vocational skills of the spouses; (10) the employability of the spouses; (11) the estate, liabilities, and needs of each spouse and the opportunity of each for further acquisition of capital assets and income; (12) liabilities of the spouses; (13) any prior marriage of each spouse; (14) whether the property award is instead of or in addition to maintenance; (15) how and by whom the property was acquired; and (16) any custodial provisions for the children.

**Alimony/Spousal Support/Maintenance:**
The court may award support to either spouse if the spouse: (1) lacks sufficient property, even after dividing the marital property, to support himself or herself; (2) is dependent on the other spouse; (3) lacks the appropriate earning skills; or (4) is unable to work because he or she is the custodial parent and the child requires special care. Either spouse may be awarded alimony for no longer than a period of time equal 50% of the length of the marriage. There is, however, no time limit if the marriage lasted for over 20 years.

**Child Custody and Visitation:**
Either parent may be awarded custody. Joint or sole child custody may be awarded based on the following factors: (1) the child's wishes; (2) the parents' wishes; (3) the bond between the child and each parent and any siblings; (4) the child's adjustment to his or her home, school, and community; (5) the mental and physical health of all individuals involved; and (6) the past and present compliance by both parents with the duty to support the child. The conduct of the proposed guardian is to be considered only as is bears on his or her relationship with the child. No preference to be given because of parent's sex. Also the petitioner must submit a signed affidavit stating that he or she has read and understands the children's rights. A list of the children's rights is available at the county clerk's office.

**Child Support:**
The court may order either parent to pay child support based on the following: (1) age and health of the child and parent; (2) the financial resources of the child and parents; (3) earning abilities of the parents; (4) the standard of living the child would have enjoyed if the marriage was not dissolved; (5) the age, health, or station of the child; (6) the estate and needs of the child; ..nd (7) the relative financial means of the parents.

**Rights to Maiden Name:**
The wife may restore her former name upon request.

# DISTRICT OF COLUMBIA

**Residence Requirements:**
Either spouse must have resided in the District of Columbia for 6 months before filing. Military personnel are eligible to file if they have been stationed in the District of Columbia for 6 months.

| Where to File: | Name of Court: | Title of Divorce Action: |
|---|---|---|
| Superior Court, Family Division | "In the Superior Court of the District of Columbia—Family Division." | Complaint for Divorce |

| Party Filing: | Other Party: | Title of Final Papers: |
|---|---|---|
| Plaintiff | Defendant | Final Decree of Divorce |

**Approved Grounds for Divorce:**
No-fault: (1) mutual voluntary separation without cohabitation for 6 months; or (2) living separate and apart without cohabitation for 1 year.

**General Divorce Procedures:**
There are no legal provisions in the District of Columbia for a simplified divorce.

**Mediation or Counseling Requirements:**
The court may order either or both spouses to attend parenting classes in those cases in which child custody is an issue.

**Legal Separation Provisions:**
Legal separation (from bed and board) will be awarded if grounded on the following: (1) adultery; (2) cruel and inhuman treatment; or (3) living separate and apart without cohabitation. One of the spouses must have been a resident for six months prior to filing for legal separation. Military personnel are considered residents if they have been stationed in Washington D.C. for six months.

**Property Distribution:**
The District of Columbia is an "equitable distribution" jurisdiction. Separate property acquired before the marriage and property acquired by gift or inheritance will be retained by each spouse. All marital property, regardless of how title is held, will be divided in an equitable manner based on the following: (1) any prior marriage of each spouse; (2) whether property awarded is in lieu of or in addition to spousal support; (3) each spouse's contribution to the acquisition of the marital property, including non-monetary contributions, i.e. homemaking; (4) earning ability of each spouse; (5) occupation of each spouse; (6) length of the marriage; (7) any and all sources of income of each spouse; (8) which spouse retains custody of the child(ren); (9) age and physical and mental health of each spouse; (10) the vocational skills of the spouses; (11) the employability of the spouses; (12) the estate, liabilities, and needs of each spouse and the opportunity of each for further acquisition of capital assets and income; and (13) the assets and debts of the spouses

**Alimony/Spousal Support/Maintenance**
Either spouse may be awarded alimony. Marital misconduct may be considered in awarding alimony. No other specific factors are listed in the statute.

**Child Custody and Visitation:**
Child custody may be granted to either parent. Custody is granted according to the best interest of the child based on the following: (1) the child's wishes; (2) the wishes of the parents; (3) the bond between the child and each parent and any siblings; (4) the mental and physical health of the parties; (5) the child's adjustment to his or her home, school and community; (6) the willingness of the parents to share custody; (7) the prior involvement of the parent in the child's life; (8) the geographical proximity of the parents; (9) the sincerity of the parent's request; (10) the age and number of children; (11) the demands of parental employment; (12) the impact on any welfare benefits; and (13) evidence of spousal or child abuse. There is a rebuttable presumption that joint interest is in the best interests of the child; unless child abuse, neglect, parental kidnapping or other intrafamily violence has occurred. The court may order the parents to submit a written parenting plan for custody.

**Child Support:**
The court may order either parent to pay child support. The court will use specific child support guidelines in awarding child support. However, the court can deviate from the guidelines if there are extraordinary factors that warrant the court to do so. Child support may be ordered paid through the court.

**Rights to Maiden Name:**
The former or maiden name will be restored upon request.

# FLORIDA

**Residence Requirements:**
Either spouse must be a resident of Florida for 6 months before filing.

| Where to File: | Name of Court: | Title of Divorce Action: |
|---|---|---|
| In the county where the respondent lives or in the county where spouses lived together before separating. | Circuit Court. "In the Circuit Court in and for the County of _____, Florida." | Petition for Dissolution of Marriage. NOTE: Disclosure from Nonlawyers: If a person who is a nonlawyer helps you fill out these forms, that person must give you a copy of Family Law Form 12.900, Disclosure from Nonlawyer, before they help you. |

| Party Filing: | Other Party: | Title of Final Papers: |
|---|---|---|
| Petitioner | Respondent | Final Judgment of Dissolution of Marriage |

**Approved Grounds for Divorce:**
No-fault: Irretrievable breakdown of the marriage. Fault-based: Mental incapacity for 3 years.

**General Divorce Procedures:**
A simplified dissolution of marriage can be used if: (1) there are no minor children and the wife is not pregnant; (2) the spouses have agreed to a fair division of property and payment of their debts; (3) the resident requirement has been satisfied; and (4) the marriage is irretrievably broken. The spouses must testify in court to the above and submit a certificate of corroborating witness as to the residency requirement. In addition, each spouse must attach a financial affidavit to the petition for dissolution of marriage.

**Mediation or Counseling Requirements:**
If one spouse disputes that the marriage is irretrievably broken or if there are minor children involved, then the court may delay the proceeding for up to 3 months, during which time the spouses will be ordered to attempt reconciliation or attend mediation sessions.

**Legal Separation Provisions:**
A spouse may file for separate maintenance and support.

**Property Distribution:**
Florida is an "equitable distribution" state. Each spouse will retain his or her separate property. Separate property is property acquired before the marriage, by gift or inheritance, or considered separate according to a written agreement. All marital property will be divided equitably based on the following factors: (1) each spouse's contribution to the acquisition of the marital property, including any non-monetary contribution, i.e. homemaking; (2) the length of the marriage; (3) standard of living during the marriage; (4) any and all sources of income of each spouse; (5) the financial resources of each spouse and ability to increase resources; (6) the age and health of each spouse; (7) the time and expense of each spouse will incur to receive sufficient education or training for appropriate employment; and (8) any other relevant factor.

**Alimony/Spousal Support/Maintenance:**
Either spouse may be awarded alimony on a rehabilitative or permanent basis. The award may be a lump sum, a periodic payment or both. Adultery may be a factor in the award. The court will also consider the same factors as listed under Property Distribution.

**Child Custody and Visitation:**
Either parent may be awarded custody. However, joint custody, referred to as "shared parental responsibility," may also be awarded. The court will base its decision on: (1) the moral fitness of the parents; (2) the child's wishes; (3) the amount of time the child has lived in a particular environment and the desirability of maintaining continuity; (4) the bond between the child and each parent; (5) any domestic violence; (6) the desire and ability of each parent to allow a loving and open relationship between the child and the other parent; (7) the material needs of the child; (8) the capability and desire of each parent to meet the child's needs; (9) the child's adjustment to his or her home, school, and community; (10) the stability of the home environment likely to be offered by each parent; (11) any evidence of spouse abuse; and (12) any other relevant factor.

**Child Support:**
Either parent may be ordered to pay child support. The court will use the official child support guidelines in awarding child support.

**Rights to Maiden Name:**
No legal provision addresses restoration of former name, however, a general statute provides for a petition for a name change.

**Disclosure from Nonlawyers:**
If a person who is a nonlawyer helps you fill out these forms, that person must give you a copy of Family Law Form 12.900, Disclosure from Nonlawyer, before they help you.

# GEORGIA

**Residence Requirements:**
One spouse must have been a resident of Georgia for at least 6 months before filing.

**Where to File:**
In the county where the resident spouse resides. The non-resident (resident in Georgia less than 6 months) may file in his or her county.

**Name of Court:**
Superior Court. "In the Superior Court of _____ County, Georgia."

**Title of Divorce Action:**
Petition for Divorce

**Party Filing:**
Petitioner

**Other Party:**
Respondent

**Title of Final Papers:**
Final Judgment and Decree of Divorce

**Approved Grounds for Divorce:**
No-fault: Irretrievable breakdown of the marriage. Fault-based: (1) adultery; (2) impotence; (3) conviction and imprisonment of over 2 years for an offense involving moral turpitude; (4) drunkenness or drug abuse; (5) separation caused by mental illness; (6) confinement for incurable insanity; (7) alcoholism; (8) fraud, duress, or force into marriage; (9) lack of mental capacity to consent to marriage; (10) cruel and inhuman treatment; (11) wife was pregnant with a child of another unknown to the husband; (12) willful desertion; (13) consent to marriage was obtained by fraud, duress, or force; or (14) incest.

**General Divorce Procedures:**
There are no simplified divorce procedures in Georgia.

**Mediation or Counseling Requirements:**
There are no legal provisions which directly address divorce mediation in Georgia.

**Legal Separation Provisions:**
A spouse may file for separate maintenance.

**Property Distribution:**
Georgia is an "equitable distribution" state. The court will divide all marital property, including any gifts and inheritances, in an equitable manner.

**Alimony/Spousal Support/Maintenance:**
The court may award permanent or temporary alimony to either spouse, unless the separation was due to that spouse's desertion or adultery. The court will consider the following factors: (1) each spouse's contribution to the acquisition of the marital property, including all non-monetary contributions; (2) length of the marriage; (3) age and health of each spouse; (4) the value of each spouse's separate property; (5) earning ability of each spouse; (6) the standard of living during the marriage; (7) the time a spouse spends obtaining sufficient education or training for appropriate employment; (8) any fixed liabilities of either spouse; and (9) the financial resources of each spouse.

**Child Custody and Visitation:**
Child custody is based on the circumstances of the case. Custody is awarded based on the best interest of the child in consideration of the following factors: (1) the suitability of each parent as custodian; (2) the psychological, emotional and developmental needs of the child; (3) the ability of the parents to communicate with each other; (4) the prior and continuing care that the parents have given the child; (5) parental support for the other parent's relationship with the child; (6) the wishes of the child (considering the child's age and maturity); (7) the safety of the child; (8) the geographic proximity of the parents; (9) any custodial agreements of the parents; and (10) any history of domestic abuse. There is a presumption against awarding joint custody in Georgia when there is a history of domestic abuse.

**Child Support:**
Either parent may be ordered to pay child support. The court will follow official child support guidelines in awarding child support payments if the parents cannot reach an agreement. The court will consider the following: (1) the cost of education; (2) day care cost; (3) income of the custodial parent; (4) a parent's obligation to provide support to other dependents; (5) shared physical custody arrangements; (6) hidden income of a parent; (7) contributions of the parents; (8) extreme economic circumstances; (9) a parent's own extraordinary needs; (10) historic spending levels of the family; (11) the cost of health and accident insurance coverage for the child; and (12) any extraordinary visitation travel expenses.

**Rights to Maiden Name:**
The former name of a spouse will be restored upon request.

# HAWAII

**Residence Requirements:**
The filing spouse must have resided in Hawaii for 3 months. However, a final judgment of divorce will not be granted unless one spouse has been a resident for 6 months.

**Where to File:**
In the judicial district where the plaintiff lives or in the judicial district where the spouses last resided together.

**Name of Court:**
Family Court

**Title of Divorce Action:**
Complaint for Divorce

**Party Filing:**
Plaintiff

**Other Party:**
Defendant

**Title of Final Papers:**
Decree of Divorce

**Approved Grounds for Divorce:**
No-fault: (1) irretrievable breakdown of the marriage; and (2) living separate and apart without cohabitation for 2 years, and it would not be harsh or oppressive to the defendant to grant the divorce. Fault-based: Legal separation and there has been no reconciliation.

**General Divorce Procedures:**
Proof of an irretrievable breakdown of the marriage may be shown by both spouses stating so in an affidavit, or by one spouse stating so in an affidavit, and the other spouse not denying it. The court may then waive any hearing and grant the divorce based on the affidavit submitted.

**Mediation or Counseling Requirements:**
The court may delay the proceedings for 60 days if one spouse disputes that there has been an irretrievable breakdown of the marriage.

**Legal Separation Provisions:**
Legal separation may be granted for up to 2 years on the grounds that the marriage is temporarily disrupted and the filing spouse has been a resident for at least 3 months.

**Property Distribution:**
Hawaii is an "equitable distribution" state. The court will divide in an equitable manner all of the spouses' property, including marital and separate property. The factors considered will be: (1) the financial position of each spouse after the divorce; (2) the burdens imposed on each spouse for the benefit of the children; (3) the earning capability of each spouse; and (4) all relevant factors.

**Alimony/Spousal Support/Maintenance:**
Either spouse may be awarded alimony based on the following: (1) length of the marriage; (2) the financial resources of each spouse; (3) earning ability of each spouse; (4) age and health of each spouse; (5) the standard of living during the marriage; (6) the length of time the spouse will need alimony; (7) the financial position the spouses will be left in after the marriage has been dissolved; (8) the ability of the spouse seeking maintenance to meet his or her needs independently; (9) the comparative financial resources of the spouses; (10) the needs and obligations of each spouse; (11) the usual occupation of the spouses during the marriage; (12) the vocational skills and employability of the spouse seeking support and maintenance; (13) any custodial and child support responsibilities; (14) the ability of the spouse from whom support is sought to meet his or her own needs while meeting the needs of the party seeking support; (15) other factors which measure the financial condition in which the spouses will be left as a result of the divorce; and (16) any other factor which measures the financial condition in which the spouses will be left in as a result of any award of maintenance.

**Child Custody and Visitation:**
Either parent may be awarded custody. In addition, joint custody may be awarded. Custody will be awarded in the best interest of the child and upon the child's preference.

**Child Support:**
Either or both parents may be ordered to pay child support. Child support is awarded in a just and equitable manner. In addition, the court will use the official child support guidelines in setting the payments for child support.

**Rights to Maiden Name:**
The wife's maiden name will be restored upon request.

# IDAHO

**Residence Requirements:**

The filing spouse must have been a resident of Idaho for 6 full weeks before filing for a divorce.

**Where to File:**

In the county where defendant resides, or, if a non-resident, in the county where the plaintiff resides.

**Name of Court:**

"In the District Court of the _____ Judicial District for the State of Idaho, In and for the County of _____."

**Title of Divorce Action:**

Complaint for Divorce

**Party Filing:**

Plaintiff

**Other Party:**

Defendant

**Title of Final Papers:**

Decree of Divorce

**Approved Grounds for Divorce:**

No-fault: (1) irreconcilable differences and living separate and apart without cohabitation for 5 years. Fault-based: (1) adultery; (2) permanent insanity; (3) convicted felon; (4) willful desertion for 1 year; (5) cruel treatment to spouse; (6) willful neglect for 1 year; and (7) drunkenness.

**General Divorce Procedures:**

A divorce may still be granted if the defendant fails to answer the complaint for divorce (default judgment). Marital settlement agreements are authorized. These agreements must be in writing and notarized. If the marital settlement agreement contains any provisions dealing in real estate, then the agreement must be recorded in the county recorder's office.

**Mediation or Counseling Requirements:**

Idaho has a mandatory 20-day waiting period before granting a divorce, unless the spouses agree differently. Either spouse can request a meeting to determine whether there can be reconciliation. If it is determined that there may be a practical chance for reconciliation and there are minor children, the court will delay the proceedings for 90 days.

**Legal Separation Provisions:**

There are no provisions for legal separation.

**Property Distribution:**

Idaho is a "community property" state. Separate property, which is property acquired: (1) prior to the marriage; (2) by gift or inheritance; or (3) by individual gift before or during the marriage, will be retained by that spouse. All other property acquired during the marriage will be divided equally, unless there are compelling circumstances to do otherwise. The court will consider the following: (1) the duration of the marriage; (2) marital misconduct; (3) the earning capability of each spouse; (4) any and all sources of income of each spouse; (5) whether property awarded is in lieu of or in addition to spousal support; (6) occupation of each spouse; (7) any premarital agreement; (8) any debts of each spouse; (9) the needs of each spouse; (10) age and health of each spouse; (11) the vocational skills of the spouses; and (12) the employability of the spouses.

**Alimony/Spousal Support/Maintenance:**

Either spouse may be awarded maintenance if such spouse: (1) lacks sufficient property to provide for his or her own maintenance; and (2) cannot support himself or herself through appropriate employment. The court will consider the following factors when awarding maintenance: (1) the time and expense a spouse will incur to obtain sufficient education or training for appropriate employment; (2) the length of the marriage; (3) age and health of each spouse; (4) the cause that led to the breakdown of the marriage; (5) the needs of the spouse seeking maintenance and the ability of the other spouse to make such payments while meeting his or her own needs; (6) the financial assets of the spouse seeking maintenance; and (7) the tax consequences to each spouse.

**Child Custody and Visitation:**

Child custody is determined according to the best interest of the child. Joint or sole custody may be awarded. The court will consider the following: (1) the wishes of the child; (2) the wishes of the parents; (3) the mental and physical health of the parents and the child; (4) the bond between the child, the parents and any siblings; (5) the child's adjustment to his or her home, school, and community; (6) a need to promote continuity and stability in the life of the child; and (7) domestic violence, whether or not in the presence of the child. Joint custody is allowed if it can be arranged to assure the child with frequent and continuing contact with both parents. Unless shown otherwise, it is presumed that joint custody is in the best interests of the child.

**Child Support:**

The court may order either parent to pay child support based on the following: (1) financial resources of the child and the parents; (2) standard of living the child would have enjoyed if the marriage was not dissolved; (3) the physical and emotional conditions and educational needs of the child; (4) the financial resources, needs and obligations of both the noncustodial and the custodial parent (normally, not including the parent's community property share of the financial resources or obligations with a new spouse); (5) the availability of reasonable medical insurance coverage for the child; (6) and the actual tax benefits achieved by the parent claiming the federal dependency exemption for income tax purposes. Child support may be paid through the clerk of the court, unless the court orders otherwise. There are official child support guidelines which the court will use unless it is shown that such amount will be unjust or inappropriate. All child support orders allow the court to enforce child support payments by withholding the income of the "paying" spouse.

**Rights to Maiden Name:**

No legal provision addresses restoration of former name; however, a general statute provides for a petition for name change.

# ILLINOIS

**Residence Requirements:**

The filing spouse must have been a resident of Illinois for 90 days before filing for a dissolution of marriage.

**Where to File:**

In the county in which either spouse resides.

**Name of Court:**

"In the Circuit Court of the _____ Judicial District, _____ County, Illinois."

**Title of Divorce Action:**

Petition for Dissolution of Marriage

**Party Filing:**

Petitioner

**Other Party:**

Respondent

**Title of Final Papers:**

Judgment for Dissolution of Marriage

**Approved Grounds for Divorce:**

No-fault: Irreconcilable differences and reconciliation has failed or further attempts will be impractical and the spouses have lived separate and apart without cohabitation for 2 years. However, if both spouses agree, the time period becomes 6 months. Fault-based: (1) adultery; (2) bigamy; (3) felony; (4) impotence; (5) drunkenness for 2 years; (6) drug abuse; (7) cruel and inhuman treatment; (8) willful desertion for 1 year; and (9) infection of the other spouse with a communicable disease.

**General Divorce Procedures:**

To speed up the divorce process, marital separation agreements are encouraged.

**Mediation or Counseling Requirements:**

If the court or either spouse requests, the court may order a conciliation conference if there is a possibility of reconciliation.

**Legal Separation Provisions:**

The petitioner must file for legal separation in the county where the respondent lives. The petitioner may seek reasonable support and maintenance if without fault and living separate and apart from the other spouse when obtaining a legal separation.

**Property Distribution:**

Illinois is an "equitable distribution" state. Each spouse will retain property acquired prior to the marriage and any property acquired by gift or inheritance. This is known as separate property. All other property and marital property will be divided, without fault, according to the following factors: (1) each spouse's contribution to the acquisition of marital property, including non-monetary contribution, i.e. homemaking; (2) the value of each spouse's separate property; (3) the financial status of each spouse and the desirability to award the family home to the custodial parent or allow that parent to live in the home until the child(ren) is grown; (4) any and all sources of income of each spouse; (5) the occupation of each spouse; (6) the financial position of each spouse, and his or her ability to acquire more capital assets and income; (7) age and health of each spouse; (8) the duration of the marriage; (9) debts of each spouse; (10) whether the property award is in lieu of or in addition to alimony; (11) the occupation of the spouses; (12) the vocational skills of the spouses; (13) the employability of the spouses; (14) the federal income tax consequences of the court's division of the property; or (15) any premarital agreement.

**Alimony/Spousal Support/Maintenance:**

Either spouse may be awarded maintenance if such spouse: (1) lacks the appropriate earning skills or is the custodial parent and unable to seek employment because the child requires special care; (2) lacks sufficient property to provide for his or her maintenance; or (3) is otherwise without sufficient income. The cause for the divorce will not be considered. The award will be based on the following: (1) age and mental and physical health of each spouse; (2) the time and expense a spouse will incur to obtain sufficient education or training for appropriate employment; (3) the needs of the spouse seeking maintenance and the ability of the other spouse to make such payments while meeting his or her own needs; (4) the standard of living established during the marriage; (5) the financial position of the spouse seeking maintenance; (6) the duration of the marriage; (7) the tax consequences to each spouse; (8) any custodial and child support responsibilities.

**Child Custody and Visitation:**

Child custody will be awarded in the best interest of the child based on the following: (1) the child's wishes; (2) the preferences of the parents; (3) mental and physical health of the child and parents; (4) domestic violence; (5) the relationship of the child with parents, siblings and other significant family members; and (6) the willingness and ability of each parent to encourage a close and continuing relationship between the child and the other parent. Joint custody may also be awarded. The court will consider the following factors: (1) the desire of each parent to cooperate in this arrangement; (2) the geographic location of each parent; and (3) any other factor the court considers relevant.

**Child Support:**

The court may order either parent to pay child support based on the following: (1) the financial resources of the child and parents; (2) the standard of living the child would have enjoyed if the marriage was not dissolved; (3) the physical and emotional conditions and educational needs of the child; and (4) the financial resources, needs and obligations of both the noncustodial and custodial parent. The support payments may include payment for the child's health insurance. There are official child support guidelines which help the court establish the amount of child support.

**Rights to Maiden Name:**

The wife may restore her former name upon request.

---

This product does not constitute the rendering of legal advice or services. This product is intended for informational use only and is not a substitute for legal advice. State laws vary, so consult an attorney on all legal matters. This product was not prepared by a person licensed to practice law in this state.

# INDIANA

**Residence Requirements:**
Either spouse must have been a resident of Indiana for 6 months before filing for a dissolution of marriage.

**Where to File:**
In the county in which one of the spouses has been a resident for at least 3 months.

**Name of Court:**
Superior Court, Circuit Court, or Domestic Relations Court. "_____ Court of _____ County, Indiana."

**Title of Divorce Action:**
Petition for Dissolution of Marriage

**Party Filing:**
Petitioner

**Other Party:**
Respondent

**Title of Final Papers:**
Final Dissolution of Marriage Decree

**Approved Grounds for Divorce:**
No-fault: Irretrievable breakdown of the marriage. Fault-based: (1) impotence; (2) conviction of a felony; and (3) permanent insanity for at least 2 years.

**General Divorce Procedures:**
A summary dissolution will be granted by the court if: (1) 60 days have passed since the filing for a petition for dissolution of marriage; (2) the petition was verified and signed by both spouses; (3) the petition contained a provision which waived a final hearing; and (4) the petition contains either a statement (a) that there are no contested matters; or (b) that the spouses have a written marital settlement agreement concerning any contested issues. If some issues remain contested, the court may hold a final hearing on those issues.

**Mediation or Counseling Requirements:**
If the court or either spouse requests counseling, then the court will delay the divorce proceeding for up to 45 days.

**Legal Separation Provisions:**
Legal separation may be granted on the grounds that it is currently intolerable for the spouses to live together.

**Property Distribution:**
Indiana is an "equitable distribution" state. All property acquired before or during the marriage, including gifts and inheritances, will be divided by the court in a just manner. It is presumed that equal division of the property is in a just manner. The court will consider the following: (1) each spouse's contribution to the acquisition of marital property, including non-monetary contributions; (2) the financial position of each spouse and the desirability to award the family home to the custodial parent or allow that parent to live in the home until the child(ren) is grown; (3) the present and future earning ability of each spouse; (4) the extent to which the property acquired by each spouse was acquired prior to marriage or by gift or inheritance; (5) any misconduct which relates to the disposition of any property; and (6) reimbursement for any financial contribution by one spouse toward the higher education of the other spouse.

**Alimony/Spousal Support/Maintenance:**
Either spouse may be awarded maintenance if such spouse: (1) lacks sufficient property to support himself or herself and any incapacitated child and unable to work because the child requires special care, or (2) is mentally or physically incapacitated and unable to support himself or herself. Rehabilitative maintenance may be awarded for up to 3 years based on the following: (1) the time and expense a spouse incurs to obtain sufficient education or training for appropriate employment; (2) earning ability of each spouse; (3) if there was any interruption in education, training, or employment by a spouse due to homemaking responsibilities; or (4) the educational level of each spouse at the time of the marriage and at the time the action is commenced.

**Child Custody and Visitation:**
Child custody is awarded in the best interest of the child based on the following: (1) the wishes of the child; (2) age and sex of the child; (3) the wishes of the parents; (4) the child's adjustment to his/her home, school, and community; (5) the mental and physical health of all individuals involved; and (6) the bond between the child, parents and any siblings. Joint custody may be awarded depending upon: (1) whether it is in the best interest of the child; (2) the geographic location of each parent; (3) the wishes of the child; (4) the fitness and suitability of the parents; (5) the nature of the physical and emotional environment in the home of each of the persons awarded joint custody; (6) the willingness and ability of the persons awarded joint custody to communicate and cooperate in advancing the child's welfare; and (7) whether the child has established a close and beneficial relationship with both of the persons awarded joint custody.

**Child Support:**
The court may order either parent to pay child support. The court will consider the following: (1) the financial resources of each parent; (2) the standard of living the child would have enjoyed if the marriage was not dissolved; and (3) the physical and emotional conditions and educational needs of the child. Support may include payment for medical insurance. Support payments may be required to be paid through the clerk of the court. There are official child support guidelines which the court may use.

**Rights to Maiden Name:**
The wife's former name may be restored upon her request.

# IOWA

**Residence Requirements:**
There is no residency requirement for the filing spouse if the respondent spouse is a resident of Iowa and has been personally served with the petition for dissolution of marriage. Otherwise, there is a 1-year residency requirement. In addition, there is a 90-day waiting period prior to the dissolution of marriage becoming final.

**Where to File:**
In the county where either spouse resides.

**Name of Court:**
District Court. "In the District Court for the County of _____, Iowa."

**Title of Divorce Action:**
Petition for Dissolution of Marriage

**Party Filing:**
Petitioner

**Other Party:**
Respondent

**Title of Final Papers:**
Decree of Dissolution of Marriage

**Approved Grounds for Divorce:**
No-fault: Irretrievable breakdown of the marriage. Fault-based: Irretrievable breakdown of the marriage.

**General Divorce Procedures:**
There are no simplified divorce procedures in Iowa. Both spouses must file financial affidavits with the petition for dissolution of marriage.

**Mediation or Counseling Requirements:**
If the court determines the need for or if either spouse requests counseling, the court will order it for up to 60 days.

**Legal Separation Provisions:**
Legal separation can only be grounded on irretrievable breakdown of the marriage.

**Property Distribution:**
Iowa is an "equitable distribution" state. All property acquired before or during the marriage, except any gifts or inheritances acquired prior to or during the marriage, will be divided. Marital fault will not be considered when dividing the property. The court will consider the following factors: (1) each spouse's contribution to the acquisition of marital property, including non-monetary contributions; (2) the value of any property brought into the marriage; (3) the duration of the marriage; (4) age and health of each spouse; (5) earning ability of each spouse; (6) the financial position of each spouse and the desirability to award the family home to the custodial parent or allow that parent to live in the home until the child(ren) is grown; (7) contribution by one spouse toward the higher education of the other spouse; (8) whether the property award is in lieu of or in addition to alimony; (9) the time and expense a spouse will incur to obtain sufficient education or training for appropriate employment; (10) the vocational skills of the spouses; (11) the employability of the spouses; (12) the federal income tax consequences of the court's division of the property; (13) any premarital or marital settlement agreement; (14) the total economic circumstances of the spouses, including any pension benefits; (15) any custodial provisions for the children; and (16) the amount and duration of any maintenance payments.

**Alimony/Spousal Support/Maintenance:**
Either spouse may be granted maintenance. The court will base its decision on the following factors: (1) the time and expense a spouse incurs to obtain sufficient education or training for gainful employment; (2) length of the marriage; (3) financial position of the spouse seeking alimony; (3) any premarital agreement; (4) the standard of living established during the marriage; (5) custodial and child support obligations; (6) earning ability of spouse seeking maintenance; (7) any interruption in education, training, or employment by a spouse due to homemaking responsibilities; (8) the tax consequences to each spouse; (9) the age of the spouses; (10) the physical and emotional condition of the spouses; (11) the vocational skills and employability of the spouse seeking support and alimony; (12) the probable duration of the need of the spouse seeking support and alimony; (13) the educational level of each spouse at the time of the marriage and at the time the action for support is commenced; and (14) any other factor the court deems just and equitable. Marital misconduct will not be considered by the court.

**Child Custody and Visitation:**
Either parent may be awarded custody. Joint custody may be awarded based on: (1) best interest of the child; (2) desire of the parents to allow a loving and open relationship between the child and the other parent; (3) the child's wishes if of sufficient age and capacity; (4) whether either parent opposes joint custody; (5) geographic location of the parents to each other; and (6) whether both parents took an active role in rearing the child.

**Child Support:**
Either parent may be ordered to pay child support. The court will consider the following: (1) financial resources of the child and parents; (2) the emotional and educational needs of the child; (3) the terms of any shared parental obligations; (4) the standard of living the child would have enjoyed if the marriage was not dissolved; (5) day care cost to the custodial parent, or if such parent does not work, the value of the child care performed by that parent; (6) the recognition of joint parental responsibilities for the welfare of the child; (7) the desirability of the parent having either sole custody or physical care of the child remaining in the home as a full-time parent; (8) the tax consequences to each parent; and (9) any other relevant factors.

**Rights to Maiden Name:**
Either spouse may restore their former name upon dissolution of the marriage.

# KANSAS

**Residence Requirements:**
Either spouse must have been a resident for 60 days before filing.

**Where to File:**
In the county where either spouse resides.

**Name of Court:**
District Court. "In the District Court in and for the County of _____, Kansas."

**Title of Divorce Action:**
Petition for Divorce

**Party Filing:**
Petitioner

**Other Party:**
Respondent

**Title of Final Papers:**
Final Decree of Divorce

**Approved Grounds for Divorce:**
No-fault: Incompatibility. Fault-based: (1) failure to perform a marital duty or obligation; and (2) incompatibility due to mental sickness.

**General Divorce Procedures:**
Kansas requires that only one spouse testify as to the facts in the divorce. Child custody agreements are authorized and are presumed to be in the child's best interest.

**Mediation or Counseling Requirements:**
On either spouse's request, or on its own initiative, the court may require that the spouses seek marriage counseling if marriage counseling services are available in the judicial district where the divorce is sought. Unless in emergency situations, there is a mandatory 60-day delay from the time the petition is filed until a final Decree of Divorce may be granted.

**Legal Separation Provisions:**
The grounds for legal separation are: (1) incompatibility; (2) failure to perform a marital duty or obligation; or (3) incompatibility due to mental sickness.

**Property Distribution:**
Kansas is an "equitable distribution" state. All property acquired before or during the marriage, including any gifts and inheritances, may be divided by the court. The court will consider the following factors: (1) the length of the marriage; (2) whether the property award is in lieu of or in addition to maintenance; (3) any misconduct which relates to the disposition of any property; (4) present and future earning ability of each spouse; (5) how and by whom the property was acquired; (6) age and health of each spouse; (7) the value of each spouse's personal property; (8) family ties and obligations; (9) any dissipation of assets by a spouse; (10) the tax consequences of property distribution; and (1) any other factor necessary to do equity and justice between the spouses.

**Alimony/Spousal Support/Maintenance:**
The court may award either spouse maintenance for up to 121 months. After this 121-month period, the spouse may request an extension of one more 121-month period. The amount awarded by the court will be whatever is judged to be fair, just and equitable. Marital fault is not considered.

**Child Custody and Visitation:**
If there is a child custody agreement between the parents, then the court will approve it if it is in the best interest of the child. If there is no agreement, the court will award child custody based on the following: (1) the child's wishes; (2) the wishes of the parents; (3) the bond between the child, each parent and any siblings; (4) the desire and ability of each parent to respect the relationship between the child and the other parent; (5) the length and time and circumstances under which the child may have been under the care of someone other than a parent; (6) the child's adjustment to his or her home, school and community; and (7) any evidence of spousal abuse. Joint custody may be awarded.

**Child Support:**
The court may order either or both parents to pay child support. The court will consider the following factors: (1) the financial resources of the child and both parents; (2) the physical, emotional, and educational needs of the child. Child support payments will be paid through a court trustee or through the clerk of the court. The amount of the child support may be determined by using the official child support guidelines.

**Rights to Maiden Name:**
A wife's former name will be restored upon request.

# KENTUCKY

**Residence Requirements:**
The filing spouse must have been a resident of Kentucky (or a member of the armed services stationed in Kentucky) for 180 days before filing.

**Where to File:**
In the county where either spouse resides.

**Name of Court:**
Circuit Court. "_____ Circuit Court, Kentucky."

**Title of Divorce Action:**
Petition for Dissolution of Marriage

**Party Filing:**
Petitioner

**Other Party:**
Respondent

**Title of Final Papers:**
Decree of Dissolution of Marriage

**Approved Grounds for Divorce:**
No-fault and Fault-based: Irretrievable breakdown of the marriage is the only grounds for a dissolution of marriage.

**General Divorce Procedures:**
The court will not grant a dissolution of marriage until the spouses have lived apart for 60 days. Marital settlement agreements are specifically authorized.

**Mediation or Counseling Requirements:**
If one spouse disagrees that the marriage is irretrievably broken, then the court may delay the proceedings for 60 days. In addition, the court may order a reconciliation conference.

**Legal Separation Provisions:**
The only grounds for legal separation is irretrievable breakdown of the marriage.

**Property Distribution:**
Kentucky is an "equitable distribution" state. Each spouse may retain his or her separate property (property acquired prior to marriage and any gifts or inheritances). The court will divide the marital property in just portions, without regard to marital fault. The court will consider the following: (1) each spouse's contribution to the acquisition of the marital property, including non-monetary contributions; (2) length of the marriage; (3) the financial position of each spouse and the desirability to award the family home to the custodial parent or allow that parent to live in the home until the child(ren) is grown; (4) the value of each spouse's separate property; and (5) any retirement benefits.

**Alimony/Spousal Support/Maintenance:**
Either spouse may be awarded maintenance based on that spouse's inability to provide for himself or herself. The award is based on the following: (1) length of marriage; (2) age and health of each spouse; (3) the financial resources of the spouse seeking alimony; (4) the ability of the spouse seeking maintenance to meet his or her needs; (5) the standard of living established during the marriage; (6) the needs of the spouse seeking maintenance and the ability of the other spouse to make such payments while meeting his or her own needs; (7) the time necessary to acquire sufficient education and training to enable the spouse to find appropriate employment, and that spouse's future earning capacity; and (8) the physical and emotional conditions of the spouses.

**Child Custody and Visitation:**
Either parent may be awarded custody. The court may award sole or joint custody based on the following factors: (1) the best interest of the child; (2) the child's wishes; (3) the preferences of the parents; (4) the bond between the child and the parents, and any siblings; (5) the child's adjustment to his or her home, school, and community; and (6) the mental and physical health of all individuals involved. Abandonment by a parent will not be considered if that parent left due to physical harm or threats thereof by the other spouse.

**Child Support:**
The court may order either parent to pay child support. The following factors will be considered: (1) the financial resources of the child; (2) the standard of living the child would have enjoyed if the marriage had not bee dissolved; (3) the physical and emotional conditions an educational needs of the child; and (4) the financial resources, need and obligations of both the noncustodial and the custodial parent. Kentucky has adopted official Child Support Guidelines which are contained in the statute. These guidelines are presumed to be correct, but may be adjusted based on the following considerations; (1) a child's extraordinary medical or dental needs; (2) a child's extraordinary educational, job training or special needs; (3) either parent's extraordinary needs, such as medical expenses; (4) the independent financial resources of the child; (5) the combined parental income in excess of the Kentucky child support guidelines amounts; (6) an agreement between the parents on child support, provided that no public assistance is being provided; and (7) any other extraordinary circumstance. In addition, the court may order a parent to provide health care insurance coverage for the child. The court may award an amount based on the official child support guidelines. However, the court may deviate from the guidelines if it is shown that such an amount will be unjust or inappropriate.

**Rights to Maiden Name:**
The wife's maiden name will be restored upon request if there are no minor children.

# LOUISIANA

**Residence Requirements:**

The filing spouse must have been a resident of Louisiana for 1 year before filing for a petition for divorce.

**Where to File:**

In the parish of the respondent/defendant, made in writing, signed by the party making it, and registered by the Recorder.

**Name of Court:**

District Court. "_____ Judicial District Court, Parish of _____, Louisiana."

**Title of Divorce Action:**

Petition for Divorce

**Party Filing:**

Petitioner/Plaintiff

**Other Party:**

Respondent/Defendant

**Title of Final Papers:**

Final Judgment of Divorce

**Approved Grounds for Divorce:**

No-fault-based: Living separate and apart for 6 months. Fault-based: (1) adultery; (2) convicted of a felony and sentenced to death or hard labor; or (3) that the spouses have been living separate and apart for a period of 6 months or more on the date of filing the petition.

**General Divorce Procedures:**

In Louisiana, the respondent/defendant does not need to answer the petition for divorce. In addition, a divorce will not be granted until a motion entitled "Rule to Show Cause" is filed.

**Mediation or Counseling Requirements:**

If there is a child custody dispute, the court may order mediation.

**Legal Separation Provisions:**

There are no legal grounds for separation. However, a spouse may petition the court for spousal support. This is intended for a couple who wishes to live apart but not divorce.

**Property Distribution:**

Louisiana is a "community property" state. All property acquired before the marriage or by gift or inheritance will be retained by that spouse. The community property will be equally divided between the spouses. The filing spouse will be awarded personal property, food and clothing necessary for the safety and well-being of that spouse and any child in custody of that spouse. Either spouse may request that the court allow that spouse to occupy the family residence until the community property has been divided. The court will consider the following factors in reaching its decision: (1) the value of each spouse's separate property; (2) the financial position of each spouse when the property is divided; and (3) the needs of the child. A spouse may be awarded an amount of money for his or her financial contribution to the education or training of a spouse that increased the other spouse's earning capacity.

**Alimony/Spousal Support/Maintenance:**

Either spouse may be awarded temporary alimony. Permanent alimony will be awarded to the spouse without fault and without sufficient means to provide for his or her maintenance. However, such an award will not be greater than 1/3 of the other spouse's income, unless the alimony is paid in a lump sum. The court will consider the following: (1) the time and expense a spouse incurs to obtain sufficient education or training for appropriate employment; (2) age and health of each spouse; (3) financial assets of each spouse; (4) debts of each spouse; and (5) any child custody and support responsibilities. Permanent alimony will be discontinued upon remarriage or cohabitation.

**Child Custody and Visitation:**

Joint or sole custody is awarded based on the best interests of the child. The following order of preference is established: (1) to both parents; (2) to either parent (without regard to race or sex of the parents); (3) to the person or persons with whom the child has been living; or (4) to any other person that the court feels suitable and able to provide an adequate and stable environment for the child. Unless shown otherwise or unless the parents agree otherwise, joint custody is presumed to be in the best interests of the child, and will be awarded based on the following factors: (1) physical, emotional, mental, religious, and social needs of the child; (2) capability and desire of each parent to meet the child's needs; (3) preference of the child, if the child is of sufficient age and capacity; (4) the love and affection existing between the child and each parent; (5) the length of time the child has lived in a stable, satisfactory environment and the desirability of maintaining continuity; (6) the desire and ability of each parent to allow an open and loving frequent relationship between the child and the other parent; (7) the wishes of the parents; (8) the child's adjustment to his or her home, school, and community; (9) the mental and physical health of all individuals involved; (10) the permanence as a family unit of the existing or proposed custodial home; (11) the distance between the potential residences; (12) the moral fitness of the parents, and (13) any other relevant factor. The conduct of the proposed guardian is to be considered only as it bears on his or her relationship with the child. The parents must submit a plan for joint custody which designates: (1) the child's residence; (2) the rights of access and communication between the parents and child; and (3) child support amounts. A parent not granted custody is entitled to visitation rights unless that parent has subjected the child to physical or sexual abuse.

**Child Support:**

Either parent may be ordered to pay child support based on the following factors: (1) the emotional and educational needs of the child; (2) the financial resources of each parent. Louisiana has official child support guidelines. These guidelines are presumed to be correct unless it is shown that such an amount would be unjust or not in the best interest of the child.

**Rights to Maiden Name:**

No legal provision addresses restoration of former name; however, a general statute provides for a petition for a name change.

# MAINE

**Residence Requirements:**

Either the plaintiff or defendant must have been a resident of Maine for 6 months before filing, or the marriage or grounds for divorce must have occurred in Maine. Otherwise, a person filing for divorce must be a resident of Maine for 6 months immediately prior to filing.

**Where to File:**

District Court in the county where either spouse resides. How-ever, the defendant has the right to move the proceedings to Superior Court.

**Name of Court:**

District Court or Superior Court. "State of Maine _____ Court, _____ County."

**Title of Divorce Action:**

Complaint for Divorce

**Party Filing:**

Plaintiff

**Other Party:**

Defendant

**Title of Final Papers:**

Judgment of Divorce

**Approved Grounds for Divorce:**

No-fault: Irreconcilable marital differences. Fault based: (1) adultery; (2) impotence; (3) alcoholism and/or drug abuse; (4) cruel and inhuman treatment; (5) confinement for permanent insanity for 7 consecutive years; (6) non-support to complaining spouse whereby the other spouse can provide support but refuses to do so; or (7) desertion for 3 years.

**General Divorce Procedures:**

If the complaint for divorce is uncontested, then the testimony of a corroborating witness is unnecessary.

**Mediation or Counseling Requirements:**

Mediation is mandatory if: (1) one spouse disputes that there are irreconcilable differences; or (2) it is a contested divorce and minor children are involved.

**Legal Separation Provisions:**

Legal separation will be granted if the spouses have been living apart for at least 60 days with just cause.

**Property Distribution:**

Maine is an "equitable distribution" state. All separate property, which is property acquired by gift or inheritance and by exchanging any property previously mentioned, will be retained by that spouse. The marital property will be divided between the spouses based on the following factors: (1) each spouse's contribution to the acquisition of marital property, including any non-monetary contribution, i.e. homemaking; (2) value of each spouse's separate property; (3) the financial position of each spouse, and the desirability to award the family home to the custodial parent. Marital fault is not a factor.

**Alimony/Spousal Support/Maintenance:**

Either spouse may be awarded alimony. The court will consider the following factors: (1) the length of the marriage; (2) age and health of each spouse; (3) the ability of each spouse to pay; (4) any economic misconduct which resulted in the diminution of marital property or income; (5) standard of living during the marriage; (6) earning ability of each spouse; (7) education and/or training of each spouse; (8) contributions to the education or earning potential of the other spouse; (9) any retirement and health insurance benefits of each spouse; (10) the tax consequences of the division of marital property, including the tax consequences of the sale of the marital home; (11) the tax consequences of an alimony award; (12) the contributions of either spouse as homemaker; (13) the contributions of either spouse to the education of earning potential to the other spouse; and (14) any other relevant factors. The factors to be considered are: (1) the age of the child; (2) the capability and desire of each parent to meet the child's needs; (3) the preference of the child, if the child is of sufficient age and capacity; (4) the length of time the child has lived in a stable, satisfactory environment and the desirability of maintaining continuity; (5) the desire and ability of each parent to allow an open and loving frequent relationship between the child and the other parent; (6) the child's adjustment to his or her home, school, and community; (7) the relationship of the child with parents, sibling, and other significant family members; (8) the stability of the home environment likely to be offered by each parent; (9) a need to promote continuity and stability i the life of the child; (10) the parent's capacity and willingness to cooperate; (11) methods for dispute resolution; (12) the effect on the child of one parent having sole authority over his or her upbringing; (13) the existence of any domestic violence of child abuse; (14) any other factors having a reasonable bearing on the child's upbringing. No preference is to be given because of parent's sex of because of the child;s age or sex. In any child custody case, the court may order an investigation of the parents and child by the Department of Human Services.

**Child Custody and Visitation:**

There are three types of custody which may be awarded: (1) responsibilities for the child's welfare may be divided, these are: primary physical residence, parent-child contact, support, education, medical and dental care, religious upbringing, travel boundaries and expenses; (2) parental responsibilities are shared. All or most responsibilities are joint decisions; or (3) one parent is granted exclusive responsibility for the child's welfare, except for child support.

**Child Support:**

The court may order either parent to pay child support. Such an order may include an insurance policy covering health care expenses. There are official child support guidelines which the court may use. However, the court may deviate from the guidelines if the amount is unjust and inappropriate.

**Rights to Maiden Name:**

Upon request, the wife may change her name during or after a divorce.

# MARYLAND

**Residence Requirements:**
One spouse must have been a resident of Maryland for 1 year if the grounds for divorce occurred outside of Maryland. Otherwise, either spouse may file for divorce. However, if insanity is the ground for divorce, the residency requirement is 2 years.

**Where to File:**
In the county where either spouse resides.

**Name of Court:**
Circuit Court. "In the Circuit Court for _____, Maryland."

**Title of Divorce Action:**
Bill for Divorce

**Party Filing:**
Plaintiff

**Other Party:**
Defendant

**Title of Final Papers:**
Decree of Divorce

**Approved Grounds for Divorce:**
No-fault: (1) Voluntarily lived separate and apart for 1 year without cohabitation, and there is no reasonable expectation of reconciliation; or (2) the spouses have lived separate and apart without interruption for 2 years. Fault-based: (1) adultery; (2) willful desertion for 1 year; (3) confinement for permanent insanity for at least 3 years; and (4) conviction of a felony or a misdemeanor with a minimum of a 3-year sentence and after serving 1 year.

**General Divorce Procedures:**
A default judgment will be granted only upon actual testimony of the filing spouse. Marital settlement agreements are encouraged and authorized by statute. Such an agreement can be used as corroboration of the filing spouse's testimony that the separation was voluntary if the agreement: (1) states that the separation was voluntary; and (2) was signed under oath before the application for divorce was filed. In addition, each spouse must file with the court a financial statement affidavit and a joint statement of marital and non-marital property. This form is available in Maryland Rule 9-206.

**Mediation or Counseling Requirements:**
The court will order mediation if child custody is an issue. However, the court will not order mediation if there is a history of physical or sexual abuse of the child.

**Legal Separation Provisions:**
Legal separation must be grounded on: (1) willful desertion; (2) cruel and inhuman treatment; or (3) voluntary separation and apart without cohabitation. The spouses must make a good faith effort toward reconciliation.

**Property Distribution:**
Maryland is an "equitable distribution" state. The spouses will retain any property acquired before the marriage or any gifts or inheritance (separate property). The marital property will be divided equitably based on the following: (1) each spouse's contribution to the acquisition of marital property, including any non-monetary contribution, i.e. homemaking; (2) the financial position of each spouse after the division of property; (3) the value of each spouse's separate property; (4) age and health of each spouse; (5) duration of the marriage; (6) whether the property award is in lieu of or in addition to alimony; (7) how and by whom the property was acquired, i.e. retirement plan; (8) the circumstances that led to the breakdown of the marriage. The court may award the family residence to either spouse; (9) the value of each spouse's property; (10) the length of the marriage; (11) whether the property award is instead of or in addition to alimony; and (12) any other factor necessary to do equity and justice between the spouses.

**Alimony/Spousal Support/Maintenance:**
The court may award alimony to either spouse, without regard to marital fault, based on the following: (1) the financial status of each spouse, including earning ability in the labor market; (2) the time and expense a spouse will incur to obtain sufficient education or training for appropriate employment; (3) length of the marriage; (4) the spouse's contribution to the acquisition of marital property, including any non-monetary contribution; (5) the needs of the spouse seeking maintenance and the ability of the other spouse to make such payments while meeting his or her own needs; (6) age and health of each spouse; (7) any agreement dealing with financial or service contribution by one spouse with the expectation of future reciprocation or compensation by the other spouse; (8) the standard of living established during the marriage; (9) the duration of the marriage; (10) the ability of the spouse from whom support is sought to meet his or her needs while meeting those of the spouse seeking support; (11) the age of the spouses; (12) any mutual agreement between the spouses concerning financial or service contributions by one spouse with the expectation of future reciprocation or compensation by the other; (13) the ability of the spouse seeking alimony to become self-supporting; (14) the circumstances which lead to the breakdown of the marriage; and (15) any other factor the court deems just and equitable.

**Child Custody and Visitation:**
Either or both spouses may be awarded child custody. The court will allow the child to live where the child is most familiar. In addition, the court will usually allow the custodial parent to use and possess the family home.

**Child Support:**
Either parent may be required to pay child support. There are child support guidelines the court may use. However, the court may deviate from the guidelines if the amount will be unjust or inappropriate.

**Rights to Maiden Name:**
Either spouse may restore a former name.

# MASSACHUSETTS

**Residence Requirements:**
One spouse must be a resident if the grounds for divorce occurred in Massachusetts. If the grounds for divorce occurred outside Massachusetts, then the filing spouse must have been a resident of Massachusetts for 1 year.

**Where to File:**
In the county where spouses last resided together. If neither live in such county then county where either spouse currently resides.

**Name of Court:**
"Commonwealth of Massachusetts, the Trial Court, the Probate & Family Court, Dept. _____ Division."

**Title of Divorce Action:**
No-fault: Petition for Divorce
Fault-based: Complaint for Divorce

**Party Filing:**
No-fault:(without separation agreement) Petitioner; (with separation agreement)Co-Petitioner.
Fault-based: Plaintiff

**Other Party:**
No-fault:(without separation agreement) Respondent; (with separation agreement) Co-Petitioner.
Fault-based: Defendant

**Title of Final Papers:**
Judgment of Divorce

**Approved Grounds for Divorce:**
No-fault: Irretrievable breakdown of the marriage. Fault-based: (1) adultery; (2) impotence; (3) imprisonment for over 5 years; (4) alcoholism and/or drug abuse; (5) cruel and inhuman treatment; (6) desertion without support to other spouse for 1 year; and (7) non-support to complaining spouse whereby the other spouse can provide support but refuses to do so.

**General Divorce Procedures:**
A lawsuit for divorce on the grounds of irretrievable breakdown of the marriage may be initiated by: (1) a signed petition by both spouses; (2) an affidavit that the marriage is irretrievably broken; and (3) a notarized separation agreement or marital settlement agreement signed by both spouses. No summons is required. Marital fault is not a factor to be considered in the division of property or maintenance. In every action for divorce, a financial statement and a public health statistical report must be filed by each spouse.

**Mediation or Counseling Requirements:**
The court may order counseling in cases where irreconcilable differences are used as the grounds for divorce.

**Legal Separation Provisions:**
Legal separation may be grounded on: (1) failure without cause to provide for support; (2) desertion; or (3) giving the other spouse justifiable cause to live separate and apart. The court may award support to the spouse and children living apart.

**Property Distribution:**
Massachusetts is an "equitable distribution" state. The court may divide all the spouses' property, including any gifts and inheritances. The court will consider the following factors: (1) each spouse's contribution to the acquisition, preservation, or appreciation of property, including non-monetary contribution, i.e. homemaking; (2) duration of marriage; (3) any and all sources of income of each spouse; (4) age and health of each spouse; (5) the occupation of each spouse; (6) the earning ability of each spouse in the job market; (7) the liabilities, financial resources and the ability to increase such assets by each spouse; (8) any health insurance coverage; and (9) the conduct of the parties during the marriage (if the grounds for divorce are fault-based). Fault is not considered if the grounds for divorce are irretrievable breakdown of the marriage and a separation/settlement agreement is filed with the petition.

**Alimony/Spousal Support/Maintenance:**
Either spouse may be awarded alimony. The court will consider the same factors as above, plus the present and future needs of any children of the marriage. In addition, health insurance coverage may be part of the maintenance award.

**Child Custody and Visitation:**
Either parent or a third party may be awarded child custody. Joint custody may also be awarded if it is in the best interest of the child and there is no marital misconduct. If child custody is contested and each parent wishes some form of shared custody, then a shared parenting plan must be submitted to the court.

**Child Support:**
Either parent may be ordered by the court to provide child support. There are official child support guidelines which the court will use. However, the court may deviate from such guidelines if evidence demonstrates the amount will be unjust or inappropriate.

**Rights to Maiden Name:**
The wife may restore her former name.

## MICHIGAN

**Residence Requirements:**
One spouse must have been a resident of Michigan for 180 days and a resident of the county where he or she files for 10 days.

**Where to File:**
In the county where either spouse resides.*

**Name of Court:**
Circuit Court. "State of Michigan, ____ Judicial Circuit, ____ County."

**Title of Divorce Action:**
Complaint for Divorce

**Party Filing:**
Plaintiff

**Other Party:**
Defendant

**Title of Final Papers:**
Judgment of Divorce

**Approved Grounds for Divorce:**
No-fault: Irretrievable breakdown of the marriage. Fault-based: Irretrievable breakdown of the marriage.

**General Divorce Procedures:**
The clerk of the Circuit Court in any Michigan county will supply each spouse with a book that provides additional forms. In addition, the Michigan Friend of the Court Bureau is to supply each party in a divorce case with a pamphlet discussing the court procedures, the rights and responsibilities of the parties, the availability of mediation, human services, and joint custody.

**Mediation or Counseling Requirements:**
Voluntary mediation services are available.

**Legal Separation Provisions:**
The grounds for legal separation are irretrievable breakdown of the marriage.

*However, a person may file for divorce in any county in the state without meeting the 10-day residency requirement if the defendant was born in or is a citizen of a foreign country and there are no minor children in the marriage that are at the risk of being taken out of the country by the defendant.

**Property Distribution:**
Michigan is an "equitable distribution" state. All the spouses' property, including gifts or inheritances, may be divided by the court. The court will consider the following: (1) each spouse's contribution to the acquisition of property, including non-monetary contributions; (2) the duration of the marriage; (3) the causes which led to the estrangement of the spouses and to the divorce; (4) the financial position and rights to any insurance policies; (5) any retirement benefits; and (6) any prior marriage of each spouse.

**Alimony/Spousal Support/Maintenance:**
The court may order either spouse to pay alimony. Alimony may be awarded to a spouse whose awarded property is insufficient to support him or her. The court will consider the following: (1) the ability of each spouse to pay; (2) the character and situation of each spouse; and (3) all other remaining circumstances of the case.

**Child Custody and Visitation:**
Either spouse may be awarded child custody. However, joint custody may also be awarded. The court will base its decision on the following factors: (1) the child's wishes; (2) the bond between the child and each parent; (3) the ability and desire of each parent to meet the child's needs; (4) the amount of time the child has lived in a particular environment and the desirability of maintaining continuity; (5) the desire and ability of each parent to allow a loving relationship between the child and the other parent; (6) moral character and prudence of the parents; (7) physical, emotional, mental, religious and social needs of the child; (8) the desire and ability of each parent to allow an open and loving frequent relationship between the child and the other parent; (9) the child's adjustment to his or her home, school and community; (10) the mental and physical health of all individuals involved; (11) the permanence as a family unit of the proposed custodial home or homes; and (12) any other factors.

**Child Support:**
Either parent may be required to pay child support. There are official child support guidelines which the court may use unless the amount is shown to be unjust or inappropriate. The Judgment of Divorce must contain a provision that one or both parents provide health care coverage if this coverage is available at a reasonable cost at their place of employment. In addition, each parent must keep the Michigan Friend of the Court Bureau informed of his or her address, sources of income, and health coverage.

**Rights to Maiden Name:**
Upon request by the wife, the court may restore her birth or former name.

## MINNESOTA

**Residence Requirements:**
Either spouse must have been a resident of Minnesota for at least 180 days before filing.

**Where to File:**
In the county where either spouse resides.

**Name of Court:**
County Court or District Court. "State of Minnesota, District Court, County of ____, ____ Judicial District."

**Title of Divorce Action:**
Petition for Dissolution of Marriage

**Party Filing:**
Petitioner, or Co-Petitioner if jointly filed

**Other Party:**
Respondent, or Co-Petitioner if jointly filed

**Title of Final Papers:**
Decree of Dissolution of Marriage

**Approved Grounds for Divorce:**
No-Fault: Irrevocable breakdown of the marriage shown by: (1) living separate and apart for 180 days; or (2) serious marital discord adversely affecting the attitude of one or both spouses toward the marriage. Fault-based: Irretrievable breakdown of the marriage is the only ground for a dissolution of marriage.

**General Divorce Procedures:**
The petition for dissolution of marriage may be brought jointly. This will eliminate the need for service of process or the use of a summons.

**Mediation or Counseling Requirements:**
If there is a child custody dispute, the court may order mediation, unless there is a history of physical or sexual abuse of the child.

**Legal Separation Provisions:**
Legal separation will be granted if the court finds that the spouses need a legal separation.

**Property Distribution:**
Minnesota is an "equitable distribution" state. All property acquired before the marriage and any gifts or inheritances will be retained by that spouse. All other property will be divided according to the following factors: (1) each spouse's contribution to the acquisition of property, including non-monetary contributions; (2) age and health of each spouse; (3) duration of marriage; (4) the financial resources of each spouse and the ability of each to increase resources; (5) the occupation of each spouse; (6) the employability of each spouse; (7) any prior marriage of each spouse; (8) the amount and sources of income of the spouses; (9) the vocational skills of the spouses; and (10) any other factor necessary to do equity and justice between the spouses. Marital fault will not be considered.

**Alimony/Spousal Support/Maintenance:**
The court may award maintenance to either spouse based on the following factors: (1) standard of living established during the marriage; (2) any interruption in education, training, or employment by a spouse due to homemaking responsibilities; (3) duration of the marriage; (4) the sacrifices the homemaker has made in terms of earnings, employment, experience, and opportunities; (5) the time necessary to acquire sufficient education and training to enable the spouse to find appropriate employment, and that spouse's future earning capacity and the probability of completing education and training and becoming fully or partially self-supporting; (6) the financial resources of the spouse seeking maintenance, including marital property apportioned to such spouse and such spouse's ability to meet his or her needs independently; (7) the contribution of each spouse to the marriage, including services rendered in homemaking, child care, education, and career building of the other spouse; (8) the age of the spouses; (9) the physical and emotional conditions of the spouses; (10) the needs of the spouse seeking support and the ability of the other spouse to make such payments while meeting his or her own needs; and (11) any other factor the court deems just and equitable. The court will also consider the factors listed under property distribution.

**Child Custody and Visitation:**
Either spouse may be awarded child custody based on the following factors: (1) the wishes of the child; (2) the bond between the child and each parent and any siblings; (3) any history of domestic violence; (4) the length of time the child has lived in a particular environment and the desire to maintain continuity; (5) the child's cultural background; (6) physical and mental health of all parties; (7) capability and desire of each parent to give the child love, affection and guidance, and to continue raising the child in the child's culture and religion or creed, if any; (8) the child's adjustment to his or her home, school and community; (9) the mental and physical health of all individuals involved; (10) the conduct of the proposed guardian only as it bears on his or her relationship with the child; (11) the stability of the home environment likely to be offered by each parent; (12) a need to promote continuity and stability in the life of the child; (13) the child's primary caretaker; and (14) any other factors. The primary caretaker factor is not a presumption in favor of the primary caretaker, but is only one factor in the decision. If both parents agree to joint custody, then the court will award joint custody unless there has been any spousal abuse.

**Child Support:**
The court may order either parent to pay child support. The court will consider the following factors: (1) debts of each parent; (2) financial resources of the child and custodial parents; (3) the standard of living the child would have enjoyed if the marriage was not dissolved; (4) the needs of the child; (5) the amount of public aid received by the child; and (6) any income tax consequences of the payment of support. The court may use the official child support guidelines to award support payments. However, the court may deviate from the guidelines if the amount is unjust or inappropriate.

**Rights to Maiden Name:**
Either spouse upon request may have their name changed.

# MISSISSIPPI

**Residence Requirements:**
One of the spouses must have been a resident for at least 6 months, and not have secured residency for the purpose of obtaining a divorce. A member of the armed services and his or her spouse are considered residents if stationed in Mississippi.

**Where to File:**
No-fault: County where either spouse resides, if both spouses are residents of Mississippi, or the county where one spouse resides if the other spouse is a non-resident of Mississippi. Fault-based: County where the defendant resides, unless the defendant is a non-resident, and then the action must be filed in the county where the complainant resides.

**Name of Court:**
"Chancery Court of _____ County, State of Mississippi."

**Title of Divorce Action:**
Bill of Complaint for Divorce

**Party Filing:**
Complainant

**Other Party:**
Defendant

**Title of Final Papers:**
Decree of Divorce

**Approved Grounds for Divorce:**
No-fault: Irreconcilable differences. Fault-based: (1) adultery; (2) impotence; (3) alcoholism and/or drug abuse; (4) confinement for permanent insanity for at least 3 years; (5) wife pregnant by another at the time of marriage without the husband's knowledge; (6) cruel and inhuman treatment; (7) willful desertion for 1 year or more; (8) imprisonment; (9) spouse lacked mental capacity to consent (including temporary incapacity resulting from drug or alcohol use); and (10) incest. In addition, an affidavit must be filed stating that there is no collusion between the spouses.

**General Divorce Procedures:**
A divorce grounded on irreconcilable differences will be granted if: (1) both husband and wife file jointly for divorce; or (2) a bill of complaint has been filed and the defendant (a) has entered an appearance by written waiver of process; or (b) has been personally served with the complaint. If the spouses cannot agree to child custody, or to the division of property, then the court will have a hearing 60 days after filing for divorce.

**Mediation or Counseling Requirements:**
There is no legal provision in Mississippi for mediation or counseling.

**Legal Separation Provisions:**
There are provisions for separate maintenance.

**Property Distribution:**
Mississippi is a "title" state. Each spouse will retain all property that is under his or her name. In addition, any jointly accumulated asset may be divided on an "equitable" basis.

**Alimony/Spousal Support/Maintenance:**
Marital fault is not considered. Either spouse may be awarded an equitable and just amount.

**Child Custody and Visitation:**
Either parent or a third party may be awarded child custody. If both parents are fit, and the child is 12 years or older, the child may choose with whom he or she wishes to live. If both parents agree to joint custody, then it is presumed to be in the best interest of the child.

**Child Support:**
Child support will be based on each parent's ability to pay a just and equitable amount. There are no factors for consideration specified in the statute.

**Rights to Maiden Name:**
Either spouse may request a name change.

# MISSOURI

**Residence Requirements:**
Either spouse must have been a resident of Missouri for 90 days before filing.

**Where to File:**
In the county where the petitioner resides.

**Name of Court:**
"In the Circuit Court, of _____ County, Missouri."

**Title of Divorce Action:**
Petition for Dissolution of Marriage

**Party Filing:**
Petitioner, or Co-Petitioner if jointly filed

**Other Party:**
Respondent, or Co-Petitioner if jointly filed

**Title of Final Papers:**
Decree of Dissolution of Marriage

**Approved Grounds for Divorce:**
No-fault and fault-based: Irretrievable breakdown of the marriage with no reasonable likelihood that the marriage can be preserved. This is the only grounds for a dissolution of marriage in Missouri.

**General Divorce Procedures:**
Settlement agreements are authorized. Both spouses may file jointly. Each spouse should be titled a "co-petitioner." Some counties have approved pre-printed forms which may be used for filing. These forms are available from the court clerk. In addition, there will be a 30-day waiting period before the court will grant a dissolution of marriage.

**Mediation or Counseling Requirements:**
The court, at its own initiative, may delay the proceeding for 30-180 days so the spouses may seek counseling.

**Legal Separation Provisions:**
The grounds for legal separation are an irretrievable breakdown of the marriage which may include the following: (1) adultery; (2) abandonment; (3) separation due to misconduct in the 12 months before filing the petition; (4) spousal behavior that the other spouse cannot reasonably be expected to live with; (5) living separate and apart continuously for 24 months. One of the spouses must be a resident of Missouri for 90 days before filing for legal separation.

**Property Distribution:**
Missouri is an "equitable distribution" state. Each spouse will retain all property acquired before the marriage or any property acquired by gift or inheritance. Commingled property does not become marital property solely by the act of commingling. The court will consider the following factors in dividing the marital property: (1) each spouse's contribution to the acquisition of property, including non-monetary contributions; (2) the value of each spouse's separate property; (3) the financial position of each spouse when the property division becomes effective; (4) the desirability of awarding the family residence to the custodial parent, and (5) any misconduct by the spouses during the marriage as it relates to the disposition of property.

**Alimony/Spousal Support/Maintenance:**
The court may award maintenance to either spouse if such spouse: (1) lacks sufficient property to provide for his or her needs; or (2) is the custodial parent and unable to work because the child needs care. The court will award maintenance based on the following: (1) the conduct by each spouse during the marriage; (2) the time a spouse spends obtaining sufficient education or training for appropriate work; (3) length of marriage; (4) the financial assets of the spouse seeking maintenance; (5) earning capability of each spouse; (6) age and health of each spouse; and (7) debts of each spouse.

**Child Custody and Visitation:**
Either parent may be awarded child custody based on the following factors: (1) the wishes of the child; (2) the child's adjustment to his or her home, school and community; (3) the mental and physical health of the child and the parents; (4) the desire and ability of each parent to meet the child's needs; (5) the intention of either parent to relocate his or her residence; (6) the bond between the child, the parents and any siblings. There is now a legislative encouragement of joint custody; (7) any history of child or spouse abuse; (8) the child's need for a continuing relationship with both parents; (9) the intention of either parent to relocate his or her residence outside Missouri; and (10) which parent is more likely to allow the child frequent and meaningful contact with the other parent. Domestic violence against a child is a bar to custody. An award of joint custody must include a joint custody plan. A parent not granted custody is entitled to reasonable visitation.

**Child Support:**
Either or both parents may be ordered to pay child support. The court will consider the following factors: (1) the financial resources of the child and the parents; (2) the standard of living the child would have enjoyed if the marriage was not dissolved; (3) the physical, emotional and educational needs of the child; and (4) the father's primary responsibility for the support of his child. There are official child support guidelines that the court may use.

**Rights to Maiden Name:**
Either spouse may petition the court for a change of name. A public notice of any name change should be published in a local newspaper in the county where the person resides.

# MONTANA

**Residence Requirements:**
Either spouse must have been a resident of Montana for at least 90 days before filing.

**Where to File:**
In the county where petitioner has been a resident for at least 90 days.

**Name of Court:**
District Court. "District Court for the State of Montana and for the County of _____."

**Title of Divorce Action:**
Petition for Dissolution of Marriage.

**Party Filing:**
Petitioner, or Co-Petitioner if joint

**Other Party:**
Respondent, or Co-Petitioner if joint

**Title of Final Papers:**
Decree of Dissolution of Marriage

**Approved Grounds for Divorce:**
No-fault: (1) Irretrievable breakdown of the marriage and serious marital discord, and no reasonable prospect of reconciliation; and (2) living separate and apart for 180 days prior to filing. Fault-based: Irretrievable breakdown of the marriage and living separate and apart for 180 days prior to filing.

**General Divorce Procedures:**
Both spouses may file jointly. If both spouses file jointly, each spouse should be titled as "co-petitioner." Settlement agreements are authorized by law.

**Mediation or Counseling Requirements:**
The court may delay the proceedings for 30 to 60 days if there are minor children, or if one spouse denies that the marriage is irretrievably broken. During this time the spouses will attend counseling.

**Legal Separation Provisions:**
The only grounds for legal separation is irretrievable breakdown of the marriage. One of the spouses must be resident of Montana of 90 days immediately prior to filing for legal separation.

**Property Distribution:**
Montana is an "equitable distribution" state. Marital misconduct is not considered in the division of property. All the spouses' property, including property acquired before the marriage and any gifts or inheritances, will be divided by the court. In doing so, the court will consider the following: (1) each 102 contribution to the acquisition of marital property, including non-monetary contributions, i.e. homemaking; (2) whether the property award is in lieu of or in addition to alimony; (3) any premarital agreements; (4) the occupation of each spouse; (5) length of marriage; (6) the time and expense a spouse will incur to obtain sufficient education or training for appropriate employment; (7) any and all sources of income of each spouse; (8) the age and health of the spouses; (9) the vocational skills of the spouses; (10) the employability of the spouses; (11) the liabilities and needs of each spouse and the opportunity of each for further acquisition of capital assets and income; (12) any prior marriage of each spouse; and (13) any custodial provisions for the children.

**Alimony/Spousal Support/Maintenance:**
Either spouse may be awarded maintenance if such spouse lacks sufficient property to support himself or herself or is the custodial parent and unable to work outside the home because the child needs special attention. In awarding maintenance, the court will consider the same factors as listed in the property distribution section, and also the following: (1) the standard of living established during the marriage; (2) the needs of the spouse seeking support and the ability of the other spouse to make such payments while meeting his or her own needs; (3) the financial resources of the spouse seeking maintenance; (4) the time necessary to acquire sufficient education and training to enable the spouse to find appropriate employment, and that 102 future earning capacity; (5) the duration of the marriage; (6) the age of the spouses; and (7) the physical and emotional conditions of the spouses.

**Child Custody and Visitation:**
Sole or joint custody may be awarded based on the following factors: (1) the wishes of the child and parents; (2) the bond between the child, each parent and any siblings; (3) domestic abuse; (4) which parent is more likely to allow the child and the other parent to develop a loving relationship; (5) the child's adjustment to his or her home, school and community; (6) the mental and physical health of all individuals involved; (7) the relationship of the child with parents, siblings, and other significant family members; (8) the continuity and stability of the child's care; (9) the developmental needs of the child; (10) whether a parent has failed to pay any of the child's birth-related costs; (11) whether the child has frequent and continuing contact with both parents; (12) any adverse effects on the child resulting form one parent's continuous and annoying efforts to amend parenting plans [annoying meant to refer to efforts to (a) amend a parenting plan within 6 months of a prior plan and (b) efforts to amend a final parenting plan without having made a good-faith effort to comply with the plan.

**Child Support:**
The court may order either or both parents to pay child support. The following will be considered: (1) age of the child; (2) financial resources of the child; (3) needs of others the parent is responsible to support; (4) the standard of living the child would have enjoyed if the marriage had not been dissolved; (5) the physical and emotional conditions and educational and medical needs of the child; (6) the financial resources, needs and obligations of both the noncustodial and custodial parent; (7) the cost of any day care; (8) the parenting plan for the child; (9) the provision of health and medical insurance for the child. In addition, the court will consider the uniform child support guidelines.

**Rights to Maiden Name:**
The wife may restore her former name.

# NEBRASKA

**Residence Requirements:**
Either spouse must have been a resident of Nebraska for at least 1 year, or the marriage was performed in Nebraska and one spouse has resided in the state during the entire marriage.

**Where to File:**
In the county where either spouse resides.

**Name of Court:**
"In the District Court for _____ County, Nebraska."

**Title of Divorce Action:**
Petition for Dissolution of Marriage

**Party Filing:**
Petitioner, or Co-Petitioner if jointly filed

**Other Party:**
Respondent, or Co-Petitioner if jointly filed

**Title of Final Papers:**
Decree of Dissolution of Marriage

**Approved Grounds for Divorce:**
No-fault: Irretrievable breakdown of the marriage. Fault-based: Spouse lacked mental capacity to consent.

**General Divorce Procedures:**
Both spouses may file. If both spouses file jointly, each spouse should be titled as "co-petitioner." Settlement agreements are authorized. There is a 60-day waiting period after filing before the court will grant a dissolution of marriage.

**Mediation or Counseling Requirements:**
The court will not grant a dissolution of marriage until every reasonable effort for a reconciliation has been made. The court may refer the spouses to counseling.

**Legal Separation Provisions:**
There are no residency requirements. Irretrievable breakdown of the marriage is the only grounds for legal separation.

**Property Distribution:**
Nebraska is an "equitable distribution" state. All separate property, including any gifts or inheritances acquired before the marriage, will be retained by that spouse. The marital property, including gifts and inheritances acquired during the marriage, will be divided based on the following factors: (1) the contribution of the spouses to the acquisition of the marital property, including non-monetary contributions; (2) the duration of the marriage; (3) the financial status of each spouse after the division of the property; and (4) any custodial obligations.

**Alimony/Spousal Support/Maintenance:**
The court will consider the same factors as listed in the property distribution section in addition to the following: (1) any interruption of personal careers or education; (2) the ability of the custodial parent to have gainful employment without interfering with the interest of the child.

**Child Custody and Visitation:**
Either parent may be awarded custody. Joint custody may be awarded if both parents agree to it. The court will consider the following factors: (1) the bond between the child, each parent and any siblings; (2) the child's wishes if of sufficient age; (3) the needs of the child and the ability of each parent to meet the child's needs; (4) the general health, welfare and social behavior of the child; and (5) any credible evidence of child or spousal abuse.

**Child Support:**
The amount of child support will be determined by the earning capacity of each parent. The court may use the official child support guidelines in awarding an amount.

**Rights to Maiden Name:**
Either spouse may request in the petition for dissolution of marriage that his or her former name be restored.

# NEVADA

**Residence Requirements:**
One spouse must have been a resident of Nevada for 6 weeks before filing. If the cause for divorce took place in the county of Nevada where the spouses lived at the time of the cause, there is no time requirement.

**Where to File:**
In the county where either spouse resides, where spouses last lived together, where the cause for the divorce took place, or where the plaintiff resided for 6 weeks immediately prior to filing for divorce.

**Name of Court:**
"In the District Court for _____ County, Nevada."

**Title of Divorce Action:**
Complaint for Divorce

**Party Filing:**
Plaintiff

**Other Party:**
Defendant

**Title of Final Papers:**
Decree of Divorce

**Approved Grounds for Divorce:**
No-fault: (1) Incompatibility; or (2) living separate and apart without cohabitation for 1 year. Fault-based: Insanity for at least 2 years before filing.

**General Divorce Procedures:**
A summary divorce may be granted if: (1) the residency requirement has been satisfied; (2) the spouses are incompatible, or they have lived separate and apart without cohabitation for 1 year; (3) there are no minor children, including adopted, and the wife is not pregnant, or the spouses have a written agreement regarding child custody and support; (4) there is no community property, or the spouses have a written agreement regarding the division of such property and have signed any deeds, titles or other evidences of transfer of property; (5) both spouses waive their right to spousal support; (6) both spouses waive their right to: (a) notice of entry of the final decree of divorce; (b) appeal; (c) a new trial; (d) their rights to request findings of fact and conclusions of law in the divorce proceeding; and (7) both spouses want the court to enter the decree of divorce. In addition, a spouse may seek a decree of divorce by default by affidavit. The affidavit must contain a statement that: (1) the residency requirement has been met; (2) all information in the affidavit is true and correct on the personal knowledge of the affiant; (3) gives facts to support allegations; and (4) affiant is competent to testify. Each divorce filed must also contain a Civil Cover sheet, a Verification of Pleadings, and request for submission, and an Affidavit of Residency.

**Mediation or Counseling Requirements:**
There are no legal provisions for mediation.

**Legal Separation Provisions:**
A spouse may have a suit for maintenance if he or she has been deserted for over 90 days, or if he or she has any of the grounds for a divorce.

**Property Distribution:**
Nevada is a "community property" state. Each spouse will retain all property acquired prior to the marriage and any property acquired by gift or inheritance. The court will divide the community property and any property held jointly on or after July 1, 1979, based on the following: (1) the financial status of each spouse after the division of the property; (2) how and by whom the property was obtained; (3) the merits of each spouse; and (4) any obligation imposed on each spouse for the benefit of the children. Marital fault will not be considered.

**Alimony/Spousal Support/Maintenance:**
Either spouse may be awarded alimony based on the same factors as listed in the property distribution section in addition to the following factors: (1) the time and expense a spouse will incur to obtain sufficient training for appropriate employment; and (2) reimbursement for any financial contribution by one spouse toward the higher education of the other. The alimony may be in a lump sum or periodic payments. Marital fault will not be considered.

**Child Custody and Visitation:**
Either spouse may be awarded custody based on the following factors: (1) the wishes of the child and parents, and (2) whether either parent has committed domestic violence. Joint custody may also be awarded if both parents agree.

**Child Support:**
There are official child support guidelines which the court will use, unless it is shown that the amount to be awarded would not meet the child's needs. The relative income of each parent will be considered.

**Rights to Maiden Name:**
The wife's former name may be restored.

# NEW HAMPSHIRE

**Residence Requirements:**
Both spouses must be residents when filing, or the filing spouse must have been a resident of New Hampshire for 1 year before filing and the other served process in the state, or the cause of divorce must have arisen in New Hampshire and one spouse must be residing in the state of New Hampshire when the petition is filed.

**Where to File:**
In the county where either spouse resides.

**Name of Court:**
Superior Court. "The State of New Hampshire, Superior Court in and for _____."

**Title of Divorce Action:**
Petition for Divorce

**Party Filing:**
Petitioner

**Other Party:**
Respondent

**Title of Final Papers:**
Decree of Divorce

**Approved Grounds for Divorce:**
No-fault: Irreconcilable differences which have caused the irremediable breakdown of the marriage. Fault-based: (1) adultery; (2) impotence; (3) abandonment and no communication for 2 years; (4) conviction and sentence of a felony with more than 1 year served; (5) cruel and inhuman treatment; (6) habitual drunkenness for 2 years; (7) living separate and apart without cohabitation (wife left without husband's consent for two years); (8) physical abuse or reasonable apprehension of physical abuse; (9) desertion without support of spouse by husband for 2 years; (10) mental abuse; (11) when either spouse has joined a religious society which professes that the relationship of the husband and wife is unlawful and refuses to cohabit with the other for 6 consecutive months; (12) when the wife of any citizen of New Hampshire leaves the state without her husband's consent and lives elsewhere for 10 consecutive years without returning to claim her marriage rights; and (13) when the wife lives in New Hampshire for 2 years and her husband becomes the citizen of a foreign country without supporting the wife.

**General Divorce Procedures:**
There are no provisions for simplified divorce procedures.

**Mediation or Counseling Requirements:**
At either spouse's request, or if the court determines there is a reasonable chance of reconciliation, the court will delay the proceeding and order counseling.

**Legal Separation Provisions:**
The grounds for legal separation are the same as the grounds for divorce.

**Property Distribution:**
New Hampshire is an "equitable distribution" state. The court will divide all the spouses' property based on the following factors: (1) the value of the property acquired prior to the marriage; (2) any contribution to the education or career development to the other spouse; (3) length of the marriage; (4) earning ability of each spouse; (5) the need to award the family residence to the custodial parent; (6) the conduct of each spouse during the marriage which increased or decreased the value of the property; (7) the age and health of each spouse; (8) the value of any gifts or inheritances; (9) any and all sources of income of each spouse; (10) the debts of each spouse; (11) the occupation of the spouses; (12) the vocational skills of the spouses; (13) the employability of the spouses; (14) the opportunity of each for further acquisition of capital assets and income; (15) the ability of the custodial parent to engage in gainful employment without interfering with the interests of any minor children in custody; (16) any significant disparity between the spouses in relation to the contribution of each spouse to the acquisition of the marital property, including the contribution of each spouse to the care and education of the children and the care and management of the home; (17) the expectation of any retirement or pension benefits; (18) the federal income tax consequences of the court's division of property; (19) any marital fault if such fault caused the breakdown of the marriage and caused pain and suffering or economic loss; (20) the value of any property acquired prior to marriage or exchanged for property acquired prior to marriage; (21) any interruption in education or career opportunities to benefit the other's career, the marriage, or any children; (22) the social and economic status of each spouse; and (23) any other relevant factor.

**Alimony/Spousal Support/Maintenance:**
Either spouse may be awarded alimony based on the same factors listed in the property distribution section in addition to the following: (1) the spouse lacks sufficient property to provide for his or her needs; (2) the paying spouse is able to meet his or her needs; and (3) the spouse seeking support cannot support himself or herself or is the custodial parent and unable to work outside the home because the child requires special care at home.

**Child Custody and Visitation:**
Custody will be awarded according to: (1) the child's wishes; (2) the education of the child; (3) any findings by a neutral mediator; and (4) any other factors. Joint responsibility for all parental rights, except physical custody, is presumed to be in the best interest of the child.

**Child Support:**
Either parent may be ordered to pay child support. There are official child support guidelines the court may use. The court will deviate from the guidelines if amount of the award will be unjust or inappropriate.

**Rights to Maiden Name:**
Upon request, the wife may have her former or maiden name restored.

# NEW JERSEY

**Residence Requirements:**
Either spouse must have been a resident of New Jersey for at least 1 year before filing. If the case is grounded on adultery, there is no time limit; however, one spouse must be a resident.

**Where to File:**
In any county of New Jersey.

**Name of Court:**
Superior Court. "Superior Court of New Jersey, Chancery Division, Family Part, _____ County."

**Title of Divorce Action:**
Complaint for Divorce

**Party Filing:**
Plaintiff

**Other Party:**
Defendant

**Title of Final Papers:**
Judgment of Divorce

**Approved Grounds for Divorce:**
No-fault: Living separate and apart for 18 months and no reasonable expectation of reconciliation. Fault-based: (1) adultery; (2) imprisonment for 18 months or more; (3) unnatural sexual behavior before or after marriage; (4) alcoholism or drug addiction; (5) confinement for permanent insanity; (6) cruel and inhuman treatment; (7) willful desertion for 1 year; (8) separation for 2 years caused by confinement for mental illness; or (9) extreme cruelty.

**General Divorce Procedures:**
A case information statement must be filed. The filing of an acknowledgment of service of process or appearance is permitted.

**Mediation or Counseling Requirements:**
There are no provisions for mediation.

**Legal Separation Provisions:**
The grounds for legal separation are the same as the grounds for divorce.

**Property Distribution:**
New Jersey is an "equitable distribution" state. A spouse will retain all property acquired before the marriage and any gifts or inheritances. All other property will be divided by the court based on the following factors: (1) each 102 contribution to the acquisition of marital property, including non-monetary contributions, i.e. homemaking; (2) the value of each 102 separate property; (3) the time and expense a spouse incurs to obtain sufficient education or training for appropriate employment; (4) the financial position of the spouses at the time the division of property occurs; (5) the need to award the family residence to the custodial parent; (6) length of the marriage; (7) the standard of living established during the marriage; (8) the age and health of the spouses; (9) the amount and sources of income of the spouses; (10) the liabilities and needs of each spouse and the opportunity of each for further acquisition of capital assets and income; (11) how and by whom the property was acquired; (12) the tax consequences to each spouse; (13) the contribution of each spouse to the acquisition of the marital property, including the contribution of each spouse as homemaker; (14) any written agreement between the spouses; (15) the income and earning capacity of the spouses; (16) the educational background, training, and employment skills of the spouses; (17) the need to create a trust fund for the future medical or educational needs of a spouse or children; and (18) any other factor necessary to do equity and justice between the spouses.

**Alimony/Spousal Support/Maintenance:**
The court may order either spouse to pay alimony considering: (1) length of the marriage; (2) earning ability of each spouse; (3) whether a 102 education, training, or employment was interrupted for homemaking; (4) the ability of each spouse to acquire capital and income; (5) the ability of each spouse to pay; (6) custodial obligations by the spouse seeking alimony; (7) the standard of living established during the marriage; (8) the time and expense necessary to acquire sufficient education and training to enable the spouse to find appropriate employment, and that 102 future earning capacity; (9) the age of the spouses; (10) the physical and emotional conditions of the spouses; (11) the earning capacities, educational levels, vocational skills, and employability of the spouses; (12) any child custodial responsibilities of the spouse seeking alimony; (13) the availability of training and employment; (14) the history or financial and non-financial contributions of each spouse to the marriage, including the contribution of each spouse to the care and education of children and interruption of personal careers or educational opportunities; (15) the equitable distribution of property and any payouts from this property, if a consideration of this income is fair and just (however, income from retirement benefits which are treated as an asset for purposes of equitable distribution are not to be considered); and (16) any other factor the court deems just and equitable.

**Child Custody and Visitation:**
Either parent may be awarded sole custody. Joint custody may also be awarded. The following factors will be considered: (1) the needs of the child; and (2) the child's wishes if the child is of sufficient age and capacity.

**Child Support:**
Child support will be based on the following factors: (1) the needs of the child; (2) the financial resources of the parents; (3) the earning abilities of the parents; (4) age and health of the individuals involved; (5) the need and capacity of the child for education, including higher education; (6) the income, assets and earning ability of the child; (7) the responsibility of the parents for the support of others; and (8) any other relevant factors.

**Rights to Maiden Name:**
Either spouse may restore a former name.

# NEW MEXICO

**Residence Requirements:**
Either spouse must have been a resident of New Mexico for at least 6 months before filing and have a home in the state.

**Where to File:**
In the county where either spouse resides.

**Name of Court:**
District Court. "State of New Mexico, In the District Court, _____ County."

**Title of Divorce Action:**
Petition for Dissolution of Marriage

**Party Filing:**
Petitioner

**Other Party:**
Respondent

**Title of Final Papers:**
Decree of Dissolution of Marriage

**Approved Grounds for Divorce:**
No-fault: Incompatibility such that the legitimate ends of the marriage relationship have been destroyed with no reasonable expectation of reconciliation. Fault-based: (1) adultery; (2) abandonment; (3) cruel and inhuman treatment.

**General Divorce Procedures:**
Written marital settlement agreements are authorized and such agreements should be recorded in the county where the spouses reside.

**Mediation or Counseling Requirements:**
The court may order the spouses to attend mediation.

**Legal Separation Provisions:**
Either spouse may begin the proceedings for property division, child custody, support, and maintenance without seeking a dissolution of marriage provided the spouses have permanently separated and do not cohabitate together.

**Property Distribution:**
New Mexico is a "community property" state. All property acquired before the marriage and any gifts or inheritances will be retained by that spouse. Property acquired outside of New Mexico is treated as though it was acquired in New Mexico, and it is treated as community property. Community property will be divided equally between the spouses.

**Alimony/Spousal Support/Maintenance:**
Either spouse may be awarded maintenance. The award is based on the following factors: (1) length of the marriage; (2) the needs of the spouse seeking maintenance and the ability of the other spouse to make such payments while meeting his or her needs; (3) the financial position of the spouse seeking maintenance; (4) the value of the property that each spouse owns; (5) the age and health of each spouse; (6) the good faith efforts of the spouses to maintain employment or become self-supporting; (7) the needs and obligations of each spouse; (8) the spouses' standard of living during the marriage; (9) the maintenance of medical and life insurance during the marriage; (10) the assets of the spouses, including any income-producing property; (11) each 102 liabilities; and (12) any marital separation or settlement agreements.

**Child Custody and Visitation:**
The factors considered in child custody are: (1) the child's wishes; (2) the parents' wishes; (3) the bond between the child and each parent; (4) the child's adjustment to his or her home, school, and community; and (5) the mental and physical health of all individuals involved. If a minor is 14 years old or older, the court may consider the wishes of the minor. Joint custody will be determined by the following: (1) the ability of the parents to cooperate with this arrangement; (2) the desire and ability of the parents to meet the child's needs; (3) whether each parent will accept all the responsibilities of parenting, including the willingness to accept or relinquish care; (4) the physical proximity of the parents to each other as this relates to the practical considerations of where the child will reside; (5) whether an award of joint custody will promote more frequent or continuing contact between the child and each of the parents; (6) the love, affection, and other emotional ties existing between the parents and the child; (7) whether each parent is able to allow the other to provide care without intrusion; and (8) the suitability of a parenting plan for the implementation of joint custody.

**Child Support:**
The court may order either parent to pay child support based on the parents' income. There are child support guidelines the court may use, unless evidence demonstrates the award will be unjust or inappropriate.

**Rights to Maiden Name:**
A spouse may have a former name restored.

# NEW YORK

**Residence Requirements:**
The residency requirement is 2 years if only one spouse lives in New York at the time of filing. However, the residency requirement will be 1 year if: (1) the marriage took place in New York and one spouse is still a resident; or (2) both spouses resided in New York and one spouse is still a resident; or (3) grounds for divorce arose in New York. No time requirement if the spouses were residents and grounds arose in New York.

| Where to File: | Name of Court: | Title of Divorce Action: |
|---|---|---|
| In the county where either spouse resides. | Supreme Court. "Supreme Court of the State of New York, _____ County." | Complaint for Divorce |

| Party Filing: | Other Party: | Title of Final Papers: |
|---|---|---|
| Plaintiff | Defendant | Judgment of Divorce |

**Important Note:**
Additional forms may be required. Call or visit your clerk of the court.

**Approved Grounds for Divorce:**
No-fault: (1) living separate and apart for 1 year under the provision of a written, signed and notarized separation agreement. A copy of such an agreement must be filed in the office of the clerk of the county; or (2) living separate and apart for 1 year under the terms of a judicial separation decree. Fault-based: (1) adultery; (2) abandonment for 1 year; (3) imprisonment for 3 or more years; or (4) cruel and inhuman treatment.

**General Divorce Procedures:**
Proof of performance of all the terms in a separation agreement must be filed. In addition, a summary divorce may be granted if: (1) the spouses have lived apart for 1 year according to the terms of the separation agreement or decree, and (2) proof that the terms were carried out. In addition, New York requires a financial disclosure to be filed in every divorce action.

**Mediation or Counseling Requirements:**
There are no provisions for mediation.

**Legal Separation Provisions:**
The grounds for legal separation are: (1) adultery; (2) abandonment; (3) imprisonment for 3 or more consecutive years; (4) neglect or failure to provide support to wife; and (5) cruel and inhuman treatment.

**Property Distribution:**
New York is an "equitable distribution" state. All property acquired prior to the marriage and any gifts or inheritances whenever acquired will be retained by that spouse. Marital property will be divided based on the following factors: (1) each 102 contribution to the acquisition of marital property, including non-monetary contributions, i.e. homemaking; (2) the value of the property acquired prior to the marriage; (3) length of the marriage; (4) the need to award the family residence to the custodial parent; (5) any and all sources of income of each spouse; (6) the wasteful disposition of assets; (7) age and health of each spouse; (8) any equitable claim that a spouse has in the marital property, including expenditures, contributions and services as a spouse, parent, wage earner, and homemaker; (9) the probable future economic circumstances of each spouse; (10) the age and health of the spouses; (11) the potential loss of inheritance or pension rights upon dissolution of the marriage; (12) whether the property award is instead of or in addition to maintenance; (13) the type of marital property in question (whether is is liquid or non-liquid); (14) the impossibility or difficulty of evaluating an interest in an asset such as a business, profession , or corporation and the desirability of keeping such as asset intact and free from interference by the other spouse; (15) any transfer of property made in anticipation of divorce; and (16) any other factor necessary to do equity and justice between the spouses. Marital fault may be considered. Financial disclosure of assets and income are mandatory.

**Alimony/Spousal Support/Maintenance:**
The court may award maintenance to either spouse based on the following factors: (1) the property of the spouse, including any property received as a result of the divorce; (2) any interruption in education, training, or employment by a spouse due to homemaking responsibilities; (3) the standard of living established during the marriage; (4) any transfer of property in anticipation of divorce; (5) age and health of each spouse; (6) the needs of the spouse seeking alimony and the ability of the other spouse to make such payments while meeting his or her own needs; (7) the earning capability of each spouse; (8) any custodial obligations of each spouse; (9) the duration of the marriage; (10) the wasteful dissipation of marital property; (11) the tax consequences to each spouse; (11) whether the spouse from whom maintenance is sought has sufficient property and income to provide maintenance for the other spouse; and (12) any other factor the court deems just and equitable.

**Child Custody and Visitation:**
Joint or sole child custody is awarded based on the best interests of the child. Neither parent is entitled to a preference. New York statutes do not list factors to be considered.

**Child Support:**
Either parent may be ordered to pay child support. There are official child support guidelines that the court may use. The court will deviate from the guidelines if there is a showing that the amount of the award will be unjust or inappropriate.

**Rights to Maiden Name:**
Upon request, the wife may have her former or maiden name restored.

# NORTH CAROLINA

**Residence Requirements:**
One spouse must have been a resident of North Carolina for at least 6 months prior to filing.

| Where to File: | Name of Court: | Title of Divorce Action: |
|---|---|---|
| In the county where either spouse resides. | Superior Court or District Court. "In the General Court of Justice, _____ Division, North Carolina, _____ County." | Complaint for Divorce |

| Party Filing: | Other Party: | Title of Final Papers: |
|---|---|---|
| Plaintiff | Respondent | Decree of Divorce |

**Approved Grounds for Divorce:**
No-fault: Living separate and apart without cohabitation for 1 year. Fault-based: Confinement for permanent insanity for 3 years, or incurable mental illness based on examinations for 3 years.

**General Divorce Procedures:**
There are no provisions for simplified divorce procedures.

**Mediation or Counseling Requirements:**
The court may order mediation if child custody is a contested issue.

**Legal Separation Provisions:**
The grounds for legal separation are: (1) adultery; (2) abandonment; (3) alcohol or drug abuse; (4) cruel and inhuman treatment; (5) personal indignities; and (7) evicting a spouse from the home.

**Property Distribution:**
North Carolina is an "equitable distribution" state. Property acquired before the marriage and gifts and inheritances whenever acquired will be retained by each spouse. The marital property will be divided equally unless the court determines that the division will be unfair. The court will consider the following: (1) each 102 contribution to the acquisition of marital property, including non-monetary contributions; (2) the value of the spouses' separate property; (3) the financial status of each spouse and the desirability to award the family home to the custodial parent or allow that parent to live in the home until the child(ren) is grown; (4) length of the marriage; (5) any depletion or waste of property; (6) any contribution to the career or education of the other spouse; (7) the net value of the property; (8) the liquid or non-liquid character of the property; (9) the economic circumstances of each spouse at the time the division of property is to become effective; (10) the age and health of the spouses; (11) any retirement benefits; (12) any prior alimony of child support obligations of each spouse; and (13) any other factor necessary to do equity and justice between the spouses.

**Alimony/Spousal Support/Maintenance:**
The court may award alimony to either spouse based on the following factors: (1) the financial resources of the spouses; (2) earning ability of each spouse; (3) length of the marriage; (4) the physical and mental health of each spouse; (5) the marital misconduct of the spouses; (6) the ages of the spouses; (7) the contribution of one spouse to the education, training, or earning power of the other spouse; (8) the effect of a spouse having primary custody of a child; (9) the relative education of the spouses and the time necessary for a spouse to acquire sufficient education or training to become self-sufficient; (10) the contribution of a spouse as a homemaker; (11) the tax consequences; and (12) any other just and equitable factor.

**Child Custody and Visitation:**
Joint or sole child custody is determined by the best interest of the child. There is no presumption that either parent is better suited to have custody.

**Child Support:**
Either parent may be ordered to pay child support based on the following: (1) the needs of the child; (2) the earning abilities of the parents; (3) the parent's ability to pay; (4) the child care and homemaking contributions by each parent; (5) the earnings, conditions and accustomed standard of living of the child; (6) any joint or shared custody arrangements; (7) the parent's own special needs, such as unusual medical expenses; (8) any types of other support provided to the child; (9) a parent's prior child support or alimony obligations; and (10) any other relevant factors. In addition, there are official child support guidelines.

**Rights to Maiden Name:**
Upon request, the wife may have her former or maiden name restored.

# NORTH DAKOTA

**Residence Requirements:**
The filing spouse must have been a resident of North Dakota for at least 6 months before filing for a divorce.

**Where to File:**
If defendant is a resident, file in his/her county; otherwise file in any county that plaintiff designates.

**Name of Court:**
District Court. "State of North Dakota, County of _____, In the District Court, _____ Judicial District."

**Title of Divorce Action:**
Complaint for Divorce

**Party Filing:**
Plaintiff

**Other Party:**
Defendant

**Title of Final Papers:**
Decree of Divorce

**Approved Grounds for Divorce:**
No-fault: Irreconcilable differences. Fault-based: (1) adultery; (2) confinement for 5 years because of permanent insanity; (3) conviction of a felony; (4) willful desertion; (5) cruel and inhuman treatment; (6) willful neglect; and (7) drunkenness.

**General Divorce Procedures:**
Separation agreements are authorized.

**Mediation or Counseling Requirements:**
If child custody is at issue, the court may order the parents to submit to mediation.

**Legal Separation Provisions:**
The grounds for a legal separation are: (1) adultery; (2) confinement for 5 years because of permanent insanity; (3) conviction of a felony; (4) willful desertion; (5) cruel and inhuman treatment; (6) willful neglect; and (7) drunkenness.

**Property Distribution:**
North Dakota is an "equitable distribution" state. The court will divide all of the spouses' property including gifts and inheritances, and any property acquired before the marriage.

**Alimony/Spousal Support/Maintenance:**
Either spouse may be ordered to pay maintenance. All the circumstances of the situation, including any marital fault, may be considered.

**Child Custody and Visitation:**
Child custody will be awarded in the best interest of the child based on the following: (1) the desire and ability of the parents to meet the needs of the child; (2) the mental and physical health of the parents and the child; (3) the bond between the child, the parents and any siblings; (4) any domestic violence; (5) the child's adjustment to his or her home, school, and community; (6) moral fitness of the parents; (7) preference of the child, if the child is of sufficient age and capacity; (8) the length of time the child has lived in a stable, satisfactory environment and the desirability of maintaining continuity; (9) the stability of the home environment likely to be offered by each parent; (10) the child's interaction with anyone who resides with a parent; (11) the capacity and disposition of the parents to give the child love, affection, guidance, and continue the child's education; (12) the permanence, as a family unit, of the proposed existing custodial home; (13) the making of any false accusations by one parent against the other; and (14) any other factors. If there is any evidence of sexual abuse of a child, the court is required to prohibit any visitation or contact with that parent unless the parent has completed counseling and the court determines that supervised visitation is in the best interests of the child. Both parents are considered to be equally entitled to custody of a child.

**Child Support:**
Either parent may be ordered to pay child support based on the following factors: (1) net income of the parents; (2) any other sources of income available to the parents; and (3) any circumstances which should be considered in reducing the amount of support on the basis of hardship. All child support orders are reviewed every 3 years.

**Rights to Maiden Name:**
The wife's former name may be restored.

# OHIO

**Residence Requirements:**
The filing spouse must have been a resident of Ohio for at least 6 months and a resident of the county for at least 90 days.

**Where to File:**
In the county of the filing spouse.

**Name of Court:**
"In the Court of Common Pleas of _____ County, Ohio."

**Title of Divorce Action:**
No-fault: Petition for Dissolution of Marriage. Fault-based: Complaint for Divorce

**Party Filing:**
Petitioner; (Fault-based: Plaintiff)

**Other Party:**
Co-Petitioner; (Fault-based: Defendant)

**Title of Final Papers:**
No-fault: Decree of Dissolution of Marriage Fault-based: Decree of Divorce

**Approved Grounds for Divorce:**
No-fault: (1) incompatibility, or (2) living separate and apart without cohabitation and without interruption for 1 year. Fault-based: (1) adultery; (2) imprisonment; (3) confinement for 4 years due to permanent insanity; (4) willful desertion for 1 year; (5) cruel and inhuman treatment; (6) drunkenness; (7) neglect; or (8) bigamy; (9) when a final divorce decree has been obtained outside of the state of Ohio that does not release the other spouse from the obligations of the marriage inside the state of Ohio; or (10) fraud.

**General Divorce Procedures:**
Both spouses may file jointly. The petition for dissolution of marriage must contain the signatures of both spouses and an attached settlement agreement with provisions for: (1) division of property; (2) spousal support, including, if the spouses desire, that the court may modify the support terms; and (3) if there are minor children, provisions for custody, visitation and child support. Both spouses must then appear in court between 30 and 90 days after filing to testify to the following: (1) each spouse voluntarily signed the agreement; (2) each is satisfied with the agreement; and (3) each is seeking a dissolution of marriage.

**Mediation or Counseling Requirements:**
At the request of either spouse, or at the court's initiative, the court may order counseling for 90 days. In addition, the court may order mediation when there are child custody and visitation issues in dispute.

**Legal Separation Provisions:**
The grounds for legal separation are: (1) adultery; (2) imprisonment; (3) when a final divorce decree has been obtained outside of the state of Ohio that does not release the other spouse from the obligations of the marriage inside the state of Ohio; (4) fraud; (5) living separate and apart without cohabitation and without interruption for 1 year; (6) willful desertion for 1 year; (7) cruel and inhuman treatment; (8) drunkenness; (9) neglect; or (10) bigamy.

**Property Distribution:**
Ohio is an "equitable division" state. All the separate property, including gifts or inheritances, will be retained by each spouse. The court will divide the marital property based on the following factors: (1) the desirability to award the family residence to the custodial parent; (2) the length of marriage; (3) the financial resources of each spouse; (4) the needs and obligations of each spouse; (5) the economic desirability of keeping the assets intact; (6) the costs of any sale of an asset; (7) the liquidity of the property to be distributed; (8) the tax consequences of the division; and (9) any other relevant factor.

**Alimony/Spousal Support/Maintenance:**
Either spouse may be awarded maintenance based on the same factors listed above in addition to the following: (1) standard of living during the marriage; (2) the lost income capacity of a spouse due to homemaking responsibilities; (3) age and health of each spouse; (4) the educational level of each spouse; (5) the earning capability of each spouse; (6) the value of the property that each spouse received in the division of the marital property; (7) any contribution by one spouse to the education or training of the other; Either parent may be ordered to pay child support. There are official child support guidelines that the court may use. The court will deviate from the guidelines if there is a showing that the amount of the award will be unjust or inappropriate.

**Child Custody and Visitation:**
Sole or joint custody may be awarded based on the following: (1) the child's wishes; (2) the child's adjustment to his or her home, school, and community; (3) the bond between the child, the parents and any siblings; (4) the mental and physical health of all individuals involved; (5) whether one parent has willfully denied visitation to the other parent; (6) any child or spousal abuse; (7) whether either parent lives or intends to live outside of Ohio; (8) the ability of the parents to cooperate and make joint decisions; (9) the health and safety of the child; (10) any history of child abuse, spouse abuse, domestic violence by a parent or anyone who is or will be a member of the household where the child will reside, or parental kidnapping; (11) the geographic proximity of the parents to each other as it relates to shared parenting; (12) the child's and parent's available time; (13) the child's available time to spend with any siblings; and (14) any other relevant factors. Both parents are considered to have equal rights to custody. In addition, for shared parenting to be awarded, both parents must request it and submit a plan for shared parenting. The financial status of a parent is not to be considered for allocating any parental rights and responsibilities. The court may require an investigation of the parents and any evidence of neglect or child or spousal abuse will be considered against the granting of shared parenting or such parent being granted the status as residential parent. For shared parenting to be awarded, both parents must request it and submit a plan.

**Child Support:**
Either parent may be ordered to pay child support. There are official child support guidelines that the court may use. The court will deviate from the guidelines if there is a showing that the amount of the award will be unjust or inappropriate.

**Rights to Maiden Name:**
The former or maiden name will be restored upon request.

# OKLAHOMA

**Residence Requirements:**
One spouse must have been a resident of Oklahoma for 6 months before filing for a divorce.

**Where to File:**
In the county of the plaintiff if the plaintiff has been a resident for 30 days, or in the defendant's county.

**Name of Court:**
"State of Oklahoma, In the District Court, _____ County."

**Title of Divorce Action:**
Petition for Divorce

**Party Filing:**
Plaintiff

**Other Party:**
Defendant

**Title of Final Papers:**
Decree of Divorce

**Approved Grounds for Divorce:**
No-fault: Incompatibility. Fault-based: (1) adultery; (2) impotence; (3) abandonment for 1 year; (4) imprisonment; (5) confinement for five years for permanent insanity; (6) cruel and inhuman treatment; (7) drunkenness; (8) wife was pregnant by another at the time of marriage; (9) gross neglect; (10) fraud; or (11) a foreign divorce which is not valid in Oklahoma.

**General Divorce Procedures:**
Separation agreements are authorized.

**Mediation or Counseling Requirements:**
The court may appoint an arbitrator if there is a joint custody dispute after the divorce takes place.

**Legal Separation Provisions:**
Either spouse may file for alimony without seeking a divorce on the following grounds: (1) adultery; (2) impotence; (3) abandonment for 1 year; (4) imprisonment; (5) confinement for permanent insanity for 5 years; (6) cruel and inhuman treatment; (7) drunkenness; (8) wife was pregnant by another at the time of marriage; (9) gross neglect; or (10) fraud.

**Property Distribution:**
Oklahoma is an "equitable distribution" state. Each spouse will retain all property acquired prior to the marriage and any gifts or inheritances whenever acquired. All the marital property will be divided in a just and reasonable manner.

**Alimony/Spousal Support/Maintenance:**
Either spouse may be awarded alimony. The award may be a lump sum or in installments. There are no other factors listed in the statute.

**Child Custody and Visitation:**
Child custody is awarded in the best interests of the child and based on the following: (1) that the child has frequent contact with both parents; and (2) that each parent be responsible in the rearing of the child. There is no preference for or against joint custody.

**Child Support:**
The court may order either parent to pay child support. The court will look at the income and property assets of each parent. There are official child support guidelines in Oklahoma.

**Rights to Maiden Name:**
A wife may have her former or maiden name restored.

# OREGON

**Residence Requirements:**
If the marriage took place in Oregon and one spouse is a resident of Oregon, then there is no residency time limit. If the marriage was not performed in Oregon, then one spouse must have been a resident of Oregon for 6 months before filing.

**Where to File:**
In the county where either spouse resides.

**Name of Court:**
"In the Circuit Court for the State of Oregon for the County of _____."

**Title of Divorce Action:**
Petition for Dissolution of Marriage

**Party Filing:**
Petitioner (Joint: Co-Petitioner)

**Other Party:**
Respondent (Joint: Co-Petitioner)

**Title of Final Papers:**
Decree of Dissolution of Marriage

**Important Note:**
Additional forms may be required. Call or visit your clerk of the court.

**Approved Grounds for Divorce:**
No-fault-based: Irreconcilable differences between the spouses which have caused the irretrievable breakdown of the marriage. Fault-based: (1) consent to marriage was obtained by fraud, duress, or force; (2) minor married without lawful consent; or (3) lacked mental capacity to consent. Misconduct of the spouses will only be considered when child custody is an issue.

**General Divorce Procedures:**
A summary dissolution of marriage may be granted if: (1) the residency requirement has been satisfied; (2) there are no minor children and the wife is not pregnant; (3) the marriage is not more than 10 years in duration; (4) neither spouse owns real estate; (5) there are no debts over $15,000 incurred by the spouses; (6) the total value of the spouses' personal property is less than $30,000, excluding any unpaid balances on loans; (7) waiver of spousal support; (8) waiver of pendente lite orders, except for spousal abuse; and (9) the Petitioner knows of no other pending domestic suit. In addition, there will be a 90-day waiting period before a hearing will be held.

**Mediation or Counseling Requirements:**
The court may order conciliation services. In addition, if there is a child custody or support dispute, the court may order mediation.

**Legal Separation Provisions:**
The grounds for legal separation are irreconcilable differences between the spouses which have caused the irretrievable breakdown of the marriage.

**Property Distribution:**
Oregon is an "equitable distribution" state. All the spouses' property can be divided by the court. There is a presumption that the spouses equally contributed to the acquisition of property, unless shown otherwise. The court will consider the following: (1) each 102 contribution to the acquisition of marital property, including non-monetary contributions; (2) any retirement benefits; (3) the cost of selling any assets; (4) the amount of taxes or liens on the property; (5) whether the property award is in lieu of or in addition to maintenance; and (6) any life insurance coverage.

**Alimony/Spousal Support/Maintenance:**
The court may award support to either spouse. The spouse receiving support must make a reasonable effort in becoming self-supportive or the court will terminate spousal support. The court will consider the following factors: (1) the time and expense a spouse incurs to obtain sufficient education or training for gainful employment; (2) length of marriage; (3) any interruption in a 102 education, training, or employment due to homemaking responsibilities; (4) standard of living during the marriage; (5) occupation of each spouse; (6) earning ability of each spouse; (7) any custodial support obligations; (8) financial resources of each spouse; (9) the tax consequences to each spouse; (10) the age of the spouses; (11) the physical and emotional conditions of the spouses; (12) the vocational skills and employability of the spouse seeking support; (13) the educational level of each spouse at the time of the marriage and at the time the divorce is filed for; (14) any life insurance; (15) the costs of health care; (16) the extent that a 102 earning capacity is impaired due to absence from the job market to be homemaker and the extent that job opportunities are unavailable considering the age of the spouse and the anticipated length of time for appropriate training; (17) the contribution of each spouse to the marriage; (18) any long term financial obligations, including legal fees; and (19) any other factor the court deems just and equitable.

**Child Custody and Visitation:**
Marital misconduct will be considered. The court will base its decision on the following factors: (1) the bond between the child, the parents and any siblings; (2) any domestic abuse; (3) the amount of time the child has lived in a particular environment, and the desirability of maintaining continuity; and (4) the child's attitude and the parents' attitude.

**Child Support:**
Either parent may be ordered to pay child support based on the following factors: (1) the financial resources of both parties; (2) the parent's ability to pay; (3) the needs of the child or other dependent; (4) the desirability of the custodial parent to remain at home as a full-time parent; (4) the standard of living the child would have enjoyed if the marriage were not dissolved; (5) the potential earnings of the parents; (6) the cost of day care to the parent having custody or physical care of the home if that parent works outside the home, or the value of the child care services performed by that parent if the parent remains in the home; (7) the tax consequences to each parent; and (8) any other relevant factors.

**Rights to Maiden Name:**
Either spouse may have a former name restored.

# PENNSYLVANIA

**Residence Requirements:**

One spouse must have been a resident of Pennsylvania for at least 6 months before filing for a divorce.

**Where to File:**

In the county where (1) the defendant re-sides; (2) where the defendant resides if plaintiff lives outside the state; (3) where marriage home was if plaintiff continuously resided in the same county; (4) prior to 6 months after separation, and if the defendant agrees, where the plaintiff resides; (5) prior to 6 months after separation, and if neither spouse lives in the county of the marriage home, where either spouse lives; or (6) after 6 months after separation, where either spouse lives.

**Name of Court:**

Court of Common Pleas. "Court of Common Pleas, _____ County, Pennsylvania."

**Party Filing:**

Plaintiff

**Other Party:**

Defendant

**Title of Divorce Action:**

Complaint for Divorce

**Title of Final Papers:**

Decree of Divorce

**Approved Grounds for Divorce:**

No-fault: (1) irretrievable breakdown of the marriage with spouses living separate and apart without cohabitation for 2 years, or (2) irretrievable breakdown of the marriage and the spouses have signed and filed affidavits stating that they consent to the divorce. Fault-based: (1) adultery; (2) imprisonment for 2 or more years; (3) confinement for 18 months due to permanent insanity; (4) willful desertion for 1 year; (5) cruel and inhuman treatment; (6) bigamy; or (7) personal indignities.

**General Divorce Procedures:**

There are no official forms for a complaint for divorce on the grounds of irretrievable breakdown of the marriage.

**Mediation or Counseling Requirements:**

The court may order counseling for reconciliation for a period of between 90 and 120 days. Either spouse may request counseling, in which case three counseling sessions may be ordered.

**Legal Separation Provisions:**

Separation agreements are binding if the terms are reasonable.

**Property Distribution:**

Pennsylvania is an "equitable distribution" state. Each spouse will retain any property acquired before the marriage and any gift or inheritance whenever acquired. The court will divide the marital property based on the following factors: (1) the value of each 102 separate property; (2) each 102 contribution to the acquisition of marital property, including non-monetary contributions; (3) the length of the marriage; (4) any and all sources of income of each spouse; (5) any debts of each spouse; (6) the earning capability of each spouse; (7) occupation of each spouse; (8) the standard of living established during the marriage; (9) the financial position of each spouse after the division of the property; (10) the tax consequences to each spouse; (11) the vocational skills of the spouses; (12) the employability of each spouses; (13) any premarital agreement; (14) any contributions toward the education, training, or increased earning power of the other spouse; (15) any prior marital obligations; and (16) any other factor necessary to do equity and justice between the spouses.

**Alimony/Spousal Support/Maintenance:**

The court may award alimony to either spouse based on the following factors: (1) any marital misconduct; (2) the time and expense a spouse will incur to obtain sufficient education or training for appropriate employment; (3) the needs of the spouse seeking alimony and the ability of the other spouse to make such payments while meeting his or her own needs; (4) age and health of each spouse; (5) the earning capability of each spouse; (6) the financial resources of each spouse; (7) the probable length of time a spouse will need alimony. There are official spousal support guidelines; (8) whether the spouse seeking alimony lacks sufficient property to provide for his or her own needs; (9) whether the spouse is unable to be self-supporting through appropriate employment; (10) whether the spouse seeking alimony is the custodian of a child; (11) any tax consequences; (12) the standard of living established during the marriage; (13) the duration of the marriage; (14) the comparative financial resources of the spouses, including their comparative earning abilities in the labor market; (15) the needs and obligations of each spouse; (16) the contribution of each spouse to the marriage, including services rendered in homemaking, child care, education, and career building of the other spouse; (17) the educational level of each spouse at the time of the marriage and at the time the action for alimony is commenced; (18) the conduct of the spouses during the marriage; and (19) any other factor the court deems just and equitable.

**Child Custody and Visitation:**

Joint or shared child custody will be determined on the best interest of the child, and upon a consideration of the following factors: (1) which parent is more likely to encourage, permit, and allow frequent and continuing contact, including physical access between the other parent and the child, and (2) whether either parent has engaged in any violent, criminally sexual, abusive, or harassing behavior. The court may require a written plan to be submitted in a shared/joint custody situation.

**Child Support:**

The court may order either parent to pay child support based on the following factors: (1) the net income of the parents; (2) the financial resources of the parents; (3) the earning capabilities of the parents; (4) any extraordinary expenses; and (5) any unusual needs of the child or the parents. There are official child support guidelines.

**Rights to Maiden Name:**

Either spouse may have a former or maiden name restored upon written notice filed with the prothonotary (chief clerk) of the court granting the divorce.

# RHODE ISLAND

**Residence Requirements:**

One spouse must have been a resident of Rhode Island for 1 year before filing.

**Where to File:**

In county of defendant if residency requirement is met, otherwise in plaintiff's county.

**Name of Court:**

Family Court. "State of Rhode Island, Family Court _____ Division."

**Party Filing:**

Plaintiff

**Other Party:**

Defendant

**Title of Divorce Action:**

Complaint for Divorce

**Title of Final Papers:**

Final Judgment of Divorce

**Approved Grounds for Divorce:**

No-fault: (1) irreconcilable differences which have caused the irremediable breakdown of the marriage, or (2) living separate and apart without cohabitation for 3 years. Fault-based: (1) adultery; (2) impotence; (3) alcoholism or drug abuse; (4) abandonment and presumed dead; (5) failure to consummate marriage; (6) willful desertion for 5 years (or less within the discretion of the court); (7) gross neglect; (8) cruel and inhuman treatment; (9) bigamy; (10) life imprisonment; (11) spouse is of unsound mind; and (12) incest.

**General Divorce Procedures:**

An official financial statement must be filed by each spouse. An official child support guidelines form must be filed in cases involving minor children. In addition, there must be a court hearing in all divorce cases.

**Mediation or Counseling Requirements:**

A family court counseling form must be filed with the complaint for divorce.

**Legal Separation Provisions:**

The grounds for legal separation are: (1) adultery; (2) impotence; (3) alcoholism or drug abuse; (4) abandonment and presumed dead; (5) failure to consummate marriage; (6) willful desertion for 5 years or less (within the discretion of the court); (7) gross neglect; (8) confinement for incurable insanity; (9) bigamy; (10) life imprisonment; (11) spouse is of unsound mind; (12) incest; (13) irreconcilable differences which have cause the irremediable breakdown of the marriage; (14) living separate and apart without cohabitation for 3 years; and (15) any other cause which may seem to require a divorce from bed and board (legal separation).

**Property Distribution:**

Rhode Island is an "equitable distribution" state. All property acquired prior to the marriage and any gift or inheritance whenever acquired will be retained by each spouse. The court will divide the remaining property based on the following factors: (1) each 102 contribution to the acquisition of marital property, including non-monetary contributions; (2) the length of the marriage; (3) the conduct of the spouses during the marriage; (4) the health and ages of the spouses; (5) the amount and sources of income of the spouses; (6) the occupation and employability of each of the spouses; (7) the contribution by one spouse to the education, training, licensure, business, or increased earning power of the other; (8) the need of a custodial parent to occupy or own the marital residence and to use or own the household effects according to the best interests of any children; (9) either 102 wasteful dissipation or unfair transfer of any assets in contemplation of divorce; and (10) any other factor which is just and proper.

**Alimony/Spousal Support/Maintenance:**

The court may award alimony to either spouse based on the following factors: (1) the extent to which a spouse was absent from employment while fulfilling homemaking responsibilities; (2) the extent to which a 102 education may have become outmoded and his or her earning capacity diminished; (3) the time and expense required for a supported spouse to acquire the appropriate education and training to develop marketable skills and become employed; (4) the probability, given the 102 age and skills, of completing education and training and becoming self-supporting; (5) the standard of living during the marriage; (6) the opportunity for either spouse for the future acquisition of capital assets and income; (7) the ability of the supporting spouse to pay, taking into consideration the supporting 102 (a) earning capacity, (b) earned and unearned income, (c) assets, (d) debts and (e) standard of living; and (8) any other factors which are just and proper.

**Child Custody and Visitation:**

There are no factors listed in the statute. Child custody will be determined according to the best interest of the child.

**Child Support:**

The court may order either parent to pay child support based on the following: (1) the financial resources of the child and parents; (2) the needs of the child; (3) earning capabilities of the parents; (4) the standard of living the child would have enjoyed if the marriage was not dissolved; (5) the earning potential of the parents; (6) any other dependents of the parents; (7) the financial resources, needs and obligations of both the noncustodial and custodial parent; and (8) any other relevant factor.

**Rights to Maiden Name:**

The wife may have her former name restored.

# SOUTH CAROLINA

**Residence Requirements:**
If both spouses are residents of South Carolina, the filing spouse must only have been a resident for 3 months. Otherwise, if only the filing spouse is a resident, then he or she must have been a resident of South Carolina for at least 1 year.

**Where to File:**
In the county where the defendant resides, the county where plaintiff resides if the defendant is a non-resident, or, if both still live in the state, the county where the spouses last lived together.

**Name of Court:**
"State of South Carolina, The Family Court of the _____ Judicial Circuit."

**Title of Divorce Action:**
Complaint for Divorce

**Party Filing:**
Plaintiff

**Other Party:**
Defendant

**Title of Final Papers:**
Decree of Divorce

**Approved Grounds for Divorce:**
No-fault: Living separate and apart without cohabitation for 1 year. Fault-based: (1) adultery; (2) alcoholism or drug abuse; (3) physical abuse or reasonable apprehension of physical abuse; or (4) willful desertion for 1 year.

**General Divorce Procedures:**
The clerk of the court may have forms, which have been developed by the court, to be used in divorce matters.

**Mediation or Counseling Requirements:**
The court may order counseling to bring about a reconciliation.

**Legal Separation Provisions:**
Legal separation and separate maintenance may be obtained in South Carolina.

**Property Distribution:**
South Carolina is an "equitable distribution" state. Each spouse will retain any property acquired prior to the marriage and any gift or inheritance whenever acquired. The court will divide all other property based on the following factors: (1) any marital misconduct; (2) length of the marriage; (3) the time and expense a spouse incurs to obtain sufficient education or training for appropriate employment; (4) each 102 contribution to the acquisition of marital property; (5) the earning ability of each spouse; (6) the financial resources of each spouse and the ability to increase resources; (7) the value of the non-marital property of each spouse; (8) the debts of each spouse; (9) the desirability to award the family residence to the custodial parent; (10) the age of the spouses; (11) any marital misconduct; (12) any economic misconduct; (13) the value of the marital property; (14) the income of each spouse; (15) the physical and emotional health of each spouse; (16) any retirement benefits; (17) whether alimony has been awarded; (18) the desirability of awarding the family home to the spouse having custody of any children; (19) the tax consequences; (20) any other support obligations of either spouse; (21) any child custody arrangements; and (22) any other relevant factors.

**Alimony/Spousal Support/Maintenance:**
Either spouse may be awarded alimony. The court will consider the following: (1) the age and health of each spouse; (2) the employment history of each spouse; (3) standard of living during the marriage; (4) the earning ability of each spouse; (5) the effect of having custody of any children on the custodial parent's ability to work full time; (6) the standard of living established during the marriage; (7) the duration of the marriage and the ages of the spouses when married and when divorced; (8) the educational background of each spouse, and the need of additional training or education to reach the 102 income potential; (9) the marital and separate property of each spouse; (10) any marital misconduct; (11) any tax consequences; (12) any prior support obligations; (13) any other relevant factors.

**Child Custody and Visitation:**
Child custody is based on the following factors: (1) the circumstances of the parents; (2) the circumstances of the case; (3) the religious faith of all parties involved; (4) the child's welfare; and (5) the best spiritual and other interests of the child. The parents both have equal rights regarding any award of custody of children.

**Child Support:**
Either parent may be ordered to pay child support. There are official child support guidelines that the court may use. The court will deviate from the guidelines if there is a showing that the amount of the award will be unjust or inappropriate.

**Rights to Maiden Name:**
The wife may have her former name restored.

# SOUTH DAKOTA

**Residence Requirements:**
The filing spouse must be a resident of South Dakota, or a member of the Armed Forces stationed in South Dakota, when filing for a divorce and until the divorce is final. There is no time limit for residency requirement.

**Where to File:**
In the county where either spouse resides. However, defendant may have the case transferred to his or her county.

**Name of Court:**
"State of South Dakota, County of _____, In the Circuit Court, _____ Judicial District."

**Title of Divorce Action:**
Complaint for Divorce

**Party Filing:**
Plaintiff

**Other Party:**
Defendant

**Title of Final Papers:**
Final Decree of Divorce

**Approved Grounds for Divorce:**
No-fault: Irreconcilable differences which have caused the irretrievable breakdown of the marriage. Fault-based: (1) adultery; (2) confinement for 5 years because of permanent insanity; (3) convicted felon; (4) willful desertion; (5) cruel and inhuman treatment; (6) willful neglect; (7) separation caused by misconduct; and (8) drunkenness.

**General Divorce Procedures:**
If the spouses base the complaint for divorce on irreconcilable differences, they can submit affidavits which establish the required residency and the grounds for divorce. In such a case, the court will not generally require either spouse to personally appear in court.

**Mediation or Counseling Requirements:**
The proceeding can be delayed for up to 30 days if the court determines that there is a reasonable possibility for reconciliation between the spouses.

**Legal Separation Provisions:**
The grounds for legal separation are: (1) adultery; (2) confinement for 5 years because of permanent insanity; (3) convicted felon; (4) willful desertion; (5) cruel and inhuman treatment; (6) willful neglect; (7) separation caused by misconduct; or (8) drunkenness.

**Property Distribution:**
South Dakota is an "equitable distribution" state. All the spouses' property will be divided. The court will consider the following factors: (1) each spouse's contribution to the acquisition of the marital property, including any non-monetary contribution; (2) the duration of the marriage; (3) the age and health of each spouse; (4) the earning capability of each spouse; (5) the value of each spouse's property; and (6) the income-producing capacity of each spouse's assets.

**Alimony/Spousal Support/Maintenance:**
The court may award either spouse maintenance for life or for a shorter duration based on the following factors: (1) the length of the marriage; (2) any marital misconduct; (3) the financial resources of each spouse; (4) the age of each spouse; (5) the needs of the spouse seeking support and the ability of the other spouse to make such payments while meeting his or her own needs; (6) the health of each spouse; (7) the financial resources of the spouse seeking maintenance, including marital property apportioned to such spouse and such 102 ability to meet his or her needs independently; and (8) the fault of the spouses during the marriage.

**Child Custody and Visitation:**
Child custody is based on the best interest of the child. The preference of the child may be considered if the child is of sufficient age and capacity.

**Child Support:**
The court may order either parent to pay child support. There are official child support guidelines, however, the court may deviate from the guidelines if the amount would be unjust or inappropriate.

**Rights to Maiden Name:**
The wife may have her former or name restored.

# TENNESSEE

**Residence Requirements:**
Either spouse must have been a resident of Tennessee for 6 months before filing if the grounds for divorce arose outside Tennessee. If the grounds for divorce arose in Tennessee, then there is no time requirement.

**Where to File:**
In the county where both spouses resided at time of separation; or county where respondent resides if he or she is a resident, or the county of the petitioner if respondent is not a resident.

**Name of Court:**
Circuit Court or Chancery Court. "In the _____ Court of _____ County, Tennessee."

**Title of Divorce Action:**
Petition for Divorce

**Party Filing:**
Petitioner

**Other Party:**
Respondent

**Title of Final Papers:**
Final Decree of Divorce

**Approved Grounds for Divorce:**
No-fault: (1) irreconcilable differences, or (2) living separate and apart without cohabitation for 2 years, and there are no minor children. Fault-based: (1) adultery; (2) impotence; (3) conviction of a felony and imprisonment; (4) willful desertion for 1 year; (5) endangering the life of the spouse; (6) wife is pregnant by another at the time of marriage without husband's knowledge; (7) bigamy; (8) commission and/or conviction of an infamous crime; or (9) refusing to move to Tennessee with a spouse and willfully absenting oneself from a new residence for 2 years.

**General Divorce Procedures:**
If the divorce is based on irreconcilable differences, the spouse may enter into a settlement agreement that has been notarized. The agreement must contain the following: (1) a specific reference to the divorce case by naming the court and docket number; or (2) state that the respondent has knowledge that a divorce will be filed; and (3) that the respondent waives service of process and filing an answer. There will be a hearing in 60 days if there are no minor children, and in 90 days if there are minor children. The settlement agreement must have a provision dealing with child custody and child support. Some counties may require that the respondent sign an appearance and waiver form before the clerk of the court.

**Mediation or Counseling Requirements:**
The court may delay the proceeding upon request from either spouse to allow an attempt at reconciliation.

**Legal Separation Provisions:**
The grounds for a legal separation are: (1) cruel and inhuman treatment; (2) that the husband makes the wife's condition intolerable with personal indignities; (3) the husband has abandoned the wife; or (4) the husband has forced the wife to leave the family residence without providing for her.

**Property Distribution:**
Tennessee is an "equitable distribution" state. Each spouse will retain any property that was acquired prior to the marriage and any gift or inheritance whenever acquired. The court will divide the marital property according to the following factors: (1) the value of the separate property of each spouse; (2) each 102 contribution to the acquisition of marital property, including non-monetary contributions; (3) the length of the marriage; (4) present and future earning ability of each spouse; (5) the economic circumstances of each spouse at the time the division of property is to become effective; (6) the liabilities and needs of each spouse and the opportunity of each for further acquisition of capital assets and income; (7) the federal income tax consequences of the court's division of the property; (8) the tangible and intangible contributions made by one spouse to the education, training, or increased earning power of the other spouse; (9) the relative ability of each party for the future acquisition of capital and income; and (10) any other factor necessary to do equity and justice between the spouses.

**Alimony/Spousal Support/Maintenance:**
Either spouse may be awarded lump sum, periodic, or rehabilitative spousal support based on the following factors: (1) the value of any separate property and the value of the spouses' share of any marital property; (2) whether the spouse seeking alimony is the custodian of a child whose circumstances make it appropriate for that spouse not to seek outside employment; (3) the need for sufficient education and training to enable the spouse to find appropriate employment; (4) the standard of living during the marriage; (5) the duration of the marriage; (6) the comparative financial resources of the spouses including their comparative earning abilities in the labor market and any retirement, pension, or profit-sharing benefits; (7) the needs and obligations of each spouse; (8) the tangible and intangible contributions of each spouse to the marriage, including services rendered in homemaking, child care, and contributions to the education, earning capacity, and career building of the other spouse; (9) the relative education and training of the spouses and the opportunity of each party to secure education and training; (10) the age of the spouses; (11) the physical and mental condition of the spouses; (12) the tax consequences to each spouse; (13) the usual occupation of the spouses during the marriage; (14) the vocational skills and employability of the spouse seeking alimony; (15) the conduct of the spouses during the marriage; and (16) any other factor the court deems just and equitable.

**Child Custody and Visitation:**
Joint or sole custody is awarded according to the best interest of the child and considering the child's preference. There is no presumption that either parent is more suited to obtain custody. However, if the child is of tender years, the sex of the parent seeking custody is a factor which may be taken into consideration.

**Child Support:**
The court may order either parent to pay child support based on the following factors: (1) the financial resources of the child and parents; (2) whether the non-custodial parent's visitation is over 110 days per year or under 55 days per year; (3) the standard of living the child would have enjoyed if the marriage was not dissolved; (4) the physical and emotional conditions and educational needs of the child; (5) the earning capacity of each parent; (6) the age and health of the child; (7) the monetary and non-monetary contributions of each parent to the well-being of the child; (8) any pension or retirement benefits of the parents; and (9) any other relevant factors.

**Rights to Maiden Name:**
A wife may resume the use of her former or maiden name.

# TEXAS

**Residence Requirements:**
Either spouse must have been a resident of Texas for 6 months and a resident of the county for 90 days before filing.

**Where to File:**
In the county of the petitioner

**Name of Court:**
"In the District Court of _____ County, Texas, _____ Judicial District."

**Title of Divorce Action:**
Petition for Divorce

**Party Filing:**
Petitioner

**Other Party:**
Respondent

**Title of Final Papers:**
Decree of Divorce

**Important Note:**
Additional forms may be required. Call or visit your clerk of the court.

**Approved Grounds for Divorce:**
No-fault: (1) The marriage has become insupportable because of discord or conflict of personalities that has destroyed the legitimate ends of the marital relationship, and prevents any reasonable expectation of reconciliation, or (2) living separate and apart without cohabitation for 3 years. Fault-based: (1) adultery; (2) abandonment; (3) cruel and inhuman treatment; (4) confinement for incurable insanity for 3 years; or (5) conviction of a felony and imprisonment for over 1 year.

**General Divorce Procedures:**
Marital settlement agreements are authorized. There is a 60-day waiting period before a divorce will be granted.

**Mediation or Counseling Requirements:**
The court may order counseling. If the counselor's report states that reconciliation is possible, the court may delay the proceeding for up to 60 additional days.

**Legal Separation Provisions:**
Separation agreements are authorized.

**Property Distribution:**
Texas is a "community property" state. Only property acquired during the marriage will be equally divided unless such a division would be unjust.

**Alimony/Spousal Support/Maintenance:**
The court may award maintenance for a spouse only if (1) the spouse from whom maintenance is requested has been convicted of family violence within two years before the suit for dissolution, or (2) the duration of the marriage was 10 years or longer and the spouse seeking maintenance (a) lacks sufficient property to provide for his or her reasonable minimum needs; (b) is unable to support him or her self through employment because of an incapacitating physical or mental disability; (c) is the custodian of a child which requires substantial care and supervision because of a physical or mental disability which makes it necessary that the spouse not be employed outside the home; or (d) clearly lacks earning ability in the labor market adequate to provide for the 102 minimum reasonable needs.

**Child Custody and Visitation:**
Joint or sole managing conservatorship (custody) is determined according to the best interests of the child. The sex of the parents is not a factor for consideration. The wishes of the child may be considered. The factors to be considered in determining the terms and conditions for possession of a child by the possessory conservator (parent with visitation) are as follows: (1) the age, circumstances, needs and best interests of the child; (2) the circumstances of the parents; (3) evidence of any spouse or child abuse; and (4) any other relevant factor. The factors specified in the statute for consideration in decisions regarding joint managing conservatorship are: (1) whether the physical, psychological or emotional needs and development of the child will benefit; (2) the ability of the parents to give first priority to the welfare of the child and reach shared decisions in the child's best interests; (3) whether each parent can encourage and accept a positive relationship between the child and the other parent; (4) was entered into voluntarily and knowingly, and (5) is in the best interests of the child. In addition, there are standard terms for a court's order on a child's conservatorship set out in the statute that are presumed to be the minimum allowable time that the parent, who is not awarded the primary physical residence of the child is to have the child.

**Child Support:**
The court may order either or both parents to pay child support based on the following factors: (1) the financial resources of the parents; (2) the age and needs of the child; (3) the amount of custodial care and visitation to the child; (4) the amount of alimony being currently paid or received; (5) whether a parent has custody of another child and any child support expenses paid or received for the care of another child; (6) provisions for health care; (7) any special educational or health care needs of the child; (8) any benefits a parent receives from an employer; (9) any debts or obligations of a parent; (10) any wage or salary deductions of the parents; (11) the cost of traveling to visit the child; (12) any positive or negative cash flow from any assets; (13) any provisions for health care or insurance; (14) any special or extraordinary educational, health care, or other expenses of the parents or the child; and (15) any other relevant factor.

**Rights to Maiden Name:**
Either spouse may resume a former name.

# UTAH

**Residence Requirements:**
The filing spouse must have been a resident of Utah (or a member of the Armed Forces stationed in Utah) and a resident of the county where the divorce is filed for at least 3 months.

| Where to File: | Name of Court: | Title of Divorce Action: |
|---|---|---|
| County of the Petitioner. | District Court; may be Family Court Division of District Court. "In the District Court of the _____ Judicial District, in and for _____ County, State of Utah." | Petition for Divorce |

| Party Filing: | Other Party: | Title of Final Papers: |
|---|---|---|
| Petitioner | Respondent | Decree of Divorce |

**Approved Grounds for Divorce:**
No-fault: (1) irretrievable differences of the marriage, or (2) living separate and apart without cohabitation for 3 years under a judicial decree of separation. Fault-based: (1) adultery; (2) impotence; (3) willful desertion for 1 year; (4) willful neglect; (5) conviction of a felony; (6) drunkenness; (7) cruel and inhuman treatment; or (8) incurable insanity.

**General Divorce Procedures:**
There is a 90 day waiting period after filing before a divorce will be granted. A divorce will not be granted upon default. However, in a default case, the evidence may be contained in an affidavit of the petitioner. Evidence and testimony must be taken in every divorce case. A financial verification form is also required in child support cases.

**Mediation or Counseling Requirements:**
Upon request, the court may order counseling to attempt reconciliation.

**Legal Separation Provisions:**
The grounds for legal separation are: (1) living separate and apart without cohabitation; (2) willful desertion; or (3) gross neglect.

**Property Distribution:**
Utah is an "equitable distribution" state. All the spouses' property may be divided equitably by the court. This includes property acquired prior to the marriage and any gifts and inheritances.

**Alimony/Spousal Support/Maintenance:**
Either spouse may be ordered to pay alimony. The following factors are to be considered: (1) the financial condition and needs of the recipient spouse; (2) the recipient's earning capacity and ability to produce income; (3) the ability of the paying spouse to provide support; (4) the length of the marriage; (5) the standard of living at the time of separation; (6) any marital fault of the spouses; (7) if the marriage has been of long duration and the marriage dissolves on the threshold of a major change in the income of one of the spouses; (8) if one 102 earning capacity has been greatly enhanced by the other's efforts; and (9) any other relevant factors. In general, the court will not award alimony for a period longer than the marriage existed. Alimony terminates upon remarriage or cohabitation with another person.

**Child Custody and Visitation:**
Joint or sole child custody is determined by the following factors: (1) the child's preference if at least 12 years of age; (2) the moral fitness of the parents; (3) which parent is better suited to meet the child's needs; and (4) which parent is willing to allow frequent and continuing contact between the child and the other parent. If there is an allegation of child abuse, the court will order an investigation by the Division of Family Services. Joint custody may be ordered if (1) it will be in the best interests of the child; (2) both parents agree to joint custody; or (3) both parents appear capable of implementing joint custody.

**Child Support:**
Either parent may be ordered to pay child support. There are official child support guidelines that the court may use. The court will deviate from the guidelines if there is a showing that the amount of the award will be unjust or inappropriate.

**Rights to Maiden Name:**
There is a general statutory provision for changing a name.

# VERMONT

**Residence Requirements:**
One spouse must have been a resident of Vermont for at least 6 months before filing. In addition, one spouse must have been a resident for 1 year before a final divorce will be granted.

| Where to File: | Name of Court: | Title of Divorce Action: |
|---|---|---|
| In the county of either spouse. | "State of Vermont, Family Court, _____ County." | Complaint for Divorce |

| Party Filing: | Other Party: | Title of Final Papers: |
|---|---|---|
| Plaintiff | Defendant | Decree of Divorce |

**Approved Grounds for Divorce:**
No-fault: Living separate and apart without cohabitation for 6 consecutive months, and the resuming of marital relations is not reasonably probable. Fault-based: (1) adultery; (2) willful desertion for 7 years; (3) gross neglect; (4) cruel and inhuman treatment; or (5) incurable mental illness.

**General Divorce Procedures:**
There are no simplified divorce procedures. A hearing is required and oral testimony of witnesses is required in all divorce cases.

**Mediation or Counseling Requirements:**
The court may delay the proceedings for 30 to 60 days if one spouse denies that they have lived apart for the required time.

**Legal Separation Provisions:**
The grounds for legal separation are: (1) adultery; (2) willful desertion for 7 years; (3) gross neglect; (4) cruel and inhuman treatment; (5) living separate and apart without cohabitation for 6 months; (6) imprisonment for 3 years or more or for life; or (7) incurable mental illness.

**Property Distribution:**
Vermont is an "equitable distribution" state. All property, regardless of when it was acquired, including gifts and inheritances, can be divided by the court based on the following factors: (1) how and by whom the property was acquired; (2) the value of each 102 property; (3) the duration of the marriage; (4) each 102 contribution to the acquisition of marital property, including non-monetary contribution; (5) the financial status of each spouse and the desirability to award the family home to the custodial parent or allow that parent to live in the home until the child(ren) is grown; (6) the occupation of each spouse; (7) the age and health of each spouse; (8) conduct of spouses during the marriage; (9) the amount and sources of income of the spouses; (10) the vocational skills of the spouses; (11) the employability of the spouses; (12) the liabilities and needs of each spouse and the opportunity of each for further acquisition of capital assets and income; (13) whether the property award is instead of or in addition to maintenance; (14) the merits of each spouse; (15) the burdens imposed upon either spouse for the benefit of the children;and (16) the contribution by one spouse to the education training or increased earning power of the other.

**Alimony/Spousal Support/Maintenance:**
The court may order either spouse to pay maintenance based on the following factors: (1) the standard of living established during the marriage; (2) the financial resources of each spouse, including the value of the property awarded from the division; (3) the needs of the spouse seeking support and the ability of the other spouse to make such payments while meeting his or her own needs;(4) the time necessary to acquire sufficient education and training to enable the spouse to find appropriate employment, and that 102 future earning capacity; (5) the duration of the marriage; (6) the financial resources of the spouse seeking maintenance, including property apportioned to such spouse and such 102 ability to meet his or her needs independently; (7) the age of the spouses; (8) the physical and emotional conditions of the spouses; and (9) any effects of inflation on the cost of living.

**Child Custody and Visitation:**
Joint or sole custody may be awarded based on the following: (1) the parents' wishes; (2) the bond between the child, each parent and any siblings; (3) the desire and ability of the parents to provide for the child's needs; (4) the desire and ability of each parent to cooperate in joint custody; (5) the child's adjustment to his or her home, school and community; (6) the ability and disposition of each parent to foster a positive relationship and frequent and continuing contact with the other parent, including physical contact unless it will result in harm to the child or parent; and (7) the quality of the child's relationship with the primary care provider, given the child's age and development.

**Child Support:**
The court may order either parent to pay child support. The court will consider the following: (1) the standard of living the child would have enjoyed if the marriage was not dissolved; (2) the needs of the child; (3) the financial resources of the parents; (4) the financial resources of the child; (5) inflation with relation to the cost of living; (6) the costs of any educational needs of either parent; (7) any travel expenses related to parent-child contact; and (8) any other relevant factors.

**Rights to Maiden Name:**
The wife may have her former name restored.

# VIRGINIA

**Residence Requirements:**
Either one of the spouses must have been a resident of Virginia for at least 6 months.

**Where to File:**
In the county where spouses last resided together; where defendant resides if defendant is a resident of Virginia, or where plaintiff resides if plaintiff is a resident of Virginia and defendant is not.

**Name of Court:**
Circuit Court or Juvenile and Domestic Relations Court or Experimental Family Court. "Virginia: In the _____ Court of _____."

**Title of Divorce Action:**
Complaint for Divorce

**Party Filing:**
Plaintiff

**Other Party:**
Defendant

**Title of Final Papers:**
Decree of Divorce

**Approved Grounds for Divorce:**
No-fault: Living separate and apart without cohabitation for 1 year or; (2) living separate and apart without cohabitation for 6 months if there are no minor children, and the spouses have entered into a separation agreement. Fault-based: (1) adultery (including homosexual acts); (2) abandonment; (3) conviction of a felony and imprisonment for 1 year; (4) cruelty; or (5) willful desertion.

**General Divorce Procedures:**
A spouse may waive service of process, but it must be signed in the presence of the clerk. In addition, the testimony of the spouses must also generally be corroborated by a witness.

**Mediation or Counseling Requirements:**
There are no provisions for mediation.

**Legal Separation Provisions:**
The grounds for legal separation are: (1) cruelty; (2) willful desertion; (3) abandonment; or (4) reasonable apprehension of bodily injury.

**Property Distribution:**
Virginia is an "equitable distribution" state. Each spouse will retain property acquired prior to the marriage and any gift or inheritance whenever acquired. The marital property will be divided based on the following factors: (1) each 102 contribution to the acquisition of the marital property, including non-monetary contributions; (2) the cause that led to the divorce; (3) the length of the marriage; (4) the debts of the spouses; (5) the age and health of the spouses; (6) the liquid or non-liquid character of the property; (7) the tax consequences; (8) how and by whom the property was acquired; (9) the contributions, monetary and non-monetary, of each spouse to the well-being of the family; and (10) any other factor necessary to do equity and justice between the spouses.

**Alimony/Spousal Support/Maintenance:**
The court may award alimony to either spouse based on the following factors: (1) the time and expense a spouse will incur to obtain sufficient education or training for appropriate employment; (2) the property of the spouses; (3) the standard of living established during the marriage; (4) the duration of the marriage; (5) the financial resources of the spouse seeking maintenance, including marital property apportioned to such spouse and such 102 ability to meet his or her needs independently; (6) the contribution of each spouse to the marriage, including services rendered in homemaking, child care, education, and career building of the other spouse; (7) the tax consequences to each spouse; (8) the age of the spouses; (9) the physical and emotional conditions of the spouses; (10) the educational level of each spouse at the time of the marriage and at the time the action for support is commenced; (11) the circumstances which contributed to the divorce; and (12) any other factor the court deems just and equitable.

**Child Custody and Visitation:**
Joint or sole custody will be awarded based on the following factors: (1) the age of the child; (2) the child's wishes, needs and financial resources; (3) the bond between the child and each parent; (4) whether each parent has had an active role in rearing the child; and (5) the mental and physical health of all individuals involved.

**Child Support:**
Either parent may be ordered to pay child support based on the following factors: (1) the standard of living the child would have enjoyed if the marriage was not dissolved; (2) the division of the marital property; (3) the age and health of the child; (4) the needs of the child; and (5) the obligations and financial resources of the parents; (6) the earning capacity of each parent; (7) the monetary or non-monetary contributions of the parents to the family's well-being; (8) the education of the parents; (9) the ability of the parents to secure education and training; (10) the income tax consequences of child support; (11) any special medical, dental or child care expenses; and (13) any other relevant factors.

**Rights to Maiden Name:**
Either spouse may have a former name restored.

# WASHINGTON

**Residence Requirements:**
Filing spouse must be a resident of Washington, or a member of the Armed Forces stationed in Washington.

**Where to File:**
In the county of either spouse.

**Name of Court:**
Superior Court or Family Court. "In the _____ Court of the State of Washington, In and For the County of _____."

**Title of Divorce Action:**
Petition for Dissolution of Marriage

**Party Filing:**
Petitioner

**Other Party:**
Respondent

**Title of Final Papers:**
Decree of Dissolution of Marriage

**Important Note:**
Additional forms may be required. Call or visit your clerk of the court.

**Approved Grounds for Divorce:**
No-fault: Irretrievable breakdown of the marriage. Fault-based: Irretrievable breakdown of the marriage is the only grounds for divorce.

**General Divorce Procedures:**
All divorce cases must be filed on official Washington forms. In addition, the spouses must file a Washington Department of Health Certificate with the petition. These forms are generally available at the clerk of the court office. There is at least a 90-day waiting period after filing the divorce and the service of summons on the respondent.

**Mediation or Counseling Requirements:**
Child custody or child visitation issues in dispute will be referred to mediation. The court may order counseling for the spouses if either spouse requests counseling.

**Legal Separation Provisions:**
Irretrievable breakdown of the marriage is the only ground for a legal separation.

**Property Distribution:**
Washington is a "community property" state. Each spouse will retain any property acquired prior to marriage or any gifts or inheritances whenever acquired. The court will divide the "community property" based on the following factors: (1) the nature and value of each 102 separate property; (2) the financial status of each spouse when the property division becomes effective; (3) the length of the marriage; (4) the nature and value of the community property; and (5) the desirability of awarding the family residence to the custodial parent or allowing that parent to live in the home until the child(ren) is grown.

**Alimony/Spousal Support/Maintenance:**
The court may award alimony to either spouse based on the following factors: (1) the time and expense a spouse will incur to obtain sufficient education or training for appropriate employment; (2) the financial position of the spouse seeking alimony; (3) the needs of the spouse seeking alimony and the ability of the other spouse to make such payments while meeting his or her own needs; (4) the debts of each spouse; (5) the age and health of each spouse; (6) the standard of living established during the marriage; (7) the duration of the marriage; (8) the physical and emotional conditions of the spouses; and (9) any child support responsibilities for a child living with the parent.

**Child Custody and Visitation:**
Joint or sole custody will be determined according to the best interests of the child. Every petition for a dissolution of marriage in which a child is involved must include a proposed parenting plan. The plan should contain the following: (1) dispute resolution; (2) a residential schedule; and (3) allocation of parental rights to make decisions for the benefit of the child. The court may order an investigation concerning the proposed parenting plan.

**Child Support:**
Either parent may be ordered to pay child support. There are official child support guidelines that the court may use. The court will deviate from the guidelines if it is shown that the amount of the award will be unjust or inappropriate.

**Rights to Maiden Name:**
The wife's former name may be restored.

# WEST VIRGINIA

Residence Requirements:

There is no time-limit residency requirement if the marriage was performed in West Virginia and one spouse is a resident when filing. Otherwise, one spouse must have been a resident for at least 1 year.

| Where to File: | Name of Court: | Title of Divorce Action: |
| --- | --- | --- |
| In the county where spouses last resided together, county of defendant if a resident, or county where plaintiff lives if defendant is a non-resident. | "Circuit Court of ________ County, West Virginia." | Complaint for Divorce |

| Party Filing: | Other Party: | Title of Final Papers: |
| --- | --- | --- |
| Plaintiff | Defendant | Decree of Divorce |

Approved Grounds for Divorce:

No-fault: (1) irreconcilable differences, or (2) living separate and apart without cohabitation and without interruption for 1 year. Fault-based: (1) adultery; (2) abandonment for 6 months; (3) alcoholism or drug abuse; (4) physical abuse or reasonable apprehension of physical abuse; (5) cruel and inhuman treatment, including false accusations of adultery or homosexuality; (7) willful neglect; or (8) habitual drunkenness.

General Divorce Procedures:

A divorce will be granted if one spouse files a verified complaint for divorce on the grounds of irreconcilable differences, and the other spouse files a verified answer admitting the irreconcilable differences. The clerk of the court will have official answer forms available free of charge. No witnesses will be necessary for any proof for a divorce on the grounds of irreconcilable differences." In other cases, witnesses will be required. The court may approve or reject a marital settlement agreement of the spouses. Standard financial disclosure forms may be required to be filed.

Mediation or Counseling Requirements:

There are no provisions for mediation.

Legal Separation Provisions:

The grounds for legal separation are the same as for divorce.

Property Distribution:

West Virginia is an "equitable distribution" state. Each spouse will retain any property acquired prior to the marriage and any gifts or inheritances whenever acquired. The marital property will be divided equally, however, the court may deviate from this plan based on the following factors: (1) the value of each 102 separate property; (2) each 102 contribution to the acquisition of marital property; (3) the conduct of each spouse as it relates to the disposition of the property; (4) the contribution by one spouse to the other spouse toward his or her education or training which will increase his or her earning ability; (5) the amount and sources of income of the spouses; (6) the value of the labor performed in a family business or in the actual maintenance or improvement of tangible marital property; (7) the foregoing by either spouse of employment or other income-earning activity through an understanding of the spouses or at the insistence of the other spouse; and (8) any other factor necessary to do equity and justice between the spouses.

Alimony/Spousal Support/Maintenance:

The court may award alimony to either spouse based on the following factors: (1) length of the marriage; (2) the financial resources of the spouses; (3) whether the spouse seeking support is the custodial parent and is unable to work outside of the home; (4) age and health of the spouses; (5) the educational level of the spouses; (6) the distribution of the marital property; (7) the occupations of the spouses; (8) the time and expense necessary to acquire sufficient education and training to enable the spouse to find appropriate employment, and that 102 future earning capacity; (9) the duration of the marriage; (10) the amount of time the spouses actually lived together as wife and husband; (11) the tax consequences to each spouse; (12) the vocational skills and employability of the spouse seeking alimony; (13) any custodial and child support responsibilities; (14) the cost of education of minor children and of health care for each spouse and the minor children; (15) any legal obligations of the spouses to support themselves or others; (16) the present employment or other income of each spouse; and (17) any other factor the court deems just and equitable. The marital misconduct of the spouses will be considered and compared.

Child Custody and Visitation:

The court may award custody to either parent. There are no specific factors listed in the statute.

Child Support:

The court may order either parent to pay child support. The court will consider the following: (1) whether the spouse seeking support is the custodian of a child whose condition or circumstances make it appropriate for that spouse not to seek outside employment; (2) the time and expense necessary to acquire sufficient education and training to enable the spouse to find appropriate employment, and that 102 future earning capacity; (3) the duration of the marriage and the actual period of cohabitation as husband and wife; (4) the comparative financial resources of the spouses, including their comparative earning abilities in the labor market; (5) the needs and obligations of each spouse; (6) the tax consequences to each spouse; (7) the age of the spouses; (8) the physical and emotional conditions of the spouses; (9) the vocational skills and employability of the spouse seeking support and maintenance; (10) any custodial responsibilities; (11) the educational level of each spouse at the time of the marriage and at the time the action for divorce is commenced; (12) the cost of education of minor children and of health care for each spouse and the minor children; (13) the distribution of marital property; (14) any legal obligations of the spouses to support themselves or others; and (15) any other factor the court deems just and equitable.

Rights to Maiden Name:

Either spouse may request that he or she have former name restored.

# WISCONSIN

Residence Requirements:

Either spouse must have been a resident of Wisconsin for 6 months and a resident of the county where the divorce will be filed for 30 days prior to filing. No hearing on the divorce will be scheduled until 120 days after the defendant is served the summons or after the filing of a joint petition.

| Where to File: | Name of Court: | Title of Divorce Action: |
| --- | --- | --- |
| In the county of the filing spouse. | Circuit Court/Family Court. "State of Wisconsin: Circuit Court, ________ County." | Petition for Divorce |

| Party Filing: | Other Party: | Title of Final Papers: |
| --- | --- | --- |
| Petitioner; Joint: Co-Petitioner | Respondent; Joint: Co-Petitioner | Decree of Divorce |

Important Note:

Additional forms may be required. Call or visit your clerk of the court.

Approved Grounds for Divorce:

No-fault: Irretrievable breakdown of the marriage which can be established by either: (1) both spouses filing jointly for a divorce on these grounds; (2) living separate and apart for 12 months; or (3) at the court's discretion. Fault-based: Irretrievable breakdown of the marriage is the only ground for a divorce.

General Divorce Procedures:

If the divorce involves children, an official child support form and a financial disclosure form must be filed with the petition. These forms are available from the court clerk. A guide to Wisconsin divorce procedures will be provided to the spouse when filing for a divorce. Official forms must be used when filing for a petition for divorce.

Mediation or Counseling Requirements:

If child custody is disputed, then mediation will be ordered. In addition, the court must inform the spouses of the availability of counseling services.

Legal Separation Provisions:

The only ground for legal separation is irretrievable breakdown of the marriage.

Property Distribution:

Wisconsin is a "community property" state. Only property acquired during the marriage will be divided equally, however, the court may deviate from this plan based on the following factors: (1) whether the property award is in lieu of or in addition to spousal support; (2) the value of each 102 separate property; (3) the occupation of each spouse; (4) the length of the marriage; (5) age and health of each spouse; (6) the earning capability of each spouse; (7) the time and expense a spouse will incur to obtain sufficient education or training for appropriate employment; (8) the contribution of each spouse to the acquisition of the marital property, including the contribution of each spouse as homemaker; (9) the amount and sources of income of the spouses; (10) the vocational skills of the spouses; (11) the federal income tax consequences of the court's division of the property; (12) the standard of living established during the marriage; (13) any premarital or marital settlement agreements; (14) any retirement benefits; (15) any custodial provisions for the children; and (16) any other relevant factor. The court may also divide any separate property of the spouses to prevent hardship on a spouse or children.

Alimony/Spousal Support/Maintenance:

The court may award maintenance to either spouse based on the above factors in addition to the following: (1) the financial resources of the spouses; (2) any mutual agreement between the spouses; (3) the time necessary to acquire sufficient education and training to enable the spouse to find appropriate employment, and that 102 future earning capacity; (4) the duration of the marriage; (5) the financial resources of the spouse seeking maintenance, including marital property apportioned to such spouse and such 102 ability to meet his or her needs independently; (6) the contribution of each spouse to the marriage, including services rendered in homemaking, child care, education, and career building of the other spouse; (6) the tax consequences to each spouse; (7) the age of the spouses; (8) the physical and emotional conditions of the spouses; (9) the vocational skills and employability of the spouse seeking maintenance; (10) the length of absence from the job market; (11) the probable duration of the need of the spouse seeking maintenance; (12) any custodial and child support responsibilities; (13) the educational level of each spouse at the time of the marriage and at the time the divorce is filed for; and (14) any other relevant factor.

Child Custody and Visitation:

Legal custody and physical placement is based on the following: (1) the best interest of the child; (2) the child's wishes; (3) the bond between the parents and the child; (4) any domestic violence; (5) whether one parent will more likely interfere in the child's relationship with the other parent; (6) the child's adjustment to his or her home, school and community; (7) the mental and physical health of all individuals involved; (8) any findings or recommendations of a neutral mediator; (9) the availability of child care; (10) any significant drug or alcohol abuse; and (11) any other factors (except the sex and race of the parent).

Child Support:

The court may order either parent to pay child support based on the following factors: (1) the standard of living the child would have enjoyed if the marriage was not dissolved; (2) the cost of day care to the custodial parent; (3) the financial resources of the child and parents; (4) the child's needs; (5) the financial resources of the child; (6) the age and health of the child; (7) the desirability of the parent having custody remaining in the home as a full-time parent; (8) the tax consequences to each parent; (9) the award of substantial periods of physical placement to both parents (joint custody); (10) any extraordinary travel expenses incurred in exercising the right to periods of physical placement; (11) the best interests of the child; and (12) any other relevant factors.

Rights to Maiden Name:

Either spouse may have his or her former name restored.


This product does not constitute the rendering of legal advice or services. This product is intended for informational use only and is not a substitute for legal advice. State laws vary, so consult an attorney on all legal matters. This product was not prepared by a person licensed to practice law in this state.

# WYOMING

**Residence Requirements:**
The filing spouse must have been a resident of Wyoming for 60 days prior to filing; or the marriage was performed in Wyoming and the filing spouse must have resided in Wyoming from the time of the marriage to the time of filing.

**Where to File:**
In the county where either spouse resides.

**Name of Court:**
"In the District Court, In and For _____ County, Wyoming."

**Title of Divorce Action:**
Complaint for Divorce

**Party Filing:**
Plaintiff

**Other Party:**
Defendant

**Title of Final Papers:**
Decree of Divorce

**Approved Grounds for Divorce:**
No-fault: Irreconcilable differences. Fault-based: Confinement for incurable insanity for 2 years.

**General Divorce Procedures:**
There is a waiting period of 20 days before a divorce will be granted.

**Mediation or Counseling Requirements:**
In cases involving child custody, the court may order the parents to attend appropriate classes regarding the impact of divorce on children.

**Legal Separation Provisions:**
The grounds for legal separation are the same as for a divorce.

**Property Distribution:**
Wyoming is an "equitable distribution" state. All property of the spouses will be divided by the court in an equitable manner based on the following: (1) the financial position of each spouse when the division becomes effective; (2) the conduct of the spouses; (3) the obligations imposed on each spouse for the benefit of the children; (4) how and by whom the property was acquired; (5) the economic circumstances of each spouse at the time the division of property is to become effective; (6) the merits of each spouse; (7) any liabilities imposed upon the property; and (8) any other factor necessary to do equity and justice between the spouses.

**Alimony/Spousal Support/Maintenance:**
The court may order either spouse to pay alimony. Marital fault is not considered. The need and ability of each spouse is considered.

**Child Custody and Visitation:**
The court will award child custody according to the following: (1) the best interest of the child; (2) the child's wishes; (3) the fitness of each parent; and (4) any evidence of domestic violence.

**Child Support:**
The court may order either parent to pay child support based on the official child support guidelines. However, the court may deviate from these guidelines if the amount would be unjust or inappropriate under the particular circumstances of the case.

**Rights to Maiden Name:**
No legal provision addresses restoration of former name, however, a general statute allows a party to petition for a name change.

# How to save on attorney fees

# How to save on attorney fees

Millions of Americans know they need legal protection, whether it's to get agreements in writing, protect themselves from lawsuits, or document business transactions. But too often these basic but important legal matters are neglected because of something else millions of Americans know: legal services are expensive.

They don't have to be. In response to the demand for affordable legal protection and services, there are now specialized clinics that process simple documents. Paralegals help people prepare legal claims on a freelance basis. People find they can handle their own legal affairs with do-it-yourself legal guides and kits. Indeed, this book is a part of this growing trend.

When are these alternatives to a lawyer appropriate? If you hire an attorney, how can you make sure you're getting good advice for a reasonable fee? Most importantly, do you know how to lower your legal expenses?

## When there is no alternative

Make no mistake: serious legal matters require a lawyer. The tips in this book can help you reduce your legal fees, but there is no alternative to good professional legal services in certain circumstances:

- when you are charged with a felony, you are a repeat offender, or jail is possible

- when a substantial amount of money or property is at stake in a lawsuit

- when you are a party in an adversarial divorce or custody case

- when you are an alien facing deportation

- when you are the plaintiff in a personal injury suit that involves large sums of money

- when you're involved in very important transactions

# Are you sure you want to take it to court?

Consider the following questions before you pursue legal action:

## What are your financial resources?

Money buys experienced attorneys, and experience wins over first-year lawyers and public defenders. Even with a strong case, you may save money by not going to court. Yes, people win millions in court. But for every big winner there are ten plaintiffs who either lose or win so little that litigation wasn't worth their effort.

## Do you have the time and energy for a trial?

Courts are overbooked, and by the time your case is heard your initial zeal may have grown cold. If you can, make a reasonable settlement out of court. On personal matters, like a divorce or custody case, consider the emotional toll on all parties. Any legal case will affect you in some way. You will need time away from work. A newsworthy case may bring press coverage. Your loved ones, too, may face publicity. There is usually good reason to settle most cases quickly, quietly, and economically.

## How can you settle disputes without litigation?

Consider *mediation*. In mediation, each party pays half the mediator's fee and, together, they attempt to work out a compromise informally. *Binding arbitration* is another alternative. For a small fee, a trained specialist serves as judge, hears both sides, and hands down a ruling that both parties have agreed to accept.

# So you need an attorney

Having done your best to avoid litigation, if you still find yourself headed for court, you will need an attorney. To get the right attorney at a reasonable cost, be guided by these four questions:

## What type of case is it?

You don't seek a foot doctor for a toothache. Find an attorney experienced in your type of legal problem. If you can get recommendations from clients who have recently won similar cases, do so.

## Where will the trial be held?

You want a lawyer familiar with that court system and one who knows the court personnel and the local protocol—which can vary from one locality to another.

## Should you hire a large or small firm?

Hiring a senior partner at a large and prestigious law firm sounds reassuring, but chances are the actual work will be handled by associates—at high rates. Small firms may give your case more attention but, with fewer resources, take longer to get the work done.

## What can you afford?

Hire an attorney you can afford, of course, but know what a fee quote includes. High fees may reflect a firm's luxurious offices, high-paid staff and unmonitored expenses, while low estimates may mean "unexpected" costs later. Ask for a written estimate of all costs and anticipated expenses.

# How to find a good lawyer

Whether you need an attorney quickly or you're simply open to future possibilities, here are seven nontraditional methods for finding your lawyer:

1) **Word of mouth**: Successful lawyers develop reputations. Your friends, business associates and other professionals are potential referral sources. But beware of hiring a friend. Keep the client-attorney relationship strictly business.

2) **Directories**: The Yellow Pages and the Martin-Hubbell Lawyer Directory (in your local library) can help you locate a lawyer with the right education, background and expertise for your case.

3) **Databases**: A paralegal should be able to run a quick computer search of local attorneys for you using the Westlaw or Lexis database.

4) **State bar associations**: Bar associations are listed in phone books. Along with lawyer referrals, your bar association can direct you to low-cost legal clinics or specialists in your area.

5) **Law schools**: Did you know that a legal clinic run by a law school gives law students hands-on experience? This may fit your legal needs. A third-year law student loaded with enthusiasm and a little experience might fill the bill quite inexpensively—or even for free.

6) **Advertisements**: Ads are a lawyer's business card. If a "TV attorney" seems to have a good track record with your kind of case, why not call? Just don't be swayed by the glamour of a high-profile attorney.

7) **Your own ad**: A small ad describing the qualifications and legal expertise you're seeking, placed in a local bar association journal, may get you just the lead you need.

# How to hire and work with your attorney

No matter how you hear about an attorney, you must interview him or her in person. Call the office during business hours and ask to speak to the attorney directly. Then explain your case briefly and mention how you obtained the attorney's name. If the attorney sounds interested and knowledgeable, arrange for a visit.

# The ten-point visit

1) Note the address. This is a good indication of the rates to expect.

2) Note the condition of the offices. File-laden desks and poorly maintained work space may indicate a poorly run firm.

3) Look for up-to-date computer equipment and an adequate complement of support personnel.

4) Note the appearance of the attorney. How will he or she impress a judge or jury?

5) Is the attorney attentive? Does the attorney take notes, ask questions, follow up on points you've mentioned?

6) Ask what schools he or she has graduated from, and feel free to check credentials with the state bar association.

7) Does the attorney have a good track record with your type of case?

8) Does he or she explain legal terms to you in plain English?

9) Are the firm's costs reasonable?

10) Will the attorney provide references?

## Hiring the attorney

Having chosen your attorney, make sure all the terms are agreeable. Send letters to any other attorneys you have interviewed, thanking them for their time and interest in your case and explaining that you have retained another attorney's services.

Request a letter from your new attorney outlining your retainer agreement. The letter should list all fees you will be responsible for as well as the billing arrangement. Did you arrange to pay in installments? This should be noted in your retainer agreement.

## Controlling legal costs

Legal fees and expenses can get out of control easily, but the client who is willing to put in the effort can keep legal costs manageable. Work out a budget with your attorney. Create a timeline for your case. Estimate the costs involved in each step.

Legal fees can be straightforward. Some lawyers charge a fixed rate for a specific project. Others charge contingency fees (they collect a percentage of your recovery, usually 35-50 percent if you win and nothing if you lose). But most attorneys prefer to bill by the hour. Expenses can run the gamut, with one hourly charge for taking depositions and another for making copies.

Have your attorney give you a list of charges for services rendered and an itemized monthly bill. The bill should explain the service performed, who performed the work, when the service was provided, how long it took, and how the service benefits your case.

Ample opportunity abounds in legal billing for dishonesty and greed. There is also plenty of opportunity for knowledgeable clients to cut their bills significantly if they know what to look for. Asking the right questions and setting limits on fees is smart and can save you a bundle. Don't be afraid to question legal bills. It's your case and your money!

# When the bill arrives

- **Retainer fees**: You should already have a written retainer agreement. Ideally, the retainer fee applies toward case costs, and your agreement puts that in writing. Protect yourself by escrowing the retainer fee until the case has been handled to your satisfaction.

- **Office visit charges**: Track your case and all documents, correspondence, and bills. Diary all dates, deadlines and questions you want to ask your attorney during your next office visit. This keeps expensive office visits focused and productive, with more accomplished in less time. If your attorney charges less for phone consultations than office visits, reserve visits for those tasks that must be done in person.

- **Phone bills**: This is where itemized bills are essential. Who made the call, who was spoken to, what was discussed, when was the call made, and how long did it last? Question any charges that seem unnecessary or excessive (over 60 minutes).

- **Administrative costs**: Your case may involve hundreds, if not thousands, of documents: motions, affidavits, depositions, interrogatories, bills, memoranda, and letters. Are they all necessary? Understand your attorney's case strategy before paying for an endless stream of costly documents.

- **Associate and paralegal fees**: Note in your retainer agreement which staff people will have access to your file. Then you'll have an informed and efficient staff working on your case, and you'll recognize their names on your bill. Of course, your attorney should handle the important part of your case, but less costly paralegals or associates may handle routine matters more economically. Note: Some firms expect their associates to meet a quota of billable hours, although the time spent is not always warranted. Review your bill. Does the time spent make sense for the document in question? Are several staff involved in matters that should be handled by one person? Don't be afraid to ask questions. And withhold payment until you have satisfactory answers.

- **Court stenographer fees**: Depositions and court hearings require costly transcripts and stenographers. This means added expenses. Keep an eye on these costs.

- **Copying charges**: Your retainer fee should limit the number of copies made of your complete file. This is in your legal interest, because multiple files mean multiple chances others may access your confidential information. It is also in your financial interest, because copying costs can be astronomical.

- **Fax costs**: As with the phone and copier, the fax can easily run up costs. Set a limit.

- **Postage charges**: Be aware of how much it costs to send a legal document overnight, or a registered letter. Offer to pick up or deliver expensive items when it makes sense.

- **Filing fees**: Make it clear to your attorney that you want to minimize the number of court filings in your case. Watch your bill and question any filing that seems unnecessary.

- **Document production fee**: Turning over documents to your opponent is mandatory and expensive. If you're faced with reproducing boxes of documents, consider having the job done by a commercial firm rather than your attorney's office.

- **Research and investigations**: Pay only for photographs that can be used in court. Can you hire a photographer at a lower rate than what your attorney charges? Reserve that right in your retainer agreement. Database research can also be extensive and expensive; if your attorney uses Westlaw or Nexis, set limits on the research you will pay for.

- **Expert witnesses**: Question your attorney if you are expected to pay for more than a reasonable number of expert witnesses. Limit the number to what is essential to your case.

- **Technology costs**: Avoid videos, tape recordings, and graphics if you can use old-fashioned diagrams to illustrate your case.

- **Travel expenses**: Travel expenses for those connected to your case can be quite costly unless you set a maximum budget. Check all travel-related items on your bill, and make sure they are appropriate. Always question why the travel is necessary before you agree to pay for it.

- **Appeals costs**: Losing a case often means an appeal, but weigh the costs involved before you make that decision. If money is at stake, do a cost-benefit analysis to see if an appeal is financially justified.

- **Monetary damages**: Your attorney should be able to help you estimate the total damages you will have to pay if you lose a civil case. Always consider settling out of court rather than proceeding to trial when the trial costs will be high.

- **Surprise costs**: Surprise costs are so routine they're predictable. The judge may impose unexpected court orders on one or both sides, or the opposition will file an unexpected motion that increases your legal costs. Budget a few thousand dollars over what you estimate your case will cost. It usually is needed.

- **Padded expenses**: Assume your costs and expenses are legitimate. But some firms do inflate expenses—office supplies, database searches, copying, postage, phone bills—to bolster their bottom line. Request copies of bills your law firm receives from support services. If you are not the only client represented on a bill, determine those charges related to your case.

## Keeping it legal without a lawyer

The best way to save legal costs is to avoid legal problems. There are hundreds of ways to decrease your chances of lawsuits and other nasty legal encounters. Most simply involve a little common sense. You can also use your own initiative to find and use the variety of self-help legal aid available to consumers.

## 11 situations in which you may not need a lawyer

1) **No-fault divorce**: Married couples with no children, minimal property, and no demands for alimony can take advantage of divorce mediation services. A lawyer should review your divorce agreement before you sign it, but you will have saved a fortune in attorney fees. A marital or family counselor may save a seemingly doomed marriage, or help both parties move beyond anger to a calm settlement. Either way, counseling can save you money.

2) **Wills**: Do-it-yourself wills and living trusts are ideal for people with estates of less than $600,000. Even if an attorney reviews your final documents, a will kit allows you to read the documents, ponder your bequests, fill out sample forms, and discuss your wishes with your family at your leisure, without a lawyer's meter running.

3) **Incorporating**: Incorporating a small business can be done by any business owner. Your state government office provides the forms and instructions necessary. A visit to your state office will probably be

necessary to perform a business name check. A fee of $100-$200 is usually charged for processing your Articles of Incorporation. The rest is paperwork: filling out forms correctly; holding regular, official meetings; and maintaining accurate records.

4) **Routine business transactions**: Copyrights, for example, can be applied for by asking the U.S. Copyright Office for the appropriate forms and brochures. The same is true of the U.S. Patent and Trademark Office. If your business does a great deal of document preparation and research, hire a certified paralegal rather than paying an attorney's rates. Consider mediation or binding arbitration rather than going to court for a business dispute. Hire a human resources/benefits administrator to head off disputes concerning discrimination or other employee charges.

5) **Repairing bad credit**: When money matters get out of hand, attorneys and bankruptcy should not be your first solution. Contact a credit counseling organization that will help you work out manageable payment plans so that everyone wins. It can also help you learn to manage your money better. A good company to start with is the Consumer Credit Counseling Service, 1-800-388-2227.

6) **Small Claims Court**: For legal grievances amounting to a few thousand dollars in damages, represent yourself in Small Claims Court. There is a small filing fee, forms to fill out, and several court visits necessary. If you can collect evidence, state your case in a clear and logical presentation, and come across as neat, respectful and sincere, you can succeed in Small Claims Court.

7) **Traffic Court**: Like Small Claims Court, Traffic Court may show more compassion to a defendant appearing without an attorney. If you are ticketed for a minor offense and want to take it to court, you will be asked to plead guilty or not guilty. If you plead guilty, you can ask for leniency in sentencing by presenting mitigating circumstances. Bring any witnesses who can support your story, and remember that presentation (some would call it acting ability) is as important as fact.

8) **Residential zoning petition**: If a homeowner wants to open a home business, build an addition, or make other changes that may affect his or her neighborhood, town approval is required. But you don't need a lawyer to fill out a zoning variance application, turn it in, and present your story at a public hearing. Getting local support before the hearing is the best way to assure a positive vote; contact as many neighbors as possible to reassure them that your plans won't adversely affect them or the neighborhood.

9) **Government benefit applications**: Applying for veterans' or unemployment benefits may be daunting, but the process doesn't require legal help. Apply for either immediately upon becoming eligible. Note: If your former employer contests your application for unemployment benefits and you have to defend yourself at a hearing, you may want to consider hiring an attorney.

10) **Receiving government files**: The Freedom of Information Act gives every American the right to receive copies of government information about him or her. Write a letter to the appropriate state or federal agency, noting the precise information you want. List each document in a separate paragraph. Mention the Freedom of Information Act, and state that you will pay any expenses. Close with your signature and the address the documents should be sent to. An approved request may take six months to arrive. If it is refused on the grounds that the information is classified or violates another's privacy, send a letter of appeal explaining why the released information would not endanger anyone. Enlist the support of your local state or federal representative, if possible, to smooth the approval process.

11) **Citizenship**: Arriving in the United States to work and become a citizen is a process tangled in bureaucratic red tape, but it requires more perseverance than legal assistance. Immigrants can learn how to obtain a "Green Card," under what circumstances they can work, and what the requirements of citizenship are by contacting the Immigration Services or reading a good self-help book.

## Save more; it's E-Z

When it comes to saving attorneys' fees, E-Z Legal Forms is the consumer's best friend. America's largest publisher of self-help legal products offers legally valid forms for virtually every situation. E-Z Legal Kits and E-Z Legal Guides include all necessary forms with a simple-to-follow manual of instructions or a layman's book. E-Z Legal Books are a legal library of forms and documents for everyday business and personal needs. E-Z Legal Software provides those same forms on disk and CD for customized documents at the touch of the keyboard.

You can add to your legal savvy and your ability to protect yourself, your loved ones, your business and your property with a range of self-help legal titles available through E-Z Legal Forms. See the product descriptions and information at the back of this guide.

# E-Z LEGAL® SOFTWARE

# AS EASY AS 1,2,3!

1. Loads from 3.5" disk or CD, both included.
2. Just click on a form title to open it.
   E-Z category menu and dialog box help you find the form you need.
3. Print professional forms in minutes.

### Vital Record Keeping Made E-Z
Over 200 ready-to-use forms to organize every aspect of your life, from business and finance to health and recreation.
*3.5 disks only.*
**Item No. SW306 • $29.95**

### Accounting–Deluxe Edition
The fastest, most economical accounting system for your small business. It handles every accounting function and is ideal for any type of business.
**Item No. SW1123 • $49.95**

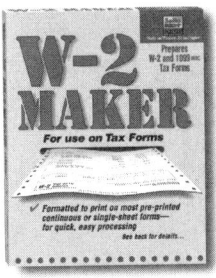 

### W-2 Maker
Saves valuable time during tax season. Quickly, accurately and easily completes stacks of W-2s, W-3s, 1099s, 1096s and more. Perfect for accounting departments.
**Item No. SW1147 • $14.95**

### Buying/Selling Your Home Made E-Z
Buy or sell almost any property with forms for listings, deeds, offers, mortgages, agreements and closing—plus helpful legal and financial tips.
**Item No. SW1111 • $29.95**

 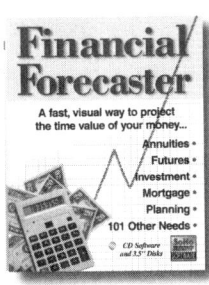

### E-Z Construction Estimator
Every Contractor can profit from this time-saving software. It automatically calculates the detailed costs of a given project, from equipment to labor.
**Item No. CD316 • $29.95**

### Financial Forecaster
The fast way to protect your financial future and make informed decisions. Easily calculate changes to your mortgage, investments, annuities, income and more!
**Item No. SW1122 • $29.95**

---

## E·Z LEGAL® SOFTWARE
*...when you need it in writing!*®

E-Z Legal Software, 384 S. Military Trail, Deerfield Beach, FL 33442
(800) 822-4566 • fax: (954) 480-8906
web site: http://www.e-zlegal.com

Microsoft, Windows, Windows NT, and the Windows logo are registered trademarks of Microsoft Corporation.

# Turn your computer into your personal lawyer

*The E-Z Way to SAVE TIME and MONEY! Print professional forms from your computer in minutes!*

### Everyday Legal Forms & Agreements Made E-Z
A complete library of 301 legal documents for virtually every business or personal situation—at your fingertips!
*Item No. CD311 • $29.95*

### Credit Repair Made E-Z
Our proven formula for obtaining your credit report, removing the negative marks, and establishing "Triple A" credit!
*Item No. SW1103 • $29.95*

### Corporate Record Keeping Made E-Z
Essential for every corporation in America. Keep records in compliance with over 170 standard minutes, notices and resolutions.
*Item No. CD314 • $29.95*

### Divorce Law Made E-Z
Couples seeking an uncontested divorce can save costly lawyers' fees by filing the forms themselves.
*Item No. SW1102 • $29.95*

### Incorporation Made E-Z
We provide all the information you need to protect your personal assets from business creditors...without a lawyer.
*Item No. SW1101 • $29.95*

### Living Trusts Made E-Z
Take steps now to avoid costly, time-consuming probate and eliminate one more worry for your family by creating your own revocable living trust.
*Item No. SW1105 • $29.95*

### Managing Employees Made E-Z
Manage employees efficiently, effectively and legally with 246 forms, letters and memos covering everything from hiring to firing.
*Item No. CD312 • $29.95*

### Last Wills Made E-Z
Ensure your property goes to the heirs you choose. Includes Living Will and Power of Attorney for Healthcare forms for each state.
*Item No. SW1107 • $14.95*

# Save On Legal Fees

with software and books from E-Z Legal available at your nearest bookstore, or call 1-800-822-4566

Stock No.: BK311
$29.95  8.5" x 11"
500 pages Soft cover
ISBN 1-56382-311-X

## Everyday Law Made E-Z
The book that saves legal fees every time it's opened.

Here, in *Everyday Law Made E-Z*, are fast answers to 90% of the legal questions anyone is ever likely to ask, such as:

- How can I control my neighbor's pet?
- Can I change my name?
- What is a common law marriage?
- When should I incorporate my business?
- Is a child responsible for his bills?
- Who owns a husband's gifts to his wife?
- How do I become a naturalized citizen?
- Should I get my divorce in Nevada?
- Can I write my own will?
- Who is responsible when my son drives my car?
- How can my uncle get a Green Card?
- What are the rights of a non-smoker?
- Do I have to let the police search my car?
- What is sexual harassment?
- When is euthanasia legal?
- What repairs must my landlord make?
- What's the difference between fair criticism and slander?
- When can I get my deposit back?
- Can I sue the federal government?
- Am I responsible for a drunken guest's auto accident?
- Is a hotel liable if it does not honor a reservation?
- Does my car fit the lemon law?

Whether for personal or business use, this 500-page information-packed book helps the layman safeguard his property, avoid disputes, comply with legal obligations, and enforce his rights. Hundreds of cases illustrate thousands of points of law, each clearly and completely explained.

**E·Z LEGAL BOOKS®**

# BE INFORMED — BE PROTECTED!

## The E-Z Legal Sexual Harassment Poster

If you do not have a well-communicated sexual harassment policy, you are vulnerable to employee lawsuits for sexual harassment.

Give your employees the information they need and protect your company from needless harassment suits by placing this poster wherever you hang your labor law poster.

BONUS! Receive our helpful manual *How to Avoid Sexual Harassment Lawsuits* with your purchase of the Sexual Harassment Poster.

## See the order form in this guide, and order yours today!

ss 1999.r1

# FEDERAL & STATE
# Labor Law Posters

## The Poster 15 Million Businesses Must Have This Year!

All businesses must display federal labor laws at each location, or risk fines and penalties of up to $7,000!
And changes in September and October of 1997 made all previous Federal Labor Law Posters obsolete;
so make sure you're in compliance—use ours!

| State | Item# |
|---|---|
| Alabama | 83801 |
| Alaska | 83802 |
| Arizona | 83803 |
| Arkansas | 83804 |
| California | 83805 |
| Colorado | 83806 |
| Connecticut | 83807 |
| Delaware | 83808 |
| Florida | 83809 |
| Georgia | 83810 |
| Hawaii | 83811 |
| Idaho | 83812 |
| Illinois | 83813 |
| Indiana | 83814 |
| Iowa | 83815 |
| Kansas | 83816 |
| Kentucky | 83817 |

| State | Item# |
|---|---|
| Louisiana | 83818 |
| Maine | 83819 |
| Maryland | 83820 |
| Massachusetts | 83821 |
| Michigan | 83822 |
| Minnesota | 83823 |
| Mississippi | 83824 |
| Missouri | 83825 |
| Montana | 83826 |
| Nebraska | 83827 |
| Nevada | 83828 |
| New Hampshire | 83829 |
| New Jersey | 83830 |
| New Mexico | 83831 |
| New York | 83832 |
| North Carolina | 83833 |
| North Dakota | 83834 |

| State | Item# |
|---|---|
| Ohio | 83835 |
| Oklahoma | 83836 |
| Oregon | 83837 |
| Pennsylvania | 83838 |
| Rhode Island | 83839 |
| South Carolina | 83840 |
| South Dakota not available | |
| Tennessee | 83842 |
| Texas | 83843 |
| Utah | 83844 |
| Vermont | 83845 |
| Virginia | 83846 |
| Washington | 83847 |
| Washington, D.C. | 83848 |
| West Virginia | 83849 |
| Wisconsin | 83850 |
| Wyoming | 83851 |

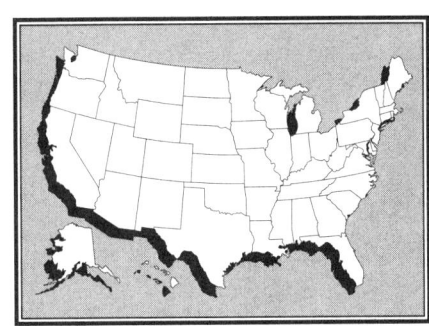

### State Labor Law Compliance Poster

Avoid up to $10,000 in fines by posting the required State Labor Law Poster available from E-Z Legal.

### $29.95

### Federal Labor Law Poster

This colorful, durable 17³/₄" x 24" poster is in full federal compliance and includes:

- The NEW Fair Labor Standards Act Effective October 1, 1996 (New Minimum Wage Act)
- The Family & Medical Leave Act of 1993*
- The Occupational Safety and Health Protection Act of 1970
- The Equal Opportunity Act
- The Employee Polygraph Protection Act

* Businesses with fewer than 50 employees should display reverse side of poster, which excludes this act.

### $11.99
Stock No. LP001

**See the order form in this guide to order yours today!**

# E·Z LEGAL® BOOKS
## ...when you need it in writing!®

# By the book...

MADE E-Z **Books** provide all the forms you need to take care of business and save on legal fees – *only $29.95 each!*

*Everyday Legal Forms & Agreements Made E-Z*  ISBN 1-56382-301-2
A do-it-yourself legal library of 301 ready-to-use perforated legal documents for virtually every personal or business need!

*Corporate Record Keeping Made E-Z*  ISBN 1-56382-304-7
Keep your own corporate records current and in compliance... without a lawyer!

*Managing Employees Made E-Z*  ISBN 1-56382-302-0
Over 240 documents to manage your employees more efficiently and legally!

*Vital Record Keeping Made E-Z*  ISBN 1-56382-300-4
201 simple and ready-to-use forms to help you keep organized records for your family, your business and yourself!

*Collecting Unpaid Bills Made E-Z*  ISBN 1-56382-309-8
Essential for anyone who extends credit and needs an efficient way to collect.

---
**Available at:**
Super Stores, Office Supply Stores, Drug Stores, Hardware Stores, Bookstores, and other fine retailers.
---

ss 1999.r1

|  | Item# | Qty. | Price Ea. |
|---|---|---|---|
| ★ **E•Z Legal Kits** | | | |
| Bankruptcy | K100 | | $21.95 |
| Incorporation | K101 | | $21.95 |
| Divorce | K102 | | $27.95 |
| Credit Repair | K103 | | $18.95 |
| Living Trust | K105 | | $18.95 |
| Living Will | K106 | | $21.95 |
| Last Will & Testament | K107 | | $16.95 |
| Small Claims Court | K109 | | $19.95 |
| Traffic Court | K110 | | $19.95 |
| Buying/Selling Your Home | K111 | | $18.95 |
| Employment Law | K112 | | $18.95 |
| Collecting Child Support | K115 | | $18.95 |
| Limited Liability Company | K116 | | $18.95 |
| ★ **E•Z Legal Software** | | | |
| Accounting-Deluxe Edition | SW1123 | | $49.95 |
| Everyday Legal Forms & Agreements Made E-Z | CD311 | | $29.95 |
| Managing Employees Made E-Z | CD312 | | $29.95 |
| Corporate Record Keeping Made E-Z | CD314 | | $29.95 |
| E-Z Construction Estimator | CD316 | | $29.95 |
| Incorporation Made E-Z | SW1101 | | $29.95 |
| Divorce Law Made E-Z | SW1102 | | $29.95 |
| Credit Repair Made E-Z | SW1103 | | $29.95 |
| Living Trusts Made E-Z | SW1105 | | $29.95 |
| Last Wills Made E-Z | SW1107 | | $14.95 |
| Buying/Selling Your Home Made E-Z | SW1111 | | $29.95 |
| W-2 Maker | SW1117 | | $14.95 |
| Asset Protection Secrets Made E-Z | SW1118 | | $29.95 |
| Solving IRS Problems Made E-Z | SW1119 | | $29.95 |
| Everyday Law Made E-Z | SW1120 | | $29.95 |
| Vital Record Keeping Made E-Z | SW306 | | $29.95 |
| ★ **E•Z Legal Books** | | | |
| Family Record Organizer | BK300 | | $24.95 |
| 301 Legal Forms & Agreements | BK301 | | $24.95 |
| Personnel Director | BK302 | | $24.95 |
| Credit Manager | BK303 | | $24.95 |
| Corporate Secretary | BK304 | | $24.95 |
| Immigration (English/Spanish) | BK305 | | $24.95 |
| E-Z Legal Advisor | LA101 | | $24.95 |
| ★ **Made E•Z Guides** | | | |
| Bankruptcy Made E-Z | G200 | | $17.95 |
| Incorporation Made E-Z | G201 | | $17.95 |
| Divorce Law Made E-Z | G202 | | $17.95 |
| Credit Repair Made E-Z | G203 | | $17.95 |
| Living Trusts Made E-Z | G205 | | $17.95 |
| Living Wills Made E-Z | G206 | | $17.95 |
| Last Wills Made E-Z | G207 | | $17.95 |
| Small Claims Court Made E-Z | G209 | | $17.95 |
| Traffic Court Made E-Z | G210 | | $17.95 |
| Buying/Selling Your Home Made E-Z | G211 | | $17.95 |
| Employment Law Made E-Z | G212 | | $17.95 |
| Trademarks & Copyrights Made E-Z | G214 | | $17.95 |
| Collecting Child Support Made E-Z | G215 | | $17.95 |
| Limited Liability Companies Made E-Z | G216 | | $17.95 |
| Partnerships Made E-Z | G218 | | $17.95 |
| Solving IRS Problems Made E-Z | G219 | | $17.95 |
| Asset Protection Secrets Made E-Z | G220 | | $17.95 |
| Immigration Made E-Z | G223 | | $17.95 |
| Buying/Selling a Business Made E-Z | G223 | | $17.95 |
| ★ **Made E•Z Books** | | | |
| Managing Employees Made E-Z | BK308 | | $29.95 |
| Corporate Record Keeping Made E-Z | BK310 | | $29.95 |
| Vital Record Keeping Made E-Z | BK312 | | $29.95 |
| Business Forms Made E-Z | BK313 | | $29.95 |
| Collecting Unpaid Bills Made E-Z | BK309 | | $29.95 |
| Everyday Law Made E-Z | BK311 | | $29.95 |
| Everyday Legal Forms & Agreements Made E-Z | BK307 | | $29.95 |
| ★ **Labor Posters** | | | |
| Federal Labor Law Poster | LP001 | | $11.99 |
| State Labor Law Poster (specify state) | | | $29.95 |
| Sexual Harassment Poster | LP003 | | $ 9.95 |
| ★ SHIPPING & HANDLING* | | | $ |
| ★ **TOTAL OF ORDER**: | | | $ |

# See an item in this book you would like to order?

To order :
1. Photocopy this order form.
2. Use the photocopy to complete your order and mail to:

**E•Z LEGAL FORMS®**

384 S Military Trail, Deerfield Beach, FL 33442
phone: (954) 480-8933 • fax: (954) 480-8906
web site: http://www.e-zlegal.com/

*Shipping and Handling:* Add $3.50 for the first item, $1.50 for each additional item.

**Florida residents add 6% sales tax.

Total payment must accompany all orders.
Make checks payable to: E•Z Legal Forms, Inc.

NAME

COMPANY

ORGANIZATION

ADDRESS

CITY     STATE     ZIP

PHONE (     )

**PAYMENT:**

❑ CHECK ENCLOSED, PAYABLE TO E-Z LEGAL FORMS, INC.

❑ PLEASE CHARGE MY ACCOUNT: ❑ MasterCard ❑ VISA   EXP.DATE

ACCOUNT NO.

Signature: _____
(required for credit card purchases)

-OR-

*For faster service, order by phone:*
**(954) 480-8933**

*Or you can fax your order to us:*
**(954) 480-8906**

# CHECK OUT THE
# E·Z LEGAL® LIBRARY

## MADE E-Z GUIDES

Each comprehensive guide contains the sample forms, information and suggestions you need to proceed.

Plus state-by-state requirements (where appropriate), an appendix of valuable resources, a handy glossary and the valuable 14-page supplement "How to Save on Attorney Fees."

## TITLES

**Asset Protection Made E-Z**
Shelter your property from financial disaster.
**Bankruptcy Made E-Z**
Take the confusion out of filing bankruptcy.
**Business Forms Made E-Z**
Organize your office's administrative and planning functions.
**Buying/Selling a Business Made E-Z**
Position your business and structure the deal for quick results.
**Buying/Selling Your Home Made E-Z**
Buy or sell your home for the right price right now!
**Collecting Child Support Made E-Z**
Ensure your kids the support they deserve.
**Collecting Unpaid Bills Made E-Z**
Get paid–and faster–every time.
**Corporate Record Keeping Made E-Z**
Minutes, resolutions, notices, and waivers for any type corporation.
**Credit Repair Made E-Z**
All the tools to put you back on track.
**Divorce Made E-Z**
Learn to proceed on your own, without a lawyer.
**Employment Law Made E-Z**
A handy reference for employers and employees.
**Everyday Law Made E-Z**
Fast answers to 90% of your legal questions.
**Everyday Legal Forms & Agreements Made E-Z**
Personal, property, and business protection for virtually any situation.

**Immigration Made E-Z**
A must-have for immigrants and aliens.
**Incorporation Made E-Z**
Information you need to get your company INC'ed.
**Last Wills Made E-Z**
Write a will the right way, the E-Z way.
**Limited Liability Companies Made E-Z**
Learn all about the hottest new business entity.
**Living Trusts Made E-Z**
Trust us to help you provide for your loved ones.
**Living Wills Made E-Z**
Take steps now to ensure Death with Dignity.
**Managing Employees Made E-Z**
Save time and money. Manage your most valuable asset–people.
**Partnerships Made E-Z**
Get your company started the right way.
**Small Claims Court Made E-Z**
Prepare for court...or explore other avenues.
**Solving IRS Problems Made E-Z**
Settle with the IRS for pennies on the dollar.
**Trademarks & Copyrights Made E-Z**
How to obtain your own copyright or trademark.
**Vital Record Keeping Made E-Z**
Preserve vital records and important information.
**Winning in Traffic Court Made E-Z**
Learn your rights on the road and in court.

## KITS

Each kit includes a clear, concise instruction manual to help you understand your rights and obligations, plus all the information and sample forms you need.

*For the busy do-it-yourselfer, it's quick, affordable, and it's E-Z.*

ss 1999.r1

# Index

## A-C

| | |
|---|---|
| Alimony | 15, 47 |
| Aid to dependent children | 115 |
| Answer and Affidavit | 82 |
| Assets, safeguarding | 30 |
| Professional licensure | 41 |
| Attorneys | 16 |
| Bank accounts | 31 |
| Child support | 52, 112 |
| Bankruptcy and child support | 116 |
| Credit, protecting | 42 |
| Community property states | 36 |
| Contempt of court | 113 |
| Corroborating witness | 96 |
| Court, preparing for | 103 |
| Credit accounts, joint | 110 |
| Custody of children | 49 |
|     Alternating | 50 |
|     Divided | 50 |
|     Joint | 49 |
|     Joint physical | 50 |
|     Jurisdiction form, about | 86 |
|     Legal | 49 |
|     Physical | 49 |
|     Shared | 49 |
|     Sole | 49-50 |
|     Split | 50 |

## D-P

| | |
|---|---|
| Debts, dividing | 42 |
| Divorce | |
|     Complaint | 76 |
|     Contested | 14 |
|     Decree of | 93 |
|     Grounds for | 24 |
|     Organizing | 25 |
|     Petition | 76 |
|     Preparing documents | 74 |
|     State requirements | 74 |
|     Uncontested | 14 |
| Equitable distribution | 36 |
| Family Support Act | 115 |
| Financial statement | 67 |
| Insurance | 30, 111 |
| Liabilities, dividing | 42 |
| Marital settlement agreement | 57 |
| Notice of hearing | 91 |
| Pensions | 40 |
| Post-divorce, checklist | 109 |
| Pre-marital agreement | 117 |
| Property | |
|     Community | 36 |
|     Dividing by agreement | 38 |
|     Marital | 36 |
|     Non-marital | 36 |

## P-W

Prosecution, criminal ............ 115
Real estate ............................. 30
Residency requirements .......... 25
Self representation ................. 17
Service by summons ............... 82
Social security benefits ........... 40
Spousal support ...................... 15
Summons ................................ 82
Valuables, safeguarding .......... 30
Visitation ....................... 50, 117
Wage garnishment ................ 113
Witnesses ............................... 10